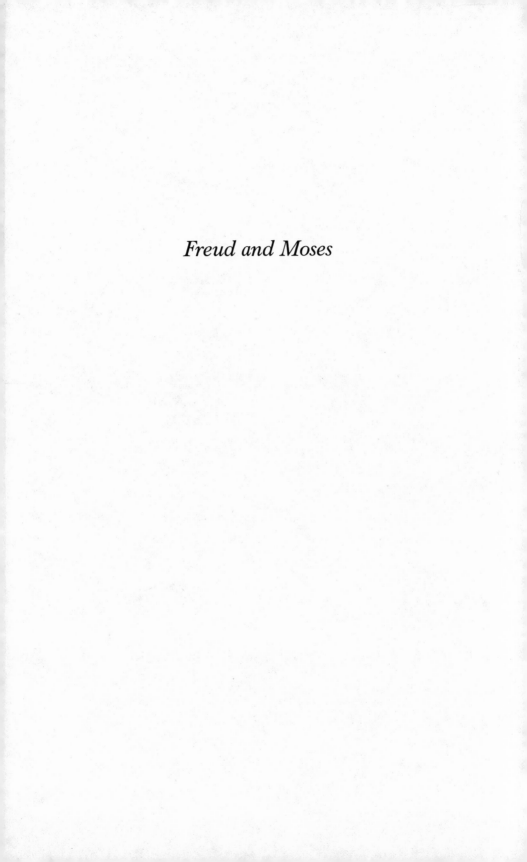

Freud and Moses

Freud and Moses

The Long Journey Home

Emanuel Rice

State University of New York Press

Published by
State University of New York Press, Albany

©1990 State University of New York

For information, address State University of New York
Press, State University Plaza, Albany, N.Y., 12216

Library of Congress Cataloging-in-Publication Data
Rice, Emanuel, 1927-
    Freud and Moses: The Long Journey Home/Emanuel Rice.
        p.   cm.
    Includes bibliographical references.
    ISBN 0-7914-0453-6 (alk. paper).—ISBN 0-7914-0454-4
(pbk.: alk. paper)
    1. Freud, Sigmund, 1857-1939—Religion.   2. Freud,
Sigmund, 1857-1939—Childhood and youth.
3. Judaism and psychoanalysis.   4. Psychoanalysts—
Austria—Biography.   I.   Title.
BF109.F74R52   1990
150.19'52—dc20   89-77695
                                                                    CIP

10 9 8 7 6 5 4 3 2 1

For Harriet

Contents

Illustrations

Preface

This book would not have been written were it not for a chance meeting, after 33 years, with my former teacher at The Rabbinical School of The Jewish Theological Seminary of America, Rabbi Robert Gordis, Emeritus Professor of Bible. A few days later he called and asked if I would write a review of Dennis B. Klein's book, *The Jewish Origins of The Psychoanalytic Movement* for *Judaism — A Quarterly Journal*, of which he is the editor. Working on this essay aroused my interest in the Jewish origins of the discoverer of psychoanalysis, and the result has turned out to be a fascinating research project, necessitating a return journey to my own and my late parents' origins.

The work could not have been done without the splendid cooperation of various individuals and institutions. Menahem Schmelzer, Professor of Medieval Hebrew Literature at The Jewish Theological Seminary of America, was unstinting in his help; always available, always the scholar and fine human being; a 'religious' individual in the truest sense of the word. He took the time from his busy schedule to decipher the difficult Hebrew script of Jacob Freud, trace its origins in the Bible, and transpose it all to Hebrew print so that as close to an unequivocal rendition could be produced for all to see and verify. Likewise, to Rabbi Jules Harlow, Director of Publications for The Rabbinical Assembly, I owe a great debt of gratitude for translating the Hebrew inscriptions. It could not have been done by a better hand. The translation is beautiful, a testimony not only to the translator's skill, but also to the mastery of the Bible by Jacob Freud. Rabbi Harlow transferred those superb skills that were so effectively used by him to produce the translation of the new Prayer Book of the Conservative Movement, *Siddur Sim Shalom*, to this task.

David L. Newlands and Steve Neufeld, then Curator and Associate Curator, respectively, Richard Wells, Director, Erica Davies and J.K. Davies — all of The Freud Museum in London — were most helpful in furnishing photographs of the Freud family Bible and other relevant data. Mark Paterson, Jo Richardson, and Thomas Roberts of The Sigmund Freud

Copyrights, Ltd. in Colchester, England were likewise most cooperative. The staff of The Gustave L. Levy Library of The Mount Sinai School of Medicine amply demonstrated their ability in tracking down, throughout this vast country, many of the articles and books that were necessary for this project. Likewise, my thanks to the staffs of the libraries of The Jewish Theological Seminary of America, The YIVO Institute for Jewish Research, The Leo Baeck Institute, and The Park Avenue Synagogue for their kind assistance.

Very special thanks are due to Leli M. Freud; to Dr. Harold P. Blum, Executive Director of The Sigmund Freud Archives; to Dr. Ronald S. Wilkinson, Manuscript Division, Library of Congress, and to his splendid staff.

My colleagues and friends were most helpful. Hans E. Schapira, Clinical Professor of Urology, and Demetrius Pertsemlides, Clinical Professor of Surgery, translated many of the German documents for me. Marsha Rozenblit, Associate Professor of History at The University of Maryland, shared her expertise in nineteenth-century Viennese Jewry. Dr. Silvia Heiman provided me with a living history of pre-world War II Vienna. John and Arlene Rosenfelder of London made some contacts for me which trans-Atlantic distance made difficult. David and Iris Freeman of London performed some valuable historical research. Joann Rosoff provided a most discerning eye for the significant detail, and her critical comments were most helpful. Thanks and appreciation are due to Ora Raphael, the daughter of the Hebrew translator of *Totem and Taboo*, Yehuda Dvosis-Dvir, for permission to publish the letters from Freud to her father.

Others who have given help and valuable suggestions are: Albert and Irena Appel, Israel Friedman, Sidney Rosoff, Ileene Smith, Donna J. Spector, Gladys Topkis, Elisabeth Young-Bruehl, and Drs. Milton C. Engel, Stuart Feder, Walter Flegenheimer, Sophie Freud, Anne Hoffman, Ruth Lubelski-Yoran, Emanuel Peterfreund, Rita M. Ransohoff, Joseph Reppen, Albert J. Solnit, Florence Vigilante, and Jack Wertheimer. Henry and Ingeborg Bondi were most gracious and helpful. Special thanks are due to the former and current chairmen of the Department of Psychiatry, Professors Marvin Stein and Kenneth L. Davis respectively, and to Edward D. Joseph, Professor of Psychiatry (and Past President of the International Psychoanalytic Association), all at The Mount Sinai School of Medicine. Jonathan Rosen was most helpful in reorganizing and editing the manuscript. His brilliant and intuitive grasp of the text resulted in a felicitous improvement of the narrative flow. The enthusiasm, graciousness, and thoughtfulness of my editor at SUNY Press, Carola F. Sautter, made for a splendid working relationship, as has the assistance of Diane Ganeles, Terry Abad, Claire Robert, and Colleen and Jerry Towle. To all of the above I owe heartfelt thanks and appreciation.

To my wife Harriet, my gratitude for her love, patience, inspiration, incisive comments, profound insights and invaluable support—all of which were indispensable in bringing this project to fruition.

CHAPTER 1

Introduction

This book is the story of an odyssey. It tells of the geographic, intellectual and religious journey that the Freud family, like thousands of other Jews, made out of the ghettoes of Eastern Europe. It is the story of how the vicissitudes of this odyssey affected Sigmund Freud, his character, genius, and creativity.

In 1956, Ernst L. Freud wrote the following on the occasion of the one-hundreth anniversary of his father's birthday:

> In the last year of my father's life, shortly after his library had been reestablished in his new Hampstead house in London, he was working at his desk while I was rummaging through the shelves. By chance, I came across an insignificant looking volume bound in black canvas, which I found to be a Bible (in Hebrew and German with a fair number of illustrations), an edition which had been very popular on the Continent about the middle of the last century. The volume had been put together from remnants of the Book of Kings, Samuel, and the nearly complete five Books of Moses. What immediately aroused my interest was the discovery of several Hebrew inscriptions on the outer pages—incidentally opening from the left and not from the right. My father, noticing my enthusiasm, presented me with the book ... The next page shows an inscription in Hebrew and this is followed by a translation into English with the first and last lines written in the shaky hand of Jacob Freud himself ... That the language of the translation should be English is most likely explained by the fact that it was made by one of Jacob's sons from his first marriage, both of whom settled in Manchester.

This Bible appears to have been a significant factor in the development of Sigmund Freud's ethnic and religious identities. In it, his father recorded notable events of the Freud family. The Bible was also one of Sigmund Freud's first textbooks in childhood, serving as a primary vehicle for his

1

introduction to the history of the Jews, to the world of antiquity, and to the origins of western civilization. It also came to symbolize a very special relationship between Jacob Freud and his son Sigmund. In presenting the family Bible as a gift to his son Ernst, Freud was reenacting the scene in which his father Jacob gave him the Bible in 1891 on the occasion of his 35th birthday.

The stories related in the Bible appear to have left an indelible imprint on Freud's mind. He repeatedly returned, in his life and work, to biblical themes and heroes which provided him with enduring models and metaphors. Joseph, the interpreter of dreams, and Moses, the first great prophet and leader of his people, are but two notable examples. The Bible also supplied some of the raw material that went into the development of Freud's character and laid the foundation of his ethnic and religious identity. This book will pursue clues to one of the most elusive aspects of Freud—the Jewish aspect— through an examination of the family Bible, his parents' origins and identity, the social, cultural and religious tenor of nineteenth-century Vienna, and Freud's own scientific and literary achievements.

It is one of the themes of this book that the relationship between Jacob and Sigmund Freud owed much more than is hitherto believed to its Jewish contexts, in all its diverse aspects, and that the family Bible, i.e., the Old Testament, was a crucial medium of its expression. As Freud himself noted:

> My deep engrossment in the Bible story (almost as soon as I had learnt the art of reading) had, as I recognized much later, an enduring effect upon the direction of my interest. (S.E. 20:8)

Increasing attention has been focused recently on the relationship between Jacob Freud and his son Sigmund, as exemplified by the work of Krull (1986). Since there is no written correspondence of Jacob Freud extant, Krull relied on other sources for her discussion. She is in agreement with all previous and current biographers, e.g., Jones (1953), Schur (1972), Clark (1980), and Gay (1987, 1988), that the tie between father and son was a close and affectionate one, unlike that with his mother which, by comparison, was somewhat distant; that Jacob and Amalia Freud (Sigmund's mother) shed their Orthodox, Ḥasidic life style by the time they were married in 1855, an initial expression of this break with the past being their marriage by a rabbi of the Reform Jewish movement; that they continued their life style as assimilated Jews, throughout the remainder of their lives, as presumably shown by the almost complete absence of the observance of religious ritual both in and out of the home.

An attempt will be made in this study to show that traditional Judaism may have played a more significant role in the Freud household than the biographers have believed. To do so, one must face the difficult task of moving beyond an image that the Freud family itself has helped to build up. Freud's daughter Anna, so long the custodian of her father's work and reputation, went so far as to suggest, in a letter to British psychoanalyst Masud Kahn (23 June 1975), the establishment of a "Defense League" to counter the injurious insinuations of unfavorable biographers. It is interesting to note that what so angered Anna in her letter to Kahn was an attempt by the biographer Marthe Robert to explore Freud's Jewish roots:

> ... she describes my father's father as an authoritarian figure, orthodox Jewish and in every respect the kind of father against whom a son revolts. The true facts are that he was a freethinker, a mild, indulgent and rather passive man, just the opposite, etc. (As quoted in Young-Bruehl, 1988, p. 431).

Though formal religion in terms of theological belief and ritual practice was not a major constituent of the family life style, it was nevertheless an important one as embodied in a home environment that was pervaded by Jewish culture and tradition. Both Jacob and Amalia Freud came from a traditional Orthodox and Hasidic background in Galicia, the Eastern European part of the Austro-Hungarian Empire, he from Tysmenitz and she from Brody. Though religion was not as all-encompassing as it was in Galicia, much of the tradition will be shown to have been retained when, after their marriage, they resided in Freiberg. Jacob Freud may well have been attracted to the enlightenment of the West and did actually become somewhat assimilated, i.e., as compared to religious life in Tysmenitz, but he never removed himself from his tradition.[1] (From 1844 to 1848 he had residences in both Tysmenitz and Freiberg and in 1848 became a permanent resident of Freiberg with his first wife Sally, who may have died in 1852 or earlier, and their two sons, Emanuel and Philipp.)

There is evidence that when Sigmund was eighteen years old the Freud family observed religious festivals and rituals. On September 18, 1874 he wrote a jocular letter to his friend Eduard Silberstein on the subject of the gratification of the senses provided by religion:

> ... even the atheist who is fortunate enough to belong to a moderately pious family cannot deny the festival when he puts a New Year's Day morsel to his lips. One might say that religion, enjoyed in moderation, stimulates the digestion, but that taken in excess it does damage to it.[2]

However one may define what Freud meant by 'a moderately pious family' observing the holiday of Rosh Hashanah (the Jewish New Year), given the context of his parents' Orthodox tradition, it is certainly not indicative of an assimilated family. The food may well have been kosher as it would have been ludicrous to associate non-kosher food in Jewish Vienna of the 1870s with religious holiday observance.

Ernest Jones (1953, I:19) noted that although Sigmund Freud's children had assured him that their grandfather had become a complete freethinker, there is some evidence to the contrary. Freud's mother, Amalia, also preserved some belief in the Deity. Judith Bernays Heller (1956), Sigmund Freud's niece, in describing the years she lived with her grandparents, noted that Jacob spent a good deal of his time studying the Talmud in the original Aramaic, the language of ancient Babylon, there being no printed translation of the Talmud in existence at the time. She also recalls the festivities of the Passover Seder, Jacob reciting the Hagaddah (the story of Passover in Hebrew) by heart and she reading parts of it. Contrast this with Martin Freud's comment (1957) that there was no religious observance in his grandparents' household. Krull (1986) notes that they also celebrated Christmas. She based this on Martin Freud's (1957) comment that the entire family gathered for dinner at the grandparents' home on Christmas and New Year's days. No other evidence is given that would substantiate the claim that it was the holiday Christmas as such that was being celebrated. The contradiction between the perception of Judith and her cousin Martin may, in part, be explainable by the difference in age, the former having been born in 1885 and the latter in 1889. Presumably Judith may have had more distinct memories of the events. Jacob Freud died in 1896 and the observance of religious ritual may have undergone some change after Amalia became a widow. Martin, for reasons unknown, may have had a need to sustain an image of the family history that would be in accord with a preconceived assimilated status.

To the contrary, Hanns W. Lange, the keeper of the family tree, has informed me (personal communication) that Freud's grandson, Walter Freud, with whom he is in close contact, has assured him that Amalia came from a strictly Orthodox household and stayed *fromm* (Orthodox and ritually observant) until her death in 1930. Given this information, it would seem absurd to claim that Jacob and Amalia, or even Amalia herself after the death of Jacob, would have celebrated Christmas.

It is indeed gratifying for an author or investigator to receive independent corroboration for his hypotheses. Such is the case with my serendipitous encounter with Henry S. Bondi. Bondi was moved to write a lengthy letter to Sophie Freud, daughter of Sigmund's son Martin, in which he stated his disillusionment and disappointment, after reading Krull's (1986) book on the Freud family, at the conspicuous omission of the extent of the Jewish dimension of Freud's life by some members of his family and biographers. He felt that before his generation, especially those who had personal intimate contact with the Freud family, pass from the scene, that the 'cover' of the secularized perspective of the Freud 'religious' story be removed so that it can be seen for what it really was.[3]

As noted above, the only surviving writings of Jacob Freud are the inscriptions written in Hebrew that are to be found within the covers of the Freud family Bible. Through a study of these inscriptions, I will attempt to show that the relationship between the biblical patriarch Jacob and his son Joseph served as a paradigm of great importance for that between Jacob and Sigmund. They both shared a fantasy based on their respective conceptualization of the Jacob and Joseph relationship.

Some comment on methodology is in order. All of Freud's writings have been examined, along with some published correspondence, as well as two of his letters to Yehuda Dvosis-Dvir, his Hebrew translator, and excerpts of letters to his childhood friend Eduard Silberstein. Most crucial are the few Hebrew inscriptions of Jacob Freud, which will be analyzed for the first time in an exegetical and dynamic manner. The Hebrew text and its origins in biblical sources, of which Jacob was apparently a master, will be used to reveal information about Jacob and his relationship with his son. From a biographical perspective, resort will be made to all available data as well as to anecdotal and previously unpublished information that has been made available to me. Jacob Freud was quite typical of that generation that was raised in the East European ghetto, was exposed to the Enlightenment, tasted of the learned fruits of the West and shed some of the restrictions of his religious past.

The dynamic and theoretical frame of reference that is used in this study is the classical psychoanalytic position; with the focus on the centrality of the Oedipal conflict in the etiology of neurotic symptoms, the partial but important role it plays in the formation of character and in the understanding of biographical and historical phenomena. This is not to lessen the contributory significance of genetic factors. Those readers who adhere to pre-Oedipal, narcissistic and object-relations approaches may endeavor to fruitfully apply them to the data and draw complementary conclusions from them. They will only serve to enrich this study.

I have not limited myself to a psychoanalytic conceptual frame of reference. Use has been made of the most recent historical and archaeological findings, especially in the last section of this book.

Sigmund Freud's journey from his Jewish origins was both universal and particular. Throughout the course of human history people have had to pass through different cultures and adapt to them. The command of God to Abraham in the Bible is a beautiful and succinct expression of this experience (Genesis 12:1-2):[4]

> *The Lord said to Abram, "Go forth from your native*
> *land and from your father's house to the land that*
> *I will show you.*

I will make of you a great nation,
And I will bless you;
I will make your name great,
And you shall be a blessing."

It is my contention that though one cannot in actuality go home again, one never really leaves it. Freud's childhood and adolescent home was typical of the East European Orthodox Jew in its transplanted character—first to Freiberg, Moravia and then to Vienna. Freud's attempt at emotional and external departure from this milieu began, rebelliously, in early adolescence. It was a long and arduous journey, but for him, most productive. The world too has been the better for it. Toward the end of his life, as so often happens, he began the return journey, first with a renewed interest in religion in general, and finally, in Judaism in particular. *Moses and Monotheism*, one of the very last creative productions of his life, exemplifies the final stages of this return.

> ... the writing of the Moses book was for Freud one last, valiant effort to set straight within his own mind the deeper conflicts and ambivalences that had plagued him all his life. His relationship to the figure of Moses and the basic psychological issues it reflected are distilled in this last flamboyant gesture of defiance. (Meissner, 1984, p. ix)

Freud's major written demonstrations of his concern for religion in general appear in *Totem and Taboo* and *Future of An Illusion*. Religion is seen as arising from the helplessness of childhood. It is the universal expression of the child's conception of the omnipotent father. Religion is seen as the vehicle for the gratification of infantile drives and yearnings in an institutionally acceptable way. This results in a conversion of inherently unacceptable thoughts and feelings to the phenomenon of a feeling of virtue and righteousness. It is also a means of resolving nearly all of the basically unresolvable fears of humankind. In short, it is a universal neurosis. It was only at the end of his life that his rebelliousness towards Judaism was particularized and he attempted to deliver what he thought would be the *coup de grace* in *Moses and Monotheism*. But, strangely enough, some of his most positive feelings about Judaism are expressed in this presumably destructive work. Hints of the emergence of positive feelings toward Judaism appear in a letter to his Hebrew translator in 1930. I will attempt to demonstrate that *Moses and Monotheism* reflects an attempt to resolve his feelings towards his father and that it is an autobiography in disguise. If East European Jewry (*Ostjuden*) is substituted for the pre-Moses Egyptian Israelites, then one will have a 'master key' to the unlocking of the 'door' leading to the latent, highly personal motivation, meaning and significance of *Moses and Monotheism*.[5] Part of my methodology will be to use Freud's own words to help in the analysis of his texts, words used in other contexts, but nevertheless, quite appropiate to the task at hand. It was, indeed, a long and tortuous voyage home and I have sought clues to this journey in many realms.

The central themes of this study which will be developed are the following:

1. That Jacob and Amalia Freud came from a strictly Orthodox Jewish background and, contrary to prevailing opinion, retained many of the traditional religious practices to the end of their lives.

2. That Jacob Freud had attended a *Yeshiva* (Talmudical academy) in his youth and was a scholar of the Holy Writ.

3. That they were not adherents of the Reform Jewish movement, nor were they assimilated Jews.

4. That Sigmund Freud himself had a more traditional upbringing than he openly admitted.

5. That Sigmund Freud and his family, either through misinterpretation, unawareness or possibly conscious misrepresentation, were somewhat less than open about the extent of the Jewishness or religiousness of his background and created an impression of an assimilated status that was not quite in accord with reality.

6. That his biographers perpetuated this myth because they appear not to have grasped the full implication of the available data.

7. That self-consciousness about one's East European origins (due to the most intense prejudice on the part of the established middle class who looked upon *Ostjuden* as primitive and inferior) motivated a pressing need on the part of the Viennese Jewish middle class to overcompensate by being as German and middle class in their cultural and intellectual interests and values as the non-Jewish middle class, if not more so. The Freud family even went so far as to create a myth, a family romance, in which their background was elevated to a most noble status.

8. That *Moses and Monotheism* was a very personal drama, and yet, though methodologically and factually flawed, a work of genius and ingenuity. It represents his attempt to come home again to his Jewish roots but on his own terms and in his own way.

I now invite the reader to join me on a voyage of a different kind, one of investigative pursuit, one that goes back to the beginning of history as expressed in the Bible and Western Civilization; to the intellectual, cultural and emotional ascent of man, all of which went ultimately into the creation of one of the great all too human geniuses of our or any age, Sigmund Freud.

CHAPTER 2

Sigmund Freud's Jewish Identity

This book tells a story that opens and shuts with the pages of a Bible. Freud's father inscribed his son's name in the family Bible when Freud was born and Freud, in a figurative sense, reinscribed his name there at the end of his life. But before we examine that book and what it represents, let us look at the Viennese world which turned Shlomo Sigismund Freud into Sigmund Freud, for Viennese culture taught a very different lesson to young, ambitious Jews like Freud from the one received by Freud's grandfather Shlomo and even by his father, Jacob.

To facilitate our understanding of the context of Freud's educational and emotional development and its effect on his Jewish identity, it would be helpful to elaborate on the historical, sociological, and cultural climate of nineteenth-century Austria. Throughout the vast area of what was to become the Austro-Hungarian Empire, Jews were treated as less than second-class citizens. They shared few, if any, rights of their Gentile neighbors.

There was, for example, the Bollete tax, which only Jews had to pay. It had been eliminated in all of the German states by the end of the eighteenth-century but persisted in Austria into the nineteenth-century. On a specified door of every police station there hung a sign, *Judenamt* (Jewish Bureau) and through its portals the richest as well as the poorest Jew had to pass to pay his Bollete tax.

Jews were not allowed to live in the cities without a special permit which had to be renewed every six months (Grunwald, 1936, p. 266). Those who had the temporary permit were known as 'Tolerated'. Before 1848, any rabbi who performed a marriage that did not have prior government approval was subject to corporal punishment. The only occupation permitted Jews was petty trading. It was not until the end of the eighteenth century that the Emperor Joseph II removed the restrictions against Jewish school attendance. Jewish youth were now permitted to attend the *Gymnasium*.[1] Since most Jews were Orthodox at the time, one can well imagine the chilling effect of compulsory

9

attendance at Saturday classes and the ubiquitous presence of the crucifix on the wall of every classroom in every school in Austria. Since the *Gymnasiums* were usually located in cities, the question can be raised about the benefits gained by the Jews who weren't allowed to live there in the first place.

In Vienna in 1784 there were 230 Jews (1.1%) out of a total population of 207,405; in 1857, there were 6,217 (2.1%) out of 284,999; in 1910, 175,318 (8.6%) out of 2,031,498 (Rozenblit, p. 17). The revolution that moved through Europe in 1848 dramatically changed the situation for Jews in Austria. They were emancipated, but emancipation in Austria did not quite yet mean what it meant in Germany or France. It had to be further elaborated and reconfirmed in 1859 and 1860; finally by 1867 it was completed. The migration of Jews from Hungary, Galicia, Bohemia and Moravia to Vienna multiplied the size of that city many times. They now had complete freedom of movement, residence and occupation. More significantly for this discussion, their children were now able to enter the public school system and religious and secular education was within the permissable reach of all. Although very few Jewish girls went to the public schools, they did attend the religious school. Strangely enough, middle-class Orthodox Jewish parents sent their daughters to Catholic girl schools for their secular education, as was the case with Bertha Pappenheim, who was a patient of Josef Breuer and who has become famous as 'Anna O', the name she is assigned in Freud and Breuer's joint publication (S.E. II, 1895).[2]

Once a group of Jews became established and assimilated in Vienna, they began to resent the newly-arrived immigrants, whom they deemed to be primitive, uncultured and uneducated. The established Jews were reminded of a past that they had struggled to disown. The following quotations from a very moving autobiography by George Clare (1982) are indicative of this phenomenon:

> In many ways the Klaars were also typical of Central European Jewry, of people who, within a short space of time, moved from the narrowness of the East-European ghettos into that wide and glamourous world of West-European culture, absorbed it, became an essential part of it, climbed to new heights during the enlightened 19th Century only to fall so deep into the dark abyss of extinction which our own century had so thoroughly prepared for them. (p. 8)

> This was why I liked Julie so much better than Adele. I was already second-generation Viennese, and Viennese-born Jews felt resentment towards the less assimilated Jews from the East. We were, or rather thought we were, quite different from that bearded, caftaned lot. We were not just Austrian, but German-Austrian. Little wonder that I resented the Yiddish singsong intonation with which Adele spoke German, a 'yoich' sigh at the start and end of almost every sentence. (p. 31)

> For years I resented the fact that my mother was born in Poland. (p. 67)

Peter Gay (1977) and his parents fled Nazi Germany just prior to the outbreak of World War II and eventually emigrated to America. He wrote of his father:

> Yet he continued to harbor one sweeping, though hardly violent, prejudice, the triumph of uninterpreted experience over cherished principles: he did not really like East European Jews. It was a symptom of remnants of insecurity, for he, like most other assimilated German Jews, feared that the invasion of Germany by *Ostjuden* must invariably feed anti-Semitism.[3]

Freud and his eldest son Martin had feelings identical to those of Clare and Gay's father on the subject of Polish Jews. Freud wrote a letter to Karl Abraham on December 25, 1918 in which he commented on Otto Rank's marital choice:

> Rank really seems to have done himself a good deal of harm with his marriage, a little Polish-Jewish wife whom no one finds congenial and who betrays no higher interests. Pretty sad and not quite comprehensible. (As quoted in Gay, 1988, p. 471)

No wonder Freud, in *An Autobiographical Study* (S.E. XX:7-8), indulged his Family Romance by positing the unsupported assumption that his family tree had deep roots in Germany:

> I have reason to believe that my father's family was settled for a long time on the Rhine (at Cologne). [See also Appendix I]

Martin Freud had difficulty accepting the Galician origins of the paternal side of his family. His verbal portrait of Amalia was, on balance, not very flattering.

> My father's father died when I was only seven years old, and although I met him often, I do not know anything about his relationship to Jewish matters. It was different with my grandmothers. My father's mother, Amalia, whom I knew very well, was a typical Polish Jewess, with all the shortcomings that that implies. She was certainly not what we would call a "lady", had a lively temper and was impatient, self-willed, sharp witted and highly intelligent.
>
> . . . There was a counterpart to my paternal grandmother, the Polish Jewess, emotional and untamed, full of life and vitality. I refer to my maternal grandmother, Emmeline Bernays. She came from a family of intellectuals; two of her uncles were well known men of letters, her grandfather had been Chief Rabbi of Hamburg, a person of historical importance, who was known as *chochem*, the wise one. I have a copy of his picture in my house, a most

impressive face, with strong and dominant features. I flattered myself when I was younger that I possessed a certain likeness to my Jewish great-grandfather, but this was possibly more a desire than a fact. Grandmother was an Orthodox Jewess, she wore a *Sheitel*, which meant that at her marriage she had sacrificed her own hair, and her head was crowned with two close-fitting artificial plaits. She was a lady through and through. I never heard her shout or scream. On Saturdays she sang Jewish prayers in a firm, melodious voice. Mild, sweet and angelic as she looked, she was always determined to have her own way, as my father experienced with grief during his engagement to my mother, which lasted for so many years.

... Two typical Jewesses, one of Ashkenasi, the other of Sephardi origin, gave the Freud family a strong Jewish background. (Martin Freud, 1967, pp. 201-203)

To cope with his ambivalence, a kind so prevalent among the second and subsequent generations of Viennese Jews, Martin created an origin for the maternal side that hints strongly of 'Family Romance'. It was a good example of an unconscious self-deception devised to repair injured self-esteem. In his eyes the Bernays' were *Sephardim*. The Bernays' being German-Jewish for several generations was not enough to undo the Galician taint of the paternal side of the Freud family. The *Sephardim* were considered to be, and also considered themselves to be, the cream of Jewish aristocracy. Rabbi Bernays was affected by the same 'virus' when he insisted on being called 'Hakham' rather than 'Rabbi'. The pathos and irony of the situation is that there is no evidence that would attest to their being *Sephardim*. It is certainly not something that would have been kept secret; to the contrary, there would have been more than ample expression of it in the family biographies if it were so.

Yet there was an underlying admiration of the bravery and aggressiveness of Galician Jews who fought back when confronted by the verbal and physical abuse of their anti-semitic classmates.

Why tolerate such indignities? I asked myself, and soon I found out that some resistance was being shown—not by Viennese students, to start with, but by boys from Galicia and Bukovina, the despised and spurned "Polish Jews". (Martin Freud, 1967, p. 207)

All of the biographies of Freud assume that the reason for the long four year engagement to Martha was Freud's impoverished financial situation. It appears from information supplied by Henry S. Bondi that this reason, though plausible, may only have been a secondary factor. The more significant motivation was the Bernays' reluctance to have their daughter marry someone from a Galician background. One of the few modes of entry, or marriage upward, for a Galician Jew into a German-Jewish family would be the shared Orthodoxy of both families. Somehow religious Orthodoxy lent itself to a degree of egalitarianism. It served as a moderate 'solvent' of geographic and cultural prejudice. The strict observance of religious ritual and the maintenance of traditional theological belief, in essence being known as an Orthodox Jewish family, had as high, if not at times higher, value in the priorities of the Orthodox Jewish community than a family's financial, cultural, geographic, or social status. Orthodox Jews who lived in Germany prior to World War II have confirmed this phenomenon.

Evidence of this egalitarian factor in religious Orthodoxy can also be seen in the choice of Rabbi by the varied houses of worship in Germany. During the period covering the second half of the nineteenth-century up to World War I, there was a serious shortage of qualified religious leaders and teachers who were born in Germany. The void was filled by the East European immigrant Jews.

There were three major Rabbinical schools in Germany. In Berlin there was the Orthodox *Hildesheimer Rabbinerseminar* and the Reform *Hochschule*. In Breslau there was the moderately Liberal or Conservative *Theologische Seminar*. During this period these three institutions ordained over forty Jews of East European origin who went on to serve in German pulpits. A much higher percentage of those East European graduates of the Orthodox and Conservative seminaries were successful in securing pulpits in Germany (35% and 36% respectively) than from the Reform (11%) (Wertheimer, 1987, pp.88-89). In his scholarly and perceptive study of the vicissitudes of East European Jewry in Germany, Wertheimer (1987) stresses the fact that the Orthodox rabbis stood a far better chance of obtaining a pulpit in the large cities of Germany whereas the Breslau graduates were forced to take positions in the smaller cities and towns. The East European graduates of the Reform seminary had to first serve an apprenticeship of many years duration in remote and sparsely populated areas before becoming eligible for employment in the larger cities.

Freud apparently never forgave the Bernays family for their prejudice. There was a story that Bondi was told by his mother, involving a painting of Ḥakham Bernays that used to hang in the hall of the Bergasse 19 apartment (probably the one referred to above by Martin Freud) (Figure 1). A little electric light beneath the painting was always kept off except when Orthodox members of the Bernays family came to visit on the Sabbath. Freud would then, apparently in spite, turn on this light. This may at first appear gracious and considerate but it should be remembered that turning on a light on the Sabbath is forbidden for the Orthodox. Bondi once asked Martin Freud, whom he knew well, about these episodes and he confirmed the story.

Figure 1. Portrait of Hakham Isaac Bernays. Reproduced by permission of A.W. Freud et al., by arrangement with Mark Paterson & Associates, Colchester.

Jones (1953, I:117) notes that Martha Freud's mother stayed with the Freuds in the spring of 1883, during the long engagement of Sigmund and Martha. As noted earlier, the biographers of Freud have created a picture of Jacob and Amalia Freud and their children as a westernized, assimilated Jewish family that no longer adhered to religious ritual practices, implying, among other things, that the Freud home was not observant of the dietary laws, i.e., not kosher. Mrs. Bernays was quite Orthodox in belief and practice (to the extent of wearing a *Sheitel*, i.e., a wig) and it is difficult to believe that she would have stayed in a home which did not adhere to the dietary laws. A woman with this degree of religious orthodoxy would not even permit herself to drink a glass of water in a non-kosher household as the glass itself would not be considered as kosher. In 1887, Sigmund wrote his sister-in-law Minna Bernays, that he and Martha were thinking of asking her and the widowed Mrs. Bernays to live with them permanently in Vienna, but they concluded that Mrs. Bernays, who was "exacting and pious" (in Gay's words [1989]), would feel uncomfortable in their nonobservant (i.e., of religious ritual) home. In addition, when one pictures the man of the house, who is capable of writing the Hebrew dedication on the occasion of his son's thirty-fifth birthday and all the while studying Talmud, then it would be inordinately incongruous to juxtapose it with an image of an assimilated, non-kosher home. Such incongruities can occur but are most unlikely.

Religious Conversion as a Vehicle for Entry—Fantasy and Reality

In America the ready availability of public education and freedom of opportunity made upward mobility an achievable goal. The intense anti-Semitism, both overt and covert, in the Austro-Hungarian Empire did not allow for similarity of ease. Complete assimilation was considered to be the only exit from a perceived restrictive Jewishness to what was thought would be complete equality and acceptance. Conversion to Christianity (usually Protestantism) was deemed to be the way out.

The names of famous Viennese Jews who took the final steps to conversion and total assimilation readily come to mind: Gustav Mahler, Arnold Schoenberg, Karl Kraus, Otto Weininger, and Victor Adler. These were joined by hundreds of others. In fact, Viennese Jews converted to Christianity at a rate higher than Jews anywhere else in the Dual Monarchy, Prague and Budapest included. To some extent the freer urban environment did accelerate disaffection from Judaism and the Jewish people. Opportunities for career and marriage available to the already baptized certainly sweetened the renunciation of Jewishness. (Rozenblit, p. 127-8)

Conversion to Christianity seldom resulted from a change in theological belief; it was, for the most part, to further one's career or facilitate marriage to a non-Jewish partner (Rozenblit, p. 136). Freud's disciple, Otto Rank, is a typical example. At the age of fifteen he had decided that he was no longer going to be Jewish and, in 1907, formally converted to Catholicism so that the courts would then allow him to change his name from Rosenfeld to Rank.[4] But, in 1918, he renounced Catholicism so that he could marry a Jewish girl.

However, most of those who converted soon found themselves players in a self-inflicted tragi-comedy. They did not give due account to the ineradicable Austrian anti-Semitism. As Rozenblit (1983) so aptly points out:

> The final ingredient in total assimilation—unprejudiced acceptance—was never widely available to the Jews in Vienna.

The converted Jews, for the most part, lived in Jewish neighborhoods, maintained the same Jewish friendships, and participated in cultural activities with other Jews.

Prior to 1848 the pathways for intellectual and emotional expression and advancement for Jewish youth were not only inhibited by political restrictions but also were limited to Judaic studies and practice. It should be noted that the only texts permitted for study were the Bible, Talmud, and commentaries related to them. The enlightenment coupled with emancipation created a vacuum in their self-image and identity. The self-hating East European identity was replaced by a new but yet very old world, that of antiquity. There were now new gods, new heroes that coexisted with those of the Bible, that pre-dated the rabbis of the Talmud.

> Though it assumed unusual proportions in Freud, this cult of antiquity was not at all unusual at the time; it was widespread among Germans and among assimilated Jews as well, for it provided neutral ground on which the two could meet. It was safer to discuss "immortal" truths than thorny questions of religion and politics. (Robert, 1976)

The central core of the curriculum in the *Gymnasium* were the courses in Greek and Latin. Every graduate had to possess a mastery of these languages and their literature. German language and literature, history, geography, mathematics, physics, religion and elective courses in French and English constituted the remainder of the curriculum. Plato, Aristotle, Sophocles, Horace, Julius Caesar and others took their places in the pantheon of heroes that was previously occupied by those of the Bible and Talmud. Ostow (1982, p. 143) is critical of Freud for choosing non-Jewish heroes such as Hannibal and Alexander, and non-Jewish classical writings over Jewish ones, but it should be remembered that this behavior was not unusual; Freud was a product of his time and place (Ellenberger, 1970; Robert, 1976). This phenomenon was true of most educated and assimilated middle-class Viennese Jews. Yet, Freud retained his underlying Jewishness. As Robert (1976) points out:

> ... it is striking to note that when writing about the more serious and more painful events of his life he drew on Jewish lore for his metaphors and illustrations, while in connection with more superficial occurrences, he tended to draw on the fund of classical quotations that every educated German has at his disposal. (p. 36)

> Whenever Freud's existence was threatened in any way, it was only in stereotyped trivial situations that he quoted his classical authors, and what he quoted always came as a surprise to him, as though he could contemplate it only at the distance imposed by respect and by the magic of foreignness. (p. 56)

Alexander the Great and Alexander Freud—Myth vs. Reality

The naming of Freud's youngest brother, Alexander, reveals a great deal of the complexity of both Jacob and Sigmund's relationship to Judaism and to each other. Freud family legend has it that young Sigmund himself selected the name Alexander. Freud's sister, Anna, whose memory has not always tallied with the facts, nevertheless provides the basis for this belief:

> My father, a self-taught scholar, was really brilliant. He would discuss with us children, especially Sigmund, all manner of questions and problems. We called these sessions "the family council." When the youngest son was born, father took Sigmund aside to consult him on the name to be given to the boy. I remember how Sigmund enthusiastically chose Alexander, basing his selection on Alexander's generosity and prowess as a general, and how he recited the whole story of the Macedonian's triumph in support of his choice. His choice of name was accepted. (Bernays, 1940)

Accepting Anna's story, biographers Shengold (1979), Krull (1986) and McGrath (1986) have attempted to explain Freud's choice of the name Alexander through a psychodynamic formulation based on the vicissitudes of the name 'Philipp'. It is based on Freud's *persons with bird beaks* dream. The dream was stimulated by the sexual stories and woodcuts in the *Philipp-son* Bible. Two of Freud's associations to the dream are to his maternal grandfather who died during Amalia's pregancy with Alexander, and that he was first informed about the facts of life by a janitor's son whose name was Philipp. In addition, it is postulated that Freud's half-brother Philipp, who was one year older than Amalia, was thought by him to have been the father of Alexander. This fantasy may have received support from the biblical story of Joseph's half-brother Reuben having had sexual intercourse with one of Jacob's concubines. Significantly, Alexander the Great was the son of a man named Philipp.

Thus Freud moved both toward and away from Judaism by selecting a name that embodied the classical culture he loved but that nevertheless contained associations to the Bible as well as to his Jewish identity. That the naming of Alexander may have been tied to Freud's association with the *Philipp*-son Bible—specifically with an illustration of Egypt—uncannily binds together Freud's concern with the biblical, the Greek, and the Egyptian which would not find direct expression until *Moses and Monotheism*.

But the choice of Alexander may have been even more overdetermined and may point even more directly to Freud's Jewish background. A document in the Sigmund Freud Archives in the Library of Congress (Figure 2) indicates that Jacob Freud may have had the name Alexander in mind from the start. Figure 2 is a copy of the page of the birth register of the *Israelitische Kultusgemeinde* (commonly called the *Gemeinde* and henceforth, in this book, to be referred to as the *IKG*) of Vienna on which is recorded the number of the birth, the date, the secular and Hebrew and/or Yiddish name of the new-born, the name of the father and mother. Note on the bottom line the date '19 April, 1866' and then the name of the newborn. The secular name is 'Alexander Gottfried Ephraim Freud and the Hebrew name is 'Alexander Hamkhunah Ziskind' which, translated, means 'Alexander, also known as, Ziskind'. In Yiddish 'Ziskind' means 'sweet child'.[5]

It has been the custom for centuries for *Ashkenazi* Jews to name their newborn after deceased relatives. The patriarch of the Freud family was Ziskind Hoffman (born 1776), Jacob Freud's maternal grandfather. He founded the textile business into which he took his grandson Jacob and which Jacob eventually took over completely after his death. Jacob's paternal grandfather was named Ephraim (Figure 4). It is thus apparent that the newborn son was named after both grandfathers. As noted in the birth announcement, written in the Freud family Bible (Figure 4), Sigmund was given the name 'Shlomo Sigismund', the first being the Hebrew and the second, either German, Polish, or Yiddish.[6]

In all the available documents the family patriarch signed his name in Hebrew as 'Ziskind Hoffman'. It is certain that all Jewish children were given more than one name, often in both the Hebrew and Yiddish languages. Gicklhorn (1969) refers to him as 'Abraham Ziskind' but gives no reference for it.[7] The pairing of the names 'Alexander Ziskind' and 'Alexander Ephraim' was fairly common among Jews for many centuries.[8] Jewish sons have been named after the Greek hero since Talmudic times. There is even a rabbi in

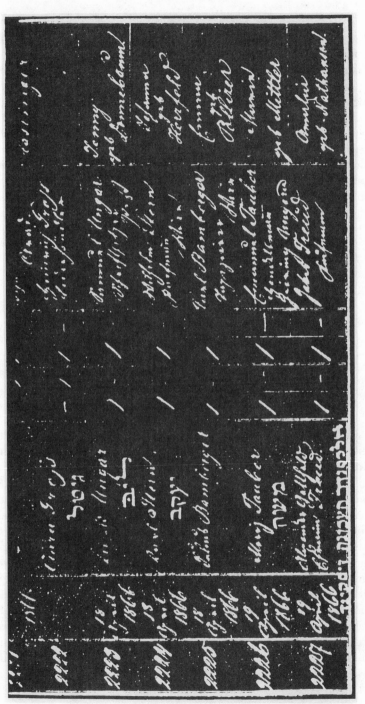

Figure 2. Birth Registry of the IKG — Alexander Freud. Courtesy of The Sigmund Freud Archives, Inc. and the Library of Congress.

the Talmud who is named Alexander. The Hungarian 'Sandor' derives from Alexander the Great.

The introduction of Greek culture into Syria and Egypt has been attributed to Alexander the Great (356-323 B.C.E.). Of all the non-Jews throughout history (leaving aside the question of Moses for the moment) he is considered to have contributed more than any other to the positive development of Judaism as exemplified (according to legend) in his attitude and numerous favors bestowed upon the Jews. The Talmud relates numerous legends about him as can be seen in Tractates *Yoma* 69a, *Ta'anit* 31b-32b, and *Sanhedrin* 91a. One legend of relevance pertains to Alexander's visit to the Temple in Jerusalem.

> Alexander's kindness to the Jews was acknowledged by them in unique fashion. Josippon says the name Alexander was given to every boy born to the priests of Judea during the year following Alexander the Great's arrival in Jerusalem. Others say it was a stratagem on the part of Simon the Just. For Alexander, perceiving the reverence in which the Temple was held by the Jews, requested of Simon that an image of himself be placed near the alter. Simon, however, explained, "Our God has prohibited all images in His Temple. But let not the king think therefore that his honor is not precious to us. We shall do something in your honor that will be an everlasting remembrance. Every son born this year to the priests, the descendants of Levi, shall be named Alexander in your honor, so that the name of Alexander will be carried forward through all future generations. (Nadich, 1983, pp. 39-40)[9]

It is indeed puzzling as to why 'Gottfried Ephraim' was not written in Hebrew in the birth register (Figure 2). The only plausible reason is that there was not enough space in the structural format of the register itself. As can be seen, the name 'Ziskind' runs into the column of the birth date.

A 'family council' may well have taken place, but Jacob Freud may have had other motivations which he apparently may not have revealed to the ten-year old Sigmund, the desire to enhance the youngster's feeling of importance. Or, he may have given the 'council' a choice of names that were all familial. But the choice must have gratified both Freuds for different yet connected reasons. Jacob Freud was fulfilling Jewish tradition, as he had in naming Freud "Shlomo," by passing on the names of his grandparents. For young Sigmund, Alexander may have been a kind of forerunner to Moses as he is depicted in *Moses and Monotheism*: a redeemer who comes from outside the tradition but who somehow becomes incorporated into it, thus providing a perfect focus for Freud's ambivalence. Like the Egyptian name Moses, the Greek name Alexander became a Jewish one.

Adolescence—Expressions of a Negative Jewish Identity

Freud was a product of times when the upwardly mobile middle class looked upon the Greek and Roman classical period with its accompanying literature with the most intense yearning and reverence. Their mastery was deemed to be an ineradicable sign of supreme intelligence and respectability. In contrast, Jacob Freud, to his son, was the expression, par excellance, of the Eastern European Jew. The pejorative significance of the geographic, religious and cultural origins of Jacob and Amalia did little to augment the self-esteem of Sigmund. I cannot completely agree with Rainey (1971) that Freud's antagonism to Judaism was limited to its religious aspects. For the most part, he was proud of being Jewish and considered himself to be a member of the Jewish community. He was not only a member of the B'nai Brith but also a dues-paying member of the IKG until his forced departure from Vienna in 1938. However, this pertains to the surface, to the conscious life of Freud. Underneath it, I believe, he had the same ambivalent conflicts about his Jewishness that others in the same class of Jews did. As I will presently demonstrate, his adolescence was marked by an ethnic self-hatred that would make an anti-Semite proud. It was only with passing age that these feelings mellowed and were replaced with a feeling of Jewish pride.

In the introduction to the Hebrew edition of *Totem and Taboo* (S.E.:13), Freud, referring to himself in the third person, wrote:

> If the question were put to him: "Since you have abandoned all these common characteristics of your countrymen, what is there left to you that is Jewish?" He would reply: "A very great deal, and probably its very essence." He could not now express that essence clearly in words; but someday, no doubt, it will become accessible to the scientific mind.

To exemplify the dilemma that faced Freud, Robert (1976) writes:

> In 1921 Franz Kafka wrote to Max Brod on the subject of a book by Karl Kraus, which, Kafka believed, revealed the ingrained defects of German-Jewish literature and on a deeper level the crisis of the assimilated Jews, corroded from within by insoluble problems of 'language': "What appeals to me more than psychoanalysis (in this book) is the observation that the father complex from which more than one Jew draws his spiritual nourishment relates not to the innocent father but to the father's Judaism. What most of those who began to write in German wanted was to break with Judaism, generally with the vague approval of their fathers (this vagueness is the revolting part of it). That is what they wanted, but their hind legs were bogged down in their father's Judaism, and their front legs could find no new ground. The resulting despair was their inspiration. (pp. 8-9)

The following are examples of Freud's feelings about his Jewish identity beginning with his stormy adolescence through the calmer perspective of older age.

At the age of sixteen, Freud went to Freiberg to visit with his childhood friend, Emil Fluss. When he returned to Vienna he wrote to Fluss on September 18, 1872:

> Our first travelling companion was a poor soul ... I ended up in the company of a most venerable old Jew and his correspondingly old wife with their melancholy languorous darling daughter and cheeky young 'hopeful' son. Their company was even more unpalatable. A casual remark I made, red with rage, could not sweeten my boredom. People are not as different as they look and they can easily be divided into definable categories by the way they think and act. This is only natural, for similar circumstances always result in similar products. (As you can see, I have not spared you my remark my original intention notwithstanding.)
>
> Now, this Jew talked in the same way as I had heard thousands of others talk before, even in Freiberg. His very face seemed familiar—he was typical. So was the boy, with whom he discussed religion. He was cut from the cloth from which fate makes swindlers when the time is ripe; cunning, mendacious, kept by his adoring relatives in the belief that he is a great talent, but unprincipled and without character. A cook from Bohemia with the most perfect pug-face I have ever seen put the lid on it. I have enough of this lot. In the course of the conversation I learned that Madame Jewess and family hailed from Meseritsch: the proper compost-heap for this sort of weed. (International Journal of Psychoanalysis, 50: 419-427, 1969; 'Some Early Unpublished Letters of Freud')

The stridency of this letter prompted Gay (1988) to comment: "A professional Jew-baiter could hardly have expressed it more forcefully." (p. 19) This overt expression of self-hatred was to re-emerge, in sublimated and projected form, towards the end of his life in *Moses and Monotheism*.

> In an enigmatic letter to Arnold Zweig [August 18, 1933], he declared Moses to have been "a strong anti-Semite" who "made no secret of it. Perhaps," Freud speculated, "he really was an Egyptian. And surely he was right." The remark, virtually unique for Freud, underscores his bitter mood in those years; he detested any signs of abject Jewish self-hatred in others and did not suspect that he was in the slightest guilty of it himself. Plainly, Moses was for Freud a dangerous figure no less than an enticing one. (Gay, 1988, p. 605)

Aside from the self-hatred so clearly evident in the letter to Fluss, there does not appear to be any conscious awareness of the significance of what was being written. The Ḥasidic family reminded him of his own parents, feelings toward whom were then projected onto them. There were many other Ortho- dox Jewish families who lived in Freiberg, though all were not Ḥasidic. In typical adolescent hyperbole, he exaggerates the number, "I had heard thou- sands of others . . ." Meseritsch is a town in Moravia on the railway line between Freiberg and Vienna. It was also the home of an important Ḥasidic dynasty.

It is important to note that this visit to Freiberg took place about seven years after a tragic scandal occurred in the Freud family. Freud referred to the event as one which made his father's hair turn gray. Jacob Freud's brother Josef was arrested, tried and convicted for the possession and sale of counterfeit money (Gicklhorn, 1976; Krull, 1986; Gay, 1988). Jones (1953, I:4) may not have been aware of the full nature of the crime when he wrote that it was a minor affair for which he received only a monetary fine as punishment. Josef was actually sentenced to ten years in jail. In response to numerous pleas by rabbis, friends, and political leaders he was released after serving four years. The counterfeit money was traced to Manchester, England, and there is some evidence that Jacob Freud and his sons Emanuel and Philipp may have been involved. No criminal charges, however, were filed against them.

The boy whom Freud describes so disparagingly may well be a projection of his own unconscious image of himself, "cunning, mendacious, kept by his adoring relatives in the belief that he is a great talent, but unprincipled and without character." After all, Freud had absolutely no way of determining whether the boy actually had these characteristics. It may also have been a case of a displacement of feelings toward Uncle Josef as well as a transference of a warded-off perception of his father and half-siblings as a result of the possible involvement in the counterfeiting scheme.

On March 17, 1873 he again wrote to Emil Fluss:

> . . . but to leave this oracular tome once and for all, I want to tell you that we had a little theatre performance at our house on the occasion of Purim (which, moreover, fell on the 13th of March, so sacred to us all; the day, too, when Caesar was murdered). A lady from the neighborhood with time hanging heavily on her hands, drilled my sisters, my little brother and a few other children into actors and actresses, thus forcing us to earn our Purim dinner (well known to be not among the worst) the hard way by an artistic treat of the strangest kind. May you never find yourself in the dilemma of being the brother of such ambitious actresses!

Freud is unforgiving of his parents, especially his father, for their Jewishness. The Oedipal conflict that motivated these comments breaks through, though in mild disguise. Of all the possible associations that he could have had to Purim, he thinks of the murder of the father of a nation,

Julius Caesar. (There may also have been some retrospective expression about his brother Julius who died when Sigmund was two years old but on a different date.) So there is Oedipal murder and castration (or death) as punishment. What is nearly always a most festive and enjoyable holiday for children is turned by the adolescent Freud into a miserable one, being 'forced' to earn the Purim dinner which, though felt to be good, is described in a negative and hostile context.

On June 16, 1873, he wrote to Fluss:

> ... Oh, Emil, why are you such a prosaic Jew? Journeymen imbued with Christian-German fervour have composed beautiful lyrical poetry in similar circumstances.

We already see here the direction Freud will later take in attempting to resolve his conflicts about his Jewish identity. In the Austria of the latter half of the nineteenth century and well into the twentieth, all things noble, pure, great, and perfect were deemed by the university-educated intelligentsia to be both Christian and German. No wonder that Richard Wagner was so popular and influential. Schopenhauer and Nietzche contributed to this mode of thought. It was not too long after this that Freud joined the *Leseverein der deutschen Studenten Wiens*, a radical society, one of whose goals was the integration of the Austro-Hungarian Empire with Germany. The ranks of this society included anti-Semites as well as Jews who rationalized their anti-Semitism by blaming it on Eastern European Jews and allying themselves with the "German" contingent.[10]

This self-hating adolescent phase eventually gave way to a somewhat more positive Jewish identity. The acquisitions of a complete set of the Talmud, in both the original language and translation, in the last decade of his life, is a striking example. His activity in the B'nai Brith, the Zionist sympathies expressed in his being named to the Board of Governors of The Hebrew University in Jerusalem, his permitting his sons to join *Kadimah* (the student Zionist organization) when they were attending the university, his profound and empathic understanding of Jewish wit, his frequent references to Jewish tradition and Biblical texts, among other manifestations, are all evidence of this change. During the Nazi occupation of Vienna, Freud made the following comment:

> After the destruction of the Temple in Jerusalem by Titus, Rabbi Jochanan ben Zakkai asked for permission to open a school at Jabneh for the study of the Torah. We are, after all, used to persecution by our history, tradition, and some of us by personal experience. (Jones, 1957, III: 221)

In May 1931 Freud wrote an addendum to a pre-printed 'Thank You' letter to Dr. David Feuchtwang in response to the latter's congratulatory note on the occasion of his seventy-fifth birthday (Figure 3). The pathos of the nostalgic, and possibly confessional, tone of this letter is remarkable. There appears to be a shared background between the avowed atheist and the Orthodox Rabbi. This was a time of his life when he was realistically concerned with his longevity as he had been suffering from, and feeling the effects of, an incurable cancer of his jaw for some time. Feuchtwang was a rabbi in Vienna from 1903 until his death in 1936. In 1927 he became the Chief Rabbi of Vienna. Nothing else is known of their relationship except that they lived near each other. Jozef Philip Hes, a psychiatrist in Israel, accidently met the daughter of this rabbi in a nursing home for the aged. She gave him a copy of this letter and the following is his translation (Hes, 1986):

> Thank you for your kind participation on my 75th birthday.
>
> Vienna, May 1931
>
> Highly esteemed Doctor,
>
> Your words aroused a special echo in me, which I do not need to explain to you. In some place in my soul, in a very hidden corner, I am a fanatical Jew. I am very much astonished to discover myself as such in spite of all efforts to be unprejudiced and impartial. What can I do against it at my age?[11]

Vitz (1988, p.201), unaware of the letter to the Chief Rabbi of Vienna, astutely observed that whenever Freud referred to his Jewish identity in his published correspondence or writings he would distance himself from it. He always used the past tense, e.g., "I was a Jew", "I became a Jew", etc. Here, in the declining years of his life, he finally affirms his identity, in the present tense, to Rabbi Feuchtwang, "I *am* a fanatical Jew" (italics mine). He was 'homeward bound'.

Shortly before leaving Vienna for London in 1938 Freud wrote to his son Ernst, who was already there (letter of May 12, 1938):

> I sometimes compare myself with the old Jacob who, when a very old man, was taken by his children to Egypt, as Thomas Mann is to describe in his next novel. Let us hope that it won't also be followed by an exodus from Egypt. It is high time Ahasverus came to rest somewhere. ('Letters of Sigmund Freud', edited by Ernst L. Freud, 1960)

Ahasverus refers to the legend of the Wandering Jew (a character in no way related to King Ahasverus in the Book of Esther). It may remotely have its basis in the Book of Matthew of The New Testament but the legend made

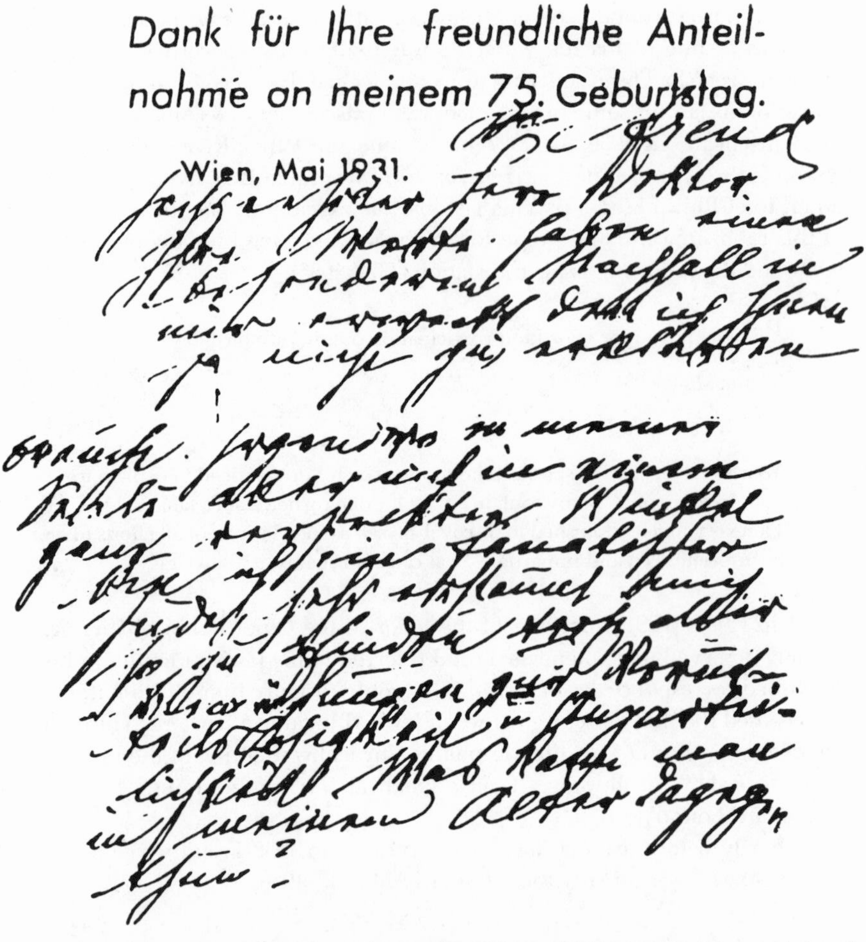

Dank für Ihre freundliche Anteil-
nahme an meinem 75. Geburtstag.

Wien, Mai 1931.

Figure 3. Sigmund Freud's letter to Chief Rabbi of Vienna, 1931. Reproduced by permission of A.W. Freud et al., by arrangement with Mark Paterson & Associates, Colchester.

its first appearance in Germany in 1602. It started with the publication of a four-leaved pamphlet, author unknown, entitled *Kurze Beschreibung und Erdzahlung von einem Juden mit Namen Ahasverus*. The legend then spread rapidly throughout Europe with many different editions and minor changes in the plot but its essence remained unaltered. Ahasverus, an imaginary figure, was a shoemaker in Jerusalem. When Jesus was on his way to the crucifixion, Ahasverus taunted him. In anger, Jesus told him to "go on forever till I return", i.e., he was condemned to wander from land to land till the Day of Judgment.

The wandering Jew was considered to be immortal and in post-Reformation Europe became the object of hate and persecution. This was the doomed sinner, the eyewitness to the crucifixion. One could see how easy it was for the superstitious believer to find a scapegoat in the nearest Jew. He was also referred to as *Der Ewige-Jude*, i.e., the immortal, or eternal Jew. (The Jewish Encyclopedia, Vol. XII: 462-3, 1906)

But more important than Freud's description of himself as the wandering Jew is his identification with the biblical Jacob. No longer the rebellious son, the dream interpreter Joseph who figured so prominently in Freud's earlier self-representations, he has become the beleagured patriarch led by his children. And like his real father Jacob, who left the city of his youth, who suffered the insults of anti-Semites, so Freud has become a wanderer, an *Ahasverus*, an object of ridicule. The reference to the wandering Jew, Freud's humorous acknowledgement of his inescapable Jewish fate, bridges the gap between Jacob the patriarch and Jacob Freud and allows Sigmund an identification with both at once. It is a faint echo of a more powerful identification enacted in *Moses and Monotheism* in which Freud projects himself into the role of Moses and at the same time the role of the slayers of Moses, the role of the father and the role of the son.

CHAPTER 3

The Freud Family Bible

The custom of recording births and deaths inside the family Bible was common among Jews and Christians throughout Europe. The practice allowed family history to intersect with the religious history of the entire people; in passing down one record the other was also preserved. As already noted, Freud maintained something of that tradition by presenting his father's Bible to his son, Ernst. But those two histories—the individual and the Biblical—would, for Freud, intersect once more toward the end of his life in a far more complicated fashion. *Moses and Monotheism*, Freud's last major work, re-imagines a biblical episode so that it takes on the personal meaning of family history. The inscription no longer stands separate from the Bible.

But that late work represents a fusion of elements Freud would struggle with for much of his life. To understand it we must first understand something of Freud's father and Freud's relationship to him. The Bible Jacob presented to his son, and the inscription it contained, becomes the Rosetta Stone whose language we must master before we can decode Freud's own ambivalent and deeply personal message in *Moses and Monotheism*.

Sigmund Freud was quite open about the importance of his father to him. In a letter to Fliess (November 2, 1896) he wrote:

> By one of those dark pathways behind the official consciousness the old man's death has affected me deeply. I valued him highly, understood him very well, and with his peculiar mixture of deep wisdom and fantastic light-heartedness he had a significant effect on my life. By the time he died, his life had long been over, but in [my]inner self the whole past has been reawakened by this event. I now feel quite uprooted.
> ('Letters', 1985)

In the preface to the second edition of *The Interpretation of Dreams* (S.E. IV:xxvi), written in 1908, he states:

For this book has a further significance for me personally—a significance which I only grasped after I had completed it. It was, I found, a portion of my own self-analysis, my reaction to my father's death—that is to say, to the most important event, the most poignant loss, of a man's life. Having discovered that this was so, I felt unable to obliterate the traces of this experience.

On February 12, 1920 Freud wrote a letter of condolence, in English, to Ernest Jones on the occasion of the death of the Jones' father:

I was about your age when my father died (43) and it revolutionized my soul.[1]

Jacob Freud was born in Tysmenitz, a city in Galicia, in 1815, into a traditional Orthodox Jewish family. He had no formal secular education (as was true of all Jews in that area and at that time) but did receive a thorough religious education, encompassing the study not only of ritual observance but also biblical and talmudic texts, at first in a *Ḥeder*, the Eastern European Jewish equivalent to a primary school, and then, almost certainly in later childhood and adolescence, in a *Yeshiva*, which is a much larger Talmudic academy. He entered the textile business of his maternal grandfather, Abraham Ziskind Hoffman, which necessitated prolonged stays in the distant city of Freiberg in order to facilitate the commercial exchange between the two cities. He eventually settled in Freiberg with his two children from his first marriage to Sally Kanner, Emanuel and Philipp, in 1852. It appears from the Freiberg city records that he arrived with a wife named Rebecca, suggesting that Sally either died prior to settling in the city and that there was a brief second marriage to Rebecca or that an error in recording was made and that Rebecca was really Sally. In any event, in the marriage certificate of Jacob and Amalia, as noted in the Vienna Israelitic Congregation in 1855, he is listed as a widower (Krull, 1986).

After the death of Sally (or Rebecca) he married Amalia Nathanson who was twenty-one years his junior. Amalia, too, came from a traditional Orthodox family that claimed a long line of prominent rabbis and talmudic scholars in the family pedigree. Her family emigrated from Brody, which was in Galicia, to Vienna when she was a young girl. It is unlikely that she had any formal education and whatever knowledge she did possess was either from her parents or self-taught. What is worthy of note was the fact that she never mastered the German language.

Theodor Reik [1971] used to visit her in the late years of her life and he observed that she spoke a Galician Yiddish and had only a rudimentary knowledge of German. This was not due to senility as her mental faculties were quite clear to the end of her life. Henry Bondi, as a child, was taken by his mother to visit Amalia and he, too, remembers her speaking only a

Galician Yiddish. This would imply that Yiddish must have been Sigmund Freud's first language as, assuredly, both parents spoke it at home. In view of this information, how are we to explain the following episode? Roback (1957, pp. 30, 34) wrote a letter to Freud in 1930 commenting: "It would please me to know that you speak, read, or at least understand Yiddish." Several weeks later Freud responded, "I have never learned or spoken Yiddish." Freud's response is perplexing and difficult to accept.

An early sign of Jacob Freud's attraction to the Haskalah, i.e., the Enlightenment as it affected the Jews of Europe, which represented the infusion of Western and Central European thought into the Eastern European traditional Orthodox way of life, was his acquisition of the Philippson Bible. Ludwig Philippson was a Reform rabbi with a thorough education in history, archaeology and classics, who translated the Old Testament into German beneath which he added commentary in German. The first edition was published between 1839 and 1854. The second and third editions were published in 1858 and 1864 respectively. In 1848, Jacob Freud obtained a copy of the first edition. In February 1856 Jacob Freud made note in this Bible, in Hebrew, of the death of his father, Shlomo. Three months later he noted the birth of his first child by Amalia, and named him Shlomo after his recently deceased father (Fig. 4-6). This first-born son was also given the secular name of Sigismund which was shortened in adolescence by the bearer himself to Sigmund. On the occasion of Sigmund's thirty-fifth birthday, Jacob had the Bible rebound, and wrote a very sensitive dedication, again in Hebrew, to his son who was now beginning to achieve fame (Fig. 7-9). It is difficult to understand why Jacob did not make any notation in the Bible of the births of any subsequent children or even of the death of Julius, who was born when Sigmund was eleven months old and died seven months later.

Several translations into English of these Hebrew inscriptions have been made. The most recent (Ernst Freud, Lucie Freud, and Ilse Grubrich-Simitis, 1978) was first translated into German and then from the German into English. Due to the difficulty in reading Jacob Freud's written Hebrew script, the translations differ from each other, resulting in somewhat different interpretations. In order to overcome this problem a new translation has been made directly from the Hebrew with the written script first transposed into print so that the informed reader can make comparisons between them. In these inscriptions Jacob Freud demonstrates a mastery of biblical texts and an attempt has been made to trace the inscriptions to their specific sources in the Bible. The last line on the page containing the death and birth announcements had never been translated because of its apparent illegibility. It has now been deciphered, transposed into Hebrew print and translated.

Such demonstrated mastery of the Bible, as manifested in these few written Hebrew texts, is not unusual in an innately intelligent man who

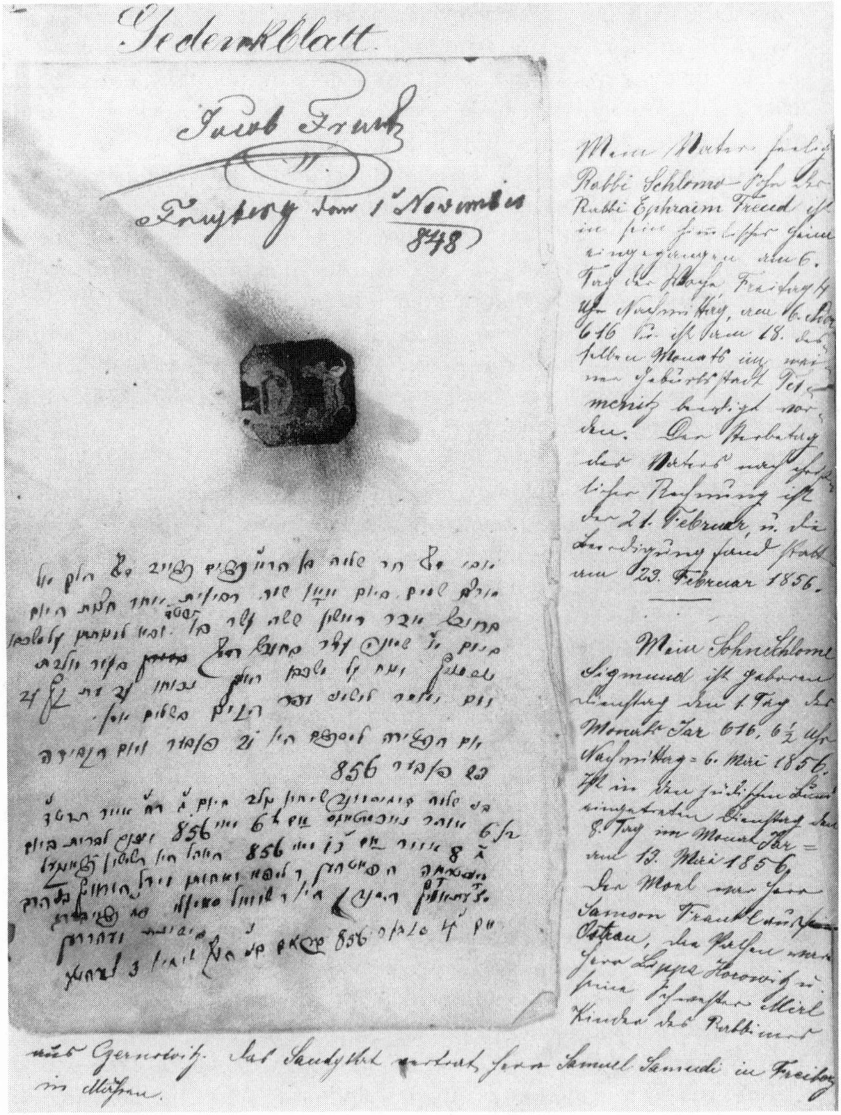

Figure 4. Gedenkblatt, death and birth announcements. Courtesy of the Freud Museum, London.

אבי ז״ל הר׳ שלמה בן הר׳ אפרים פרייד ז״ל הלך אל

ארצת שמים[1] ביום וואו שעה רביעית אחר חצות היום

בחודש אדר ראשון ששה עשר בו תרט״ז ובא למנוחתו[2] על משכבו[3]

ביום א׳ שמונה עשר בחודש הנ״ל בעיר מולדתי

טיסמיניץ   ינוח על משכבו הולך נכוחו[4] עד עת קץ[5] עד

יום יאמר לישיני עפר הקיצו[6] בשלום אמן

יום הפטירה למספרם הי׳ 21 פעבער ויום הקבורה

23 פעבער 856

בני שלמה סיגיסמונד שיחי׳ נולד ביום ג׳ ר״ח אייר תרט״ז

6/2 אוהר נאכמיטאגס אם 6 מאי 856 ונכנס לברית ביום

ג׳ 8 אייר אם 13 מאי 856 המוהל הי׳ ר׳ שמשון פראנקעל

מאסטרא הפאטהען ר׳ ליפא ואחותו מירל הורוויץ בני הרב

מצערנאוויץ הסנדק היה ר׳ שמואל סאמועלי פה פרייבורג

במדינת מעהררען

אם 4 .... 856 בעקאם בני הנ״ל שיחי׳ 3 צעהנע

[1] ארצת שמים — השו׳ ארץ חיים, תהלים כ״זי י״ג

[2] ובא למנוחתו — השו׳ והיתה מנוחתו כבוד, ישעי׳ י״א י׳:

[3] ובא למנוחתו על משכבו — השו׳ תפלת א־ל מלא רחמים: וינוח בשלום על משכבו

[4] ינוח על משכבו הולך נכוחו — ישעי׳ נ״ז ב׳

[5] עד עת קץ — דניאל י״א ל״ה, שם י״ב ד׳

[6] לישיני עפר הקיצו — ר׳ דניאל י״ב ב׳: ורבים מישני אדמת עפר יקיצו

Figure 5. Transposition of Hebrew script to print.

Commemorative Page in the Freud Family Bible

My father, of blessed memory, Reb Shlomo son of Reb Ephraim Freud, of blessed memory, went to the land of heaven[1] on the sixth day of the week [i.e., Friday] at four o'clock in the afternoon on the sixteenth day of the month of Adar I, 5616, and came to his resting place[2,3] on the first day of the week [i.e., Sunday] on the eighteenth day of the same month in the city of my birth, Tysmenitz. He who walked a straight course shall have peace on his resting place[4] until the time of the end[5], until the day when He shall say to those who sleep in dust[6]: "Awake in peace." Amen.

The day of death, according to the general calender [literally: their reckoning], was February 21 and the day of burial February 23, [1]856.

My son Shlomo Sigismund, long may he live, was born on the third day of the week [i.e., Tuesday], the first day of the month of Iyaar, 5616, at 6:30 P.M., on the sixth day of May, [1]856, and entered into the covenant on the third day of the week, the eighth day of Iyaar, the thirteenth of May, [1]856. The mohel was Reb Samson Frankl of Ostrau, the godparents were Reb Lippa and his sister of Mirl Horowitz, children of the Rabbi from Czernowitz. The sandek was Reb Samuel Samueli from here in Freiberg, Moravia.

On the fourth of [?] [1]856 my son mentioned above, long may he live, got three teeth.

Translated from Hebrew
by Rabbi Jules Harlow

Figure 6. Translation of Gedenkblatt into English.

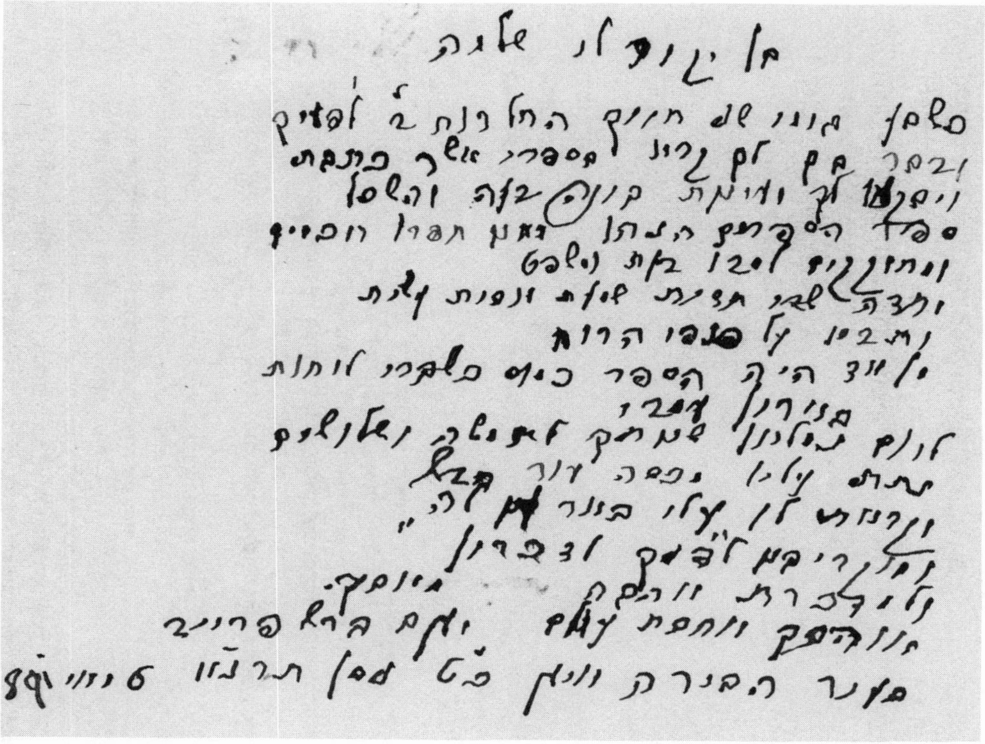

Figure 7. Jacob Freud's Hebrew dedication in honor of Sigmund's 35th birthday. Courtesy of the Freud Museum, London.

בן יקר לי שלמה[1]

כשבע בימי שני חייך[2] החל רוח ה׳ לפעמך[3]

ודבר בך: לך, קרא בספרי אשר כתבתי[4]

ויבקעו לך מעינות[5] בינה דעה והשכל[6]

ספר הספרים הנהו בארו חפרו חכמים[7]

ומחוקקים[8] למדו דעת ומשפט

מחזה שדי חזית[9] שמעת ורבות עשית[10]

ותדא על כנפי הרוח[11]

מן אז היה הספר כמוס[12] בשברי לוחות

בארון עמדי[13]

ליום נמלאו שנותיך לחמשה ושלושים

נתתי עליו מכסה עור חדש[14]

וקראתי לו עלי באר ענו לה[15]

ואקריבנו לפניך לזכרון

ולמזכרת אהבה   מאביך

אוהבך אהבת עולם[16]   יעקב בר״ש פרייד

בעיר הבירה וויען כ״ט ניסן תרנ״א 6 מאי 891

---

[1] בן יקר לי — ירמי׳ ל״א י״ט: הבן יקיר לי אפרים

[2] בימי שני חייך — בראשית מ״ז ט: ימי שני חיי (על יעקב)

[3] החל רוח ה׳ לפעמך — שופטים י״ג כ״ה: ותחל רוח ה׳ לפעמו

[4] בספרי אשר כתבתי — שמות ל״ב ל״ב: מספרך אשר כתבת

[5] ויבקעו לך מעינות — בראשית ז׳ י״א: נבקעו כל מעינות

[6] בינה דעה והשכל — ירמי׳ ג׳ ט״ו: דעה והשכיל (לשון הברכה הרביעית בשמונה עשרה)

[7] בארו חפרו חכמים — במדבר כ״א י״ח: באר חפרוה שרים

[8] ומחוקקים — שם: במחוקק

[9] מחזה שדי חזית — במדבר כ״ד ד׳: מחזה שדי יחזה

[10] רבות עשית — תהלים מ׳ ו׳: רבות עשית

[11] ותדא על כנפי רוח — תהלים י״ח י״א: וידא על כנפי רוח

[12] מן אז היה הספר כמוס — דברים ל״ב ל״ד: הלא הוא כמס עמדי

[13] בשברי לוחת בארון עמדי — דברים י׳ ב׳: הלחות הראשונים אשר שברת ושמתם בארון

[14] מכסה עור חדש — במדבר ד׳ י׳: מכסה עור תחש

[15] עלי באר ענו לה — במדבר כ״א י״ז

[16] אהבת עולם — ירמי׳ ל״א ב׳: ואהבת עולם אהבתיך

Figure 8. Transposition of Hebrew script (dedication) to print.

Jacob Freud's Family Bible Inscription To His Son

My precious son[1] Shlomo
In the seventh of the years of your life[2] the spirit of the Lord first moved you[3]
And spoke to you: Go, read in My book which I have written[4] And fountains
of knowledge, discernment, and wisdom[6] will burst open before you[5].
Behold, it is the Book of books, the well unearthed by sages[7], From which
our rulers[8] drew knowledge and justice.
A vision of the Almighty have you beheld[9]; many things have you heard and
accomplished[10],
Gliding on the wings of the wind [spirit?][11].
Since that time has the Book been sealed up[12] with me like the broken tablets
in the Ark[13].
For the day on which your years amount to thirty-five
Have I covered it with new leather[14].
Calling it: "Spring up, O well; greet it with song!"[15]
And offering it to you as a remembrance,
A reminder of love   From your father
Who loves you with love eternal[16].   Jacob son of Reb Sh. Freud.

In the capital city of Vienna, 29th of Nissan, 5651, May 6, [1]891.

Translated from Hebrew
by Rabbi Jules Harlow

Figure 9. Translation of dedication into English.

comes from a background of such intense biblical literacy and religious observance as that of Jacob Freud. We must remember that the Bible and Talmud were *the* texts for learning, especially for those who did not have the opportunity to acquire secular knowledge. Not only was the Bible taught at a very early age but study of it was expected to continue all of one's life. The entire Pentateuch (the first Five Books of the Old Testament) is divided into roughly fifty-two segments so that it is read and completed in the synagogue in one year and then begun over again. It has been the custom for centuries for Orthodox Jewish men to read and study the particular week's segment on the morning of the Sabbath prior to attending services in the synagogue. This is considered God's word and thus treated with the appropriate reverence. Portions of the weekly chapters are read in the synagogue on the Sabbath afternoon, and on Monday and Thursday mornings.[2]

The family Bible was recently taken out of storage in preparation for the opening of The Freud Museum in London in 1986. It has hitherto been thought that the Bible was from the 1858 edition (Eva Rosenfeld, 1956) but it now appears that it was the 1839 edition and acquired by Jacob Freud some time after that, possibly in 1848 when he was allowed to establish permanent residence in Freiberg. Upon opening the crates of Freud's books the curators of the museum discovered not only the family Bible but, in addition, a complete eight volume set of the 1858 edition of the Philippson Bible which, with the exception of some markings in Volume III (Trosman and Simmons, 1973), is in pristine condition. Freud or his father must have acquired it from someone else because the name of a previous owner, a Rabiner Altmann, is written on the inside cover.

The family Bible may have originally existed in the form of separate volumes but at some point in Freud's childhood or adolescence it was put away. Jacob Freud found it again in a closet and had it rebound into one volume. Presumably, it must have undergone very extensive usage. The rebinding was done poorly, not only in terms of the binding itself but also it appears that the bookbinder did not know much about the Bible. The various books of the Bible are out of their correct order. Like all Hebrew books, this Bible is read from right to left, but the *Book of Kings*, which should follow at a substantial distance in the text, actually precedes the *Book of Genesis* in the Freud family Bible. The title page is missing. This Bible is bound with the pages in the following sequence (from right to left): pp. 423-672 [*2 Samuel* 11, 11-17; to *2 Kings* 18, 28-35]; then pp. 1-966 [*Genesis*; to *Deuteronomy* 31, 3-11].[3]

The written Hebrew inscriptions are on separate sheets of paper that were kept inside the Bible covers. On the first sheet (Figure 4) the word *Gedenkblatt* (Memory Page) appears at the very top, then Jacob Freud's signature, "Freiberg, 1 November, 848". His monogram is on a small piece of paper which has been attached to a larger sheet with a translation into

German of the page's contents to the right of the Hebrew. What is most striking about the Bible is that there are many markings in it, most of them in the Hebrew text. These markings are underlined in red, blue and green pencil (Figure 10). Freud's frequent references (Roback, 1957; letter to Dvosis-Dvir, see Figure 11) to his inability to read Hebrew would appear to rule him out as the source of these markings. However, his acknowledged illiteracy in Hebrew raises more questions than it answers.

The curators of The Freud Museum observed that many of the other books in Freud's library, which according to them, only Sigmund and not Jacob could have read, were similarly underlined in red, blue and green. When Freud's desk was opened recently, red, blue and green pencils were found in the drawer. It is worth noting that this was a lifelong habit of Freud's. In addition to the underlinings in colored pencil, some of the Bible's illustrations have also been colored in by the hand of a child. It is little wonder, then, that these illustrations so impressed the young Freud that they appeared in several of his dreams.

An examination of the original manuscript of *Moses and Monotheism* in the Sigmund Freud Archives of the Library of Congress revealed numerous markings in red pencil which could only have been done by Freud himself. As Figure 4 shows, there is a handwritten German translation to the right of the two Hebrew announcements. It is not known when it was written nor who was the translator. This translation appears to be incomplete.

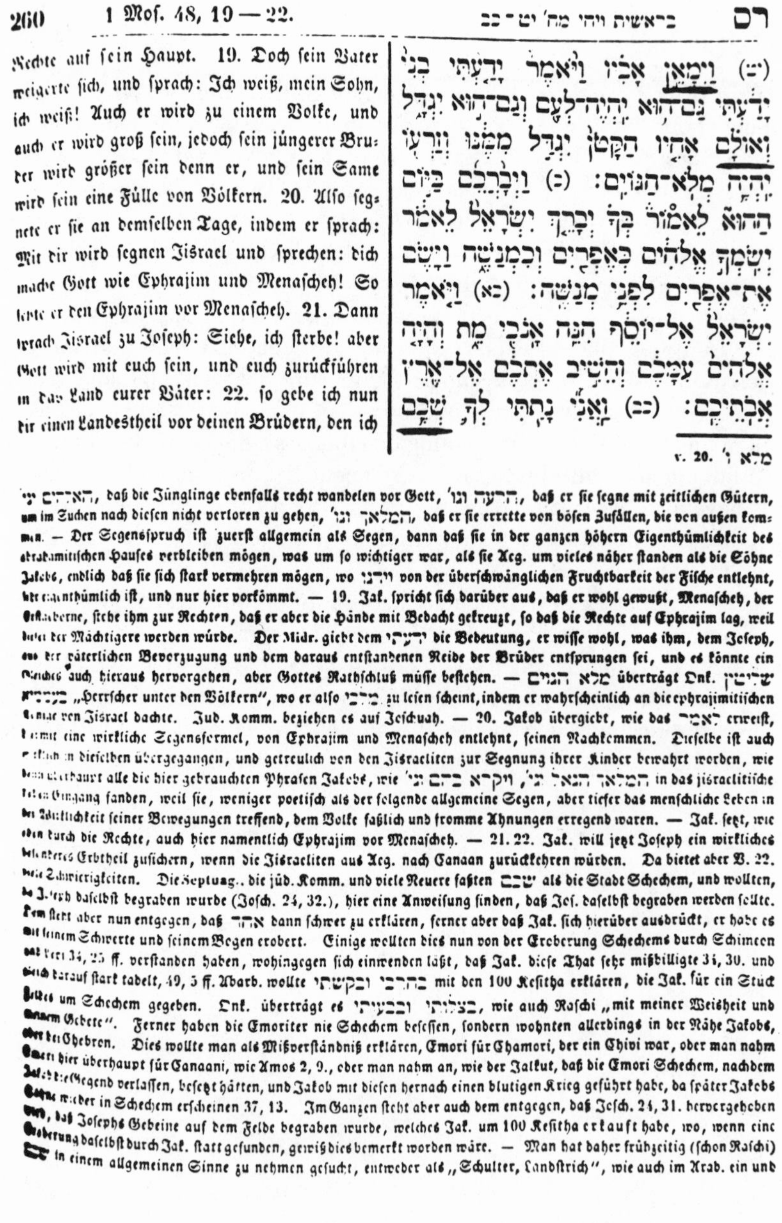

Rechte auf sein Haupt. 19. Doch sein Vater weigerte sich, und sprach: Ich weiß, mein Sohn, ich weiß! Auch er wird zu einem Volke, und auch er wird groß sein, jedoch sein jüngerer Bruder wird größer sein denn er, und sein Same wird sein eine Fülle von Völkern. 20. Also segnete er sie an demselben Tage, indem er sprach: Mit dir wird segnen Israel und sprechen: dich mache Gott wie Ephrajim und Menascheh! So setzte er den Ephrajim vor Menascheh. 21. Dann sprach Israel zu Joseph: Siehe, ich sterbe! aber Gott wird mit euch sein, und euch zurückführen in das Land eurer Väter: 22. so gebe ich nun dir einen Landestheil vor deinen Brüdern, den ich

(יט) וַיְמָאֵן אָבִיו וַיֹּאמֶר יָדַעְתִּי בְנִי
יָדַעְתִּי גַּם הוּא יִהְיֶה לְּעָם וְגַם הוּא יִגְדָּל
וְאוּלָם אָחִיו הַקָּטֹן יִגְדַּל מִמֶּנּוּ וְזַרְעוֹ
יִהְיֶה מְלֹא הַגּוֹיִם: (כ) וַיְבָרֲכֵם בַּיּוֹם
הַהוּא לֵאמוֹר בְּךָ יְבָרֵךְ יִשְׂרָאֵל לֵאמֹר
יְשִׂמְךָ אֱלֹהִים כְּאֶפְרַיִם וְכִמְנַשֶּׁה וַיָּשֶׂם
אֶת אֶפְרַיִם לִפְנֵי מְנַשֶּׁה: (כא) וַיֹּאמֶר
יִשְׂרָאֵל אֶל יוֹסֵף הִנֵּה אָנֹכִי מֵת וְהָיָה
אֱלֹהִים עִמָּכֶם וְהֵשִׁיב אֶתְכֶם אֶל אֶרֶץ
אֲבֹתֵיכֶם: (כב) וַאֲנִי נָתַתִּי לְךָ שְׁכֶם

v. 20. מלא ו'

הַקָּטֹן, daß die Jünglinge ebenfalls recht wandeln vor Gott, וגו וירעה, daß er sie segne mit zeitlichen Gütern, um im Suchen nach diesen nicht verloren zu gehen, המלאך וגו, daß er sie errette von bösen Zufällen, die von außen kommen. — Der Segensspruch ist zuerst allgemein als Segen, dann daß sie in der ganzen höhern Eigenthümlichkeit des abrahamitischen Hauses verbleiben mögen, was um so wichtiger war, als sie Aeg. von vielem näher standen als die Söhne Jakobs, endlich daß sie sich stark vermehren mögen, wo ידגו von der überschwänglichen Fruchtbarkeit der Fische entlehnt, die eigenthümlich ist, und nur hier vorkömmt. — 19. Jak. spricht sich darüber aus, daß er wohl gewußt, Menascheh, der Erstgeborne, stehe ihm zur Rechten, daß er aber die Hände mit Bedacht gekreuzt, so daß die Rechte auf Ephrajim lag, weil bei der Mächtigere werden würde. Der Midr. giebt dem ידעתי die Bedeutung, er wisse wohl, was ihm, dem Joseph, aus der väterlichen Bevorzugung und dem daraus entstandenen Neide der Brüder entsprungen sei, und es könnte ein solches auch hieraus hervorgehen, aber Gottes Rathschluß müsse bestehen. — מלא הגוים überträgt Onk. שלטין, „Herrscher unter den Völkern", wo er also ראשי zu lesen scheint, indem er wahrscheinlich an die ephrajimitischen Könige von Israel dachte. Jud. Komm. bezieht es auf Jeschuah. — 20. Jakob überträgt, wie das ראשי erweist, בך eine wirkliche Segensformel, von Ephrajim und Menascheh entlehnt, seinen Nachkommen. Dieselbe ist auch wirklich in dieselben übergegangen, und getreulich von den Israeliten zur Segnung ihrer Kinder bewahrt worden, wie überhaupt alle die hier gebrauchten Phrasen Jakobs, wie המלאך וגו' וקרא בהם וגו' in das israelitische Leben Eingang fanden, weil sie, weniger poetisch als der folgende allgemeine Segen, aber tiefer das menschliche Leben in der Wirklichkeit seiner Bewegungen treffend, dem Volke faßlich und fromme Ahnungen erregend waren. — Jak. setzt, wie schon durch die Rechte, auch hier namentlich Ephrajim vor Menascheh. — 21. 22. Jak. will jetzt Joseph ein wirkliches bestimmtes Erbtheil zusichern, wenn die Israeliten aus Aeg. nach Canaan zurückkehren würden. Da bietet aber B. 22. große Schwierigkeiten. Die Septuag. die jüd. Komm. und viele Neuere faßten שכם als die Stadt Schechem, und wollten, da Jos. daselbst begraben wurde (Josch. 24, 32.), hier eine Anweisung finden, daß Jos. daselbst begraben werden sollte. Dem steht aber nun entgegen, daß אחד dann schwer zu erklären, ferner aber daß Jak. sich hierüber ausdrückt, er habe es mit seinem Schwerte und seinem Bogen erobert. Einige wollten dies nun von der Eroberung Schechems durch Schimeon und Levi 34, 25 ff. verstanden haben, wogegen sich einwenden läßt, daß Jak. diese That sehr mißbilligte 34, 30. und sich darauf stark tadelt, 49, 5 ff. Abarb. wollte בחרבי ובקשתי mit den 100 Kesitha erklären, die Jak. für ein Stück um Schechem gegeben. Onk. überträgt es בצלותי ובבעותי, wie auch Roschi „mit meiner Weisheit und meinem Gebete". Ferner haben die Emoriter nie Schechem besessen, sondern wohnten allerdings in der Nähe Jakobs, über den Chebron. Dies wollte man als Mißverständniß erklären, Emori für Chamori, der ein Chivi war, oder man nahm Emori hier überhaupt für Canaani, wie Amos 2, 9., oder man nahm an, wie der Jalkut, daß die Emori Schechem, nachdem Jak. die Gegend verlassen, besetzt hätten, und Jakob mit diesen hernach einen blutigen Krieg geführt habe, da später Jakobs Söhne wieder in Schechem erscheinen 37, 13. Im Ganzen steht aber auch dem entgegen, daß Josch. 24, 31. hervorgehoben wird, daß Josephs Gebeine auf dem Felde begraben wurde, welches Jak. um 100 Kesitha erkauft habe, wo, wenn eine Eroberung daselbst durch Jak. stattgefunden, gewiß dies bemerkt worden wäre. — Man hat daher frühzeitig (schon Roschi) שכם in einem allgemeinen Sinne zu nehmen gesucht, entweder als „Schulter, Landstrich", wie auch im Arab. ein und

Figure 10. Photograph of page from the Book of Genesis containing underlined words by Sigmund Freud(?) Courtesy of the Freud Museum, London.

CHAPTER 4

Sigmund Freud's Knowledge of Hebrew

In 1925 Freud wrote the following letter to the editor of The Jewish Press Centre in Zurich (S.E.XIX:291):

> ... I can say that I stand apart from the Jewish religion as from all other religions: that is to say, they are of great significance to me as a subject of scientific interest, but I have no part in them emotionally. On the other hand I have always had a strong feeling of solidarity with my fellow-people, and have always encouraged it in my children as well. We have all remained in the Jewish denomination.
>
> In the time of my youth our free-thinking religious instructors set no store by their pupils' acquiring a knowledge of the Hebrew language and literature. My education in this field was therefore extremely behindhand, as I have since often regretted.

It is hoped that what has been said thus far (and in subsequent portions of this book) justifiably brings into question Freud's comment, "but I have no part in them emotionally". He is certainly correct if he is referring to theological belief, ritual observance and synagogue affiliation. However, the creator of psychoanalysis and all that it implies appears not, for whatever reasons, to have paid sufficient attention to unconscious motivation and determinism. Despite outward appearances, an attitude of complete scientific dispassion cannot be justifiably ascribed to Freud.

The term 'freethinker' has been noted earlier in this study in Jones' (1953, I:19) comment that Freud's children had assured him that Jacob Freud had become a complete freethinker but that there was evidence to the contrary. Freud here uses the term to apply to his teachers of religion. Rainey (1971, p. 22) points out that the German word *Freisinniger* can also be translated as 'liberal', but it did denote a more specific frame of reference in the second half of the nineteenth century. In the context of Viennese Jewry it was used

41

to describe the adherents of Reform Judaism in contrast to those of Orthodox Judaism. From what can be gathered from Samuel Hammerschlag's writings, though not Orthodox, he was far from a 'free-thinker'.

The following brief letter from Freud (Letters, 1960) sent to Martha could serve as a paradigm of his conflicts over his Jewish identity.[1]

Rome

September 21, 1907

E quindi uscimmo a riveder le stelle
   Who knows this? Until nightfall I was with the dead in a Roman columbarium, in Christian and Jewish catacombs. It is cold, dark and not very pleasant down there. In the Jewish ones the inscriptions are Greek, the candelabrum—I think it's called Menorah—can be seen on many tablets. The (female) guide—I was the only visitor—forgot to bring the key of the exit, so we had either to go all the way back or stay down below. I chose the former.

Affectionately

Papa

(The opening phrase in this letter is the last line from Dante's "Inferno": "And thence we came forth to see the stars again."").

There is no doubt that Freud did have Hebrew instruction in childhood and early adolescence. However, if the letters Freud wrote to his friends in mid-adolescence about his negative impressions about people and things Jewish were any indication (more on these letters later), it would appear highly unlikely that he would have agreed to continue Hebrew studies after graduating from the *Gymnasium*. Hebrew is a language that needs continued and intensified practice for one to have a reading and writing command that is workable. If the adolescent ceases to take Hebrew lessons, does not continue to read Hebrew, and if the lessons themselves were rather brief and superficial, then with advancing age knowledge of the language will fade and it will eventually appear strange. This may, in part, explain Freud's memory lapse. The doubt about the 'Menorah' however, is another matter.

What can we make of the phrase, "I think it's called Menorah?" Did he really have difficulty recalling the Hebrew word for the seven-branched candelabrum? Or was he being facetious? This lapse in memory is puzzling. Due to the Biblical injunctions against idol worship, Judaism does not have many symbols, but of the very few that do exist the most prominent and ubiquitous is the Menorah, and it has been so for close to 2,500 years. The festival of Hanukkah, in which the Menorah is rather prominent, was certainly celebrated by Freud and his family during his childhood and adolescence. The term 'Menorah', however, is applied to both the seven-branched candelabrum and to the lamp used to celebrate Hanukkah, though the latter need not look like the candelabrum depicted on the Arch of Titus. In fact, the Hanukkah lamp is an eight-branched candelabrum. The celebration of Hanukkah derives from a miracle that was supposed to have occurred after the destruction of the Temple, when a cruse of oil which was in such small quantity that it should have been exhausted after one day turned out to be sufficient to burn for eight days. If Purim was celebrated, as Freud has described, then there is no question that Hanukkah, with all its games and gifts, was likewise celebrated.

Freud certainly knew Rome and its antiquities. Can we doubt that he had seen the Arch of Titus, in reality and in depictions? This Arch was erected by the Roman Senate in the year 80 C.E. in honor of Vespasian and his son Titus for their victory over the Jews and conquest of Jerusalem. It has several bas reliefs, the best known being on the inner wall, which portrays a victory procession. It is not clear whether the figures are Jewish slaves or victorious Roman soldiers. They are carrying away the spoils from the Temple and quite conspicuous among them is the Menorah. For Jews the Arch of Titus has always symbolized Jewish defeat and tragedy.

The Jews of ancient Rome used to bury their dead in the catacombs to avoid the common custom of cremation, which was forbidden by the Jewish religion. It is assumed that the idea of using the Menorah as a symbol in the catacombs was inspired by its representation on the Arch of Titus. There is, however, a biblical reference to the Menorah as well. The prophet Zechariah (4:1-5, 10-14) writing in 519 B.C.E., describes a night vision or hallucination in which the gold menorah is used as a symbol of God's omniscience.

Freud has impressed us with his knowledge of symbols and of Latin, Greek and Jewish history and literature. His startling tentativeness about the Hebrew word for the candelabrum would appear to be an indication or expression of intense inner conflict about his identity. We can see from his letter to Martha that the catacombs made him quite anxious. Was it the omnipresence of death, the relative darkness, the claustrophobia, or being alone with the female guide that produced his anxiety and forgetfulness?

One could even ask why he had to mention the idea of 'Menorah'. Though there may well have been other underlying motivations, the inclusion of this thought may indicate that his presence in the midst of antiquity was not sufficient to comfort him or enhance his self-esteem. Thus he was unable to cope with the anxiety that was aroused. It appears that in time of real difficulty Freud returned to his Jewish roots.

Freud's 1925 statement about the inadequacy of his knowledge of Hebrew raises many questions. In a letter dated February 20, 1930, Freud wrote to

A.A. Roback (1957, p. 27) after the latter had sent him a copy of his book *Jewish Influence in Modern Thought*;

> You will be interested to learn that my father actually came from a Hasidic milieu. He was 41 years of age when I was born, and had been estranged from his home-town associations for almost 20 years. I had such a non-Jewish upbringing that today I am not even able to read your dedication which is evidently in Hebrew characters. In later years I have often regretted this gap in my education.

Roback comments that the dedication was not written in Hebrew and that Freud must have been referring to the new seal of the Sci-Art Publishers, which contained a Hebrew verse from the prophet Jeremiah: "And knowledge and enlightenment shall be your guide".

On December 15, 1930 Freud wrote to Yehuda Dvosis-Dvir, the Hebrew translator of *Totem and Taboo* who lived in the then Palestine, now Israel (Figure 11):

15 XII 1930

Wien 9, Bergasse 19

Very esteemed sir,

I am sending you herewith the two forewords you requested. The one that pertains to the lecture is cool and matter of fact, while the other one expresses warmer tones. I hope that you will find it satisfactory. It gives me extraordinary pleasure and satisfaction that some of my books will appear in the Hebrew language. My father spoke the holy language as well as German or even better. He let me grow up in perfect ignorance on everything concerning Judaism. Only as a mature man was I angry at him for it. But I felt my being Jewish earlier because of the effect of German anti-Semitism to which I was exposed during my days at the university.

Zionism evoked in me my strongest sympathy, and has had my complete loyalty up to the present time. I knew from the beginning about your great anxiety which apparently has been proven correct by the current situation. I would prefer being mistaken about this.

With the warmest thanks for your great trouble, and with cordial greetings

yours

Sigmund Freud

Of special interest in this letter is Freud's expression of anger at his father for not taking a more active role in his Hebrew education. It is indeed

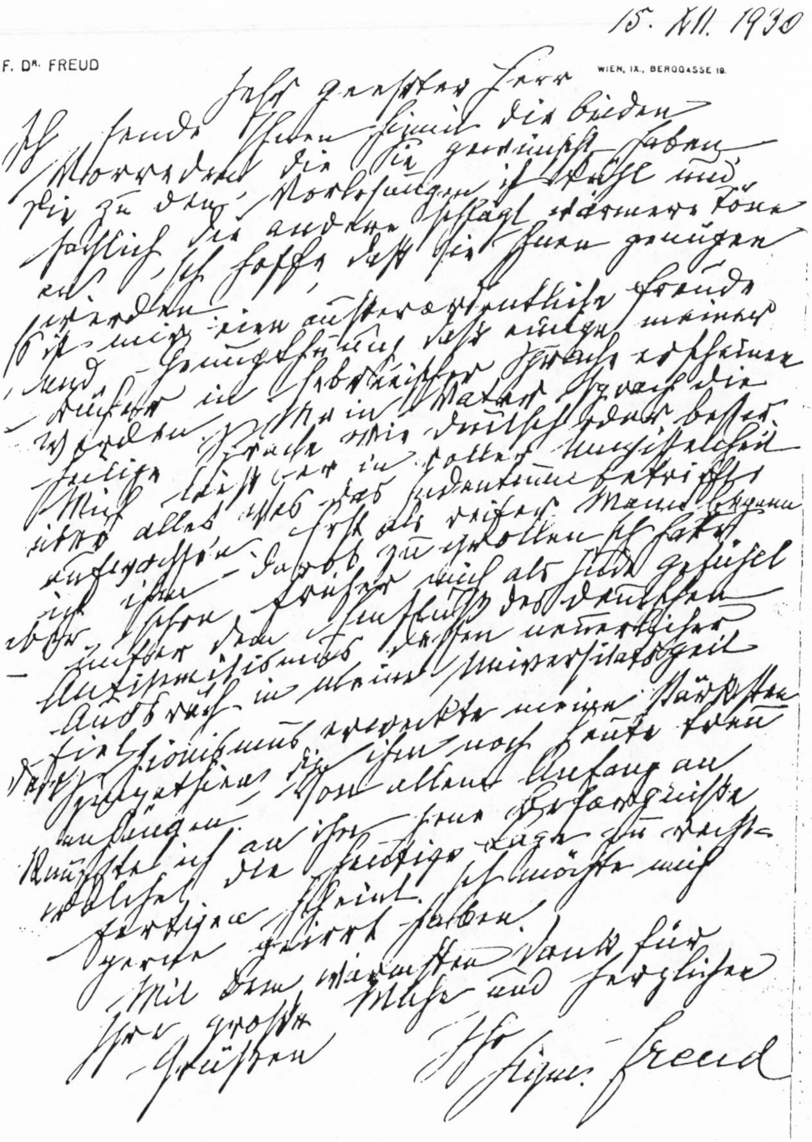

Figure 11. Sigmund Freud's letter to Hebrew translator of *Totem and Taboo*, 1930. Reproduced by permission of A.W. Freud et al., by arrangement with Mark Paterson & Associates, Colchester and courtesy of Ora Raphael.

an enigma that Jacob Freud, who appeared to be steeped in Biblical and Talmudic learning, did not take steps to educate his son in this regard. One has to wonder about the role of Amalia Freud in the decision making process about the content of their favorite son's education. Could she have been a strong factor in either the strengthening or the weakening of the religious tradition? It would be interesting to know to what extent the Jewish festivals were celebrated in the family after the death of Jacob Freud.

It is not clear what Freud was referring to in mentioning anxiety about "the current situation". Judging from the context of the letter, it may be about intensified anti-Semitism in Austria but it also may be about the situation in the then Palestine.

Eight years later, upon completion of the translation, Freud wrote another letter to the translator (Figure 12):

> 11. XII. 1938
> 20 Maresfield Gardens,
> London, N.W.3.
> Tel: Hampstead 2002

> Very esteemed sir

> I am very pleased to hear that the Hebrew edition of *Totem and Taboo* is about to appear. Since then I have also received a parcel which I believe are the proofs of the book (I, unfortunately, cannot read Hebrew). As for the foreword I have nothing to change. The mysterious sentence mentioned by you refers to the question in which form our common tradition is present in our spiritual life, which is a difficult and purely psychological problem.

> My next book *Moses and Monotheism* will appear in the spring in English and German. Its translation into the holy language would naturally afford me great pleasure. It is a continuation of the theme of *Totem and Taboo*, the application to history of the Jewish religion. I must ask you to consider that its contents might hurt Jewish sensitivity insofar as there is a reluctance to submit the subject to scientific inquiry.

> With devoted thanks and heartfelt greeting,

> yours

> Sigm. Freud

In this letter Freud again expresses his regrets about not being able to read Hebrew. The data pertaining to Freud's knowledge or ignorance of Hebrew are rather confusing. As noted earlier, Freud was exposed to Hebrew in both childhood and adolescence. Religious instruction was mandated by

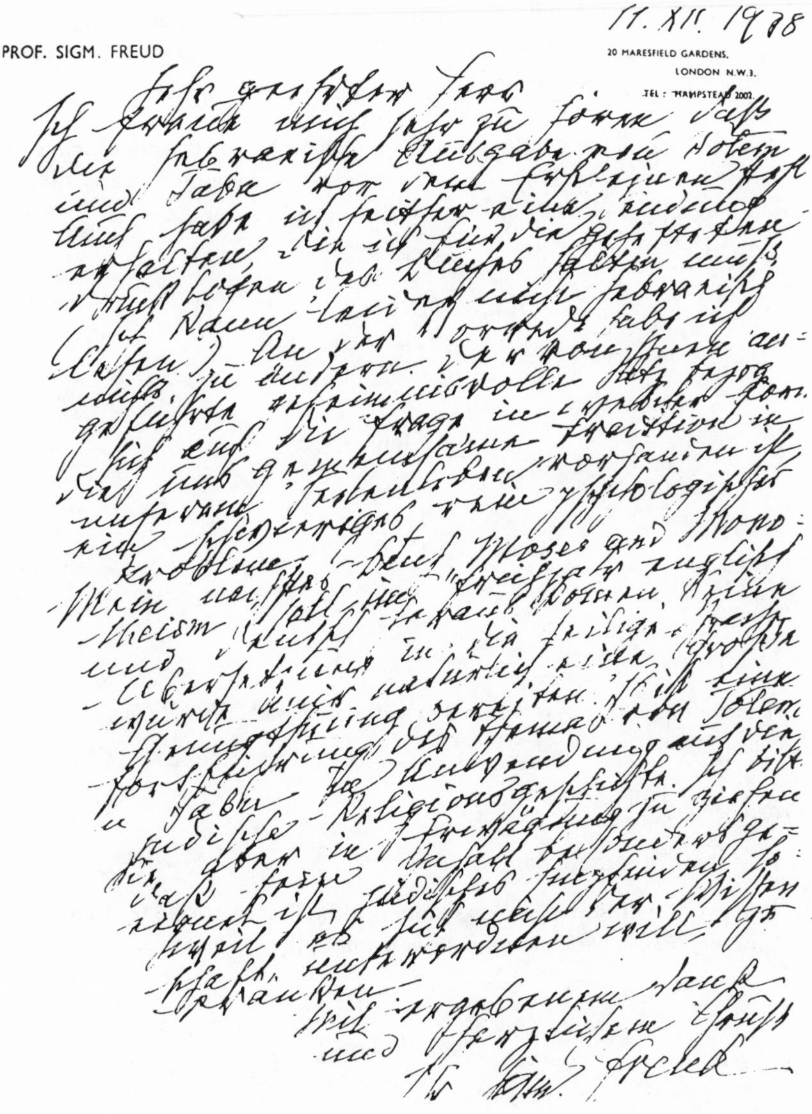

Figure 12. Sigmund Freud's letter to Hebrew translator of *Totem and Taboo*, 1938. Reproduced by permission of A.W. Freud et al., by arrangement with Mark Paterson & Associates, Colchester and courtesy of Ora Raphael.

the government starting at age six in primary school (or home tutoring) through graduation from the *Gymnasium* at age eighteen, so that Freud would have had a total of twelve years of exposure to Hebrew studies.[2] As we have shown, the instructor in all these years must have been Hammerschlag. Since Freud received the highest marks in the *Gymnasium* class, he must have attained some degree of mastery over the subject matter. Examinations and grades had to be given (Rainey, 1971; Rozenblit, 1983).

The curricula for religious instruction for the period during which time Freud attended school (1862[?]-1874) have been found and they are as follows (Wolf, 1861, pp. 144-150; 1876):

VOLKSSCHULECLASSEN
(Primary School Classes)

A. Boys

First Class

First Semester

a. Hebrew readings

b. Translation of prayers: *Shema, Veahavtah, Kedushah, Birkhat Hamazon* until *Hazon et Hakol.*

Second Semester

a. First Book of Moses (Genesis), Chapters 1, 2.

b. Prayers: Repetition of prayers taught in the first semester; translation of the prayers: *Elohai Nishmah* until *Vaihi Ratzon.*

Second Class

First Semester

a. First Book of Moses (Genesis), Chapters 3, 4 (until verse 18), 6, 7, 8, 9 (until verse 30), 21 (until verse 22), 22, 23, 24, 25, (until verse 19), 27, 28, 29 (until verse 30).

b. Prayers: *Mah Tovuh, Shemoneh Esreh—Modim* until the end; *Birkhat Hamazon* until *Uveneh Yerushalayim.*

c. Grammar: Gender, number, case, article.

Third Class

First Semester

a. First Book of Moses (Genesis), Chapters 32 (until verse 4), 33, 35 (until verse 21), 37, 39 (until verse 20), 40, 41, 42, 43, 44 (until verse 18).

b. Prayers: *Ahtah Honeyn* until *Modim; Aleynu.*

Second Semester

a. First Book of Moses (Genesis), Chapters 44 (until verse 18), 45, 46 (until verse 8, skip verses 9-27, then continue from verse 28 through to the end of the chapter), 47, 48, 49 (until verse 28), 50.
  Second Book of Moses (Exodus), Chapters 1, 2, 3, 4 (until verse 18), 5, 6 (until verse 13), 11, 12.

b. Prayers: *Barukh Sheamar* until *Melekh Mehulal Batishbakhot, Borkhu* until *Leayl Barukh.*

Fourth Class

First Semester

a. Second Book of Moses (Exodus), Chapters 13, 14, 15, 16, 17, 18, 19, 20, 21 (until verse 12), 22 (until verse 15 and then verse 19 to end), 23, 24, 31 (until verse 12), 32, 33, 34.

b. Prayers: *Adon Olam, Barukh Adonai Leaylohim, Vahyivarekh David, Ahava Rabah.*

c. Bible History: From the birth of Moses until his death.

Second Semester

a. Third Book of Moses (Leviticus), Chapters 23, 24, 25, 26 (until verse 14).
  Fourth Book of Moses (Numbers), Chapters 6 (until verse 22), 9, 10, 11, 12, 13, 14, 15 (until verse 32), 16, 17, 20, 21 (until verse 10), 22, 27, 32.

b. Prayers: *Tefilat Aravit Shel Hol, Vahyehi Binsoa.* (Open the Ark, carry out the Torah, and then return it; only those parts will be translated which will be read in the synagogue by those who pray.)

c. Grammar: Pronouns, Hitpael from the *Shlomim.*

d. Bible History: From Joshua to the Kings. (At the present time, singing will take place in the public schools and the Temple songs will be taught, depending on the ability of the students to learn them. This teaching will be done by the choir director Herr J. Sulzer.)

B. Girls

First Class

a. Bible History: From the beginning of the world to the time of the Kings. (For those girls who do not as yet read German there will be a preparation class. The course will be limited to a description of the history of the Bible and the reading of Hebrew.)

b. Hebrew lessons and the translation of prayers: *Shema, Veahavtah, Kedusha.*

Second Class

a. Bible History: From the time of the Kings to the restoration of the Second Temple.

b. Prayers *Shema, Veahavtah, Vehayah, Avot, Gevurot, Kedusha, Birkhat Hamazon* until *Hazon et Hakol.*

Third Class

a. Reading assignments in the German translations of:
Isaiah, Chapters 1, 2, 5, 6, 11, 58.
Jeremiah, Chapters 1, 8, 9, 17, 31.
Ezekiel, Chapters 17, 18, 37.
Hosea 6; Joel 3; Amos 3; Jonah 2; Micah 6; Zephaniah 3; Haggai 2; Zechariah 5, 8; Malachi 1.
At the same time, the history of the times in which the Prophets lived will be taught.

CHAPTER 5

Jacob and Amalia Freud—Orthodox or Reform Jews?

The Marriage Certificate

One reason it has been easy to dismiss or misinterpret Jacob Freud's Bible dedication in the past is that Jacob Freud's connection to Judaism was itself misunderstood. That Jacob Freud became an assimilated Jew has been taken for granted by all of Freud's biographers and family. Though Jones (1953) did express some doubt, it has never really been questioned. One document that has been cited as proof is the marriage certificate of Jacob and Amalia Freud dated July 29, 1855 and signed by Rabbi Isaac Noah Mannheimer. This rabbi has been identified by the Freud biographers as a 'Reform' rabbi, thereby putting the stamp of validity on the assimilated status of the Freud family. Further scrutiny of this marriage certificate and the historical, cultural and religious circumstances of the time will indicate that this assumption is open to serious question.

Rabbi Mannheimer was a most unusual member of the Jewish clergy. If one adheres to the idea that if a Jew were not traditionally Orthodox then he must be Reform then I presume that this appellation would apply. (Conservative Judaism as we know it today did not exist at that time; there were, however, varying gradations of Orthodoxy present in Vienna, ranging from the ultra-Orthodox Hasidic on one end of the spectrum to the more westernized Jews on the other end.) However, Rabbi Mannheimer was not considered to be a member of the classical Reform movement. Quite the contrary, he was as anti-Reform as he was anti-Orthodox. A prominent historian of Jewish literature has written:

> Isaac Noah Mannheimer was rabbi in Vienna for a period of thirty-two years from 1825 to 1857, and the influence he exerted on the Jews of the Austrian capital was exceptionally great. It was he who organized the Jewish community in that city and made it a model of Jewish organized life. He

was very conservative in his religious views, and while he was thoroughly modern and believed in beautifying the services, he did not approve of the innovations of the reformers and was a great force in reconciling the traditional type of Judaism with modern conditions. (Waxman, III:749, 1945)

Mannheimer was born in Copenhagen in 1793 and graduated from the university there. He was at first an adherent of Reform Judaism but gradually became more traditional in his conception and practice. In 1824 he was invited to be the spiritual leader of the new *Seitenstetten Synagogue* in Vienna. He averted a split between the Orthodox and Reform Jews, a phenomenon that was intensifying in Western European countries at the time, by being a strong proponent for the retention of the use of Hebrew in the prayer service, circumcision and prayers for the restoration of Zion, i.e., a Jewish homeland in Israel. He was also against the use of an organ in the synagogue to accompany the prayer service.

> Mannheimer's opinion on Orthodox and Reform Judaism, given in March 1858, and still preserved in the archives of the community, is of interest. He rejects reform insofar as it is based on rationalism, discards revelation and tradition, breaks with historical Judaism in public worship, eliminates Hebrew, excludes the messianic passages in the prayer book, eliminates or shortens the reading from the Torah, and, in its extremist form, transfers the Sabbath to Sunday. Vienna, as Mannheimer emphasizes, rests upon conservatism. (Grunwald, 1936, p. 376)

At the time of Mannheimer's arrival Jews were not permitted to form, or even be considered as, an organized entity or community. Even the sanctioning of a rabbi was not permitted so that, in the eyes of the Austrian government, Mannheimer's official status was that of headmaster of the religious school. (Church and State in Austria were inseparable and recognition of any other organized religious entity would have been perceived as a threat to the primacy of Catholicism. One of the attractions of Germany in the eyes of the middle-class enlightened Austrian was that it was a secular state.) He never used the title of 'Rabbi' but was called 'Preacher'. In 1826, on his own initiative, he introduced the keeping of records of birth, marriage and death for the Jews of Vienna. In 1831, he was formally commissioned by the government to establish and maintain a central registry for these records. He was active in the establishment of many Jewish social organizations. He was constantly active in his attempts to get the government to grant legal status to the Jewish community. He was responsible for the defeat, in 1842, of the attempt to establish a limit, or quota, on the number of Jews admitted to the medical school. He was also responsible for the abolition of the medieval Jewish oath, the *more Judaico*, and the special tax that only Jews had to pay.

In 1848, he was elected to the Austrian Reichstag and fought for the abolition of the death penalty.

What is of relevance to this study is the establishment of the central registry noted above. Mannheimer was the only person in the 1850s who could give legal sanction to a Jewish marriage because of the authorization given to him by the civil authorities to do so. He was also the only one empowered to list the marriage in the registry. Mannheimer was the official 'Preacher' of the entire Jewish Community of Vienna. Marsha Rozenblit (personal communication) has informed me that there was an Orthodox rabbi in Vienna in the 1850s, a man named Rabbi Lazar Horwitz. The civil authorities did not recognize marriages performed by him alone, but they did recognize marriages performed by him if Mannheimer was present or indicated approval in some way. Rozenblit believes that Mannheimer and Horwitz had an arrangement whereby the latter could perform marriages, but only for members of Mannheimer's synagogue. Not having Mannheimer involved in the wedding ceremony meant that the marriage would not have been recognized by the Austrian Government and that the resulting children would be considered illegitimate. The children would then have to assume their mother's maiden name and lose all rights of inheritance from their father.

The marriage certificate of Jacob and Amalia Freud has been published (Krull, 1986) and is completely in German. However, there must have been another document, the *Ketubah*, which is the traditional Jewish marriage contract. It was written on parchment or paper, in Aramaic, the language of ancient Israel and Babylon, but with Hebrew characters. This document was probably lost, but possibly may be in the possession of a member of the Freud family. In light of the knowledge that Mannheimer was the only person empowered by the government to perform Jewish marriages, it would appear that the marriage of the Freuds by Mannheimer may have had nothing to do with their religious beliefs but solely with their desire to have their marriage made legitimate. This is a matter of crucial importance in understanding the religious background of the elder Freud's family, as every biographer to date has used this marriage certificate as documentary evidence for their being Reform and/or assimilated Jews dating back to the time of their marriage in 1855.

Religious Affiliation of Emanuel and Philipp Freud

Another way of determining the extent of Jacob Freud's drift away from Orthodox Judaism would be to look at what happened to his two sons from his first marriage, Emanuel and Philipp. In 1859, when the entire Freud family left Freiberg, Jacob, Amalia and their progeny went first to Leipzig for several months and then to Vienna. Emanuel and his family, as well as his younger brother Philipp, emigrated to Manchester, England where they became successful businessmen and, according to Martin Freud (1958), perfect English gentlemen.

It would have been assumed that if Jacob Freud had begun the process of his sons' assimilation then this process would have continued and even accelerated in the democratic and egalitarian atmosphere of England. This, however, was not the case. Emanuel, Philipp, and their families, affiliated not with the Reform group of Manchester but with the Orthodox segment of the Jewish population. As in Vienna, but even more so in aristocratic England, class aspiration and status influenced the choice of association. The Orthodox group in Manchester was split not only along religious lines but also according to economic, cultural and educational status. Those who had been in Manchester for some time or who had achieved some success eschewed the newly arrived Eastern European Jews (exactly as had occurred among the established middle-class Jews in Vienna). The new arrivals had their own synagogues while the established Jews belonged to the *Great Synagogue* which was also Orthodox but with a pattern of assembly and decorum closer to its Reform or Anglican counterparts.

In the late 1860s there was a migration southward of successful Jews to a part of Manchester too distant (i.e., for walking on the Sabbath) from the Great Synagogue to permit membership. There were also some Jews who were displeased by the snobbishness of some of the *Great Synagogue* membership. Emanuel and Philipp Freud were among those who moved to this new area and were among the founding members of the new Orthodox institution, to be called the *South Manchester Synagogue*.

At the open meeting of September 8, 1872, it was declared that the new synagogue's affairs should be "marked by that thoroughly conciliatory and inaggressive spirit, which at all times has been the standard of a truly Jewish movement" and that a "gentle reform" be instituted (Williams, 1976. p. 319)."Gentle reform" meant only a slight change in the inner architecture of the synagogue and an increased use of English in the prayer service. The change in the internal layout involved the moving of the pulpit from the center to the front of the synagogue. As the historian of Manchester Jewry writes, "It was the social quality of the new congregation, not its religious novelty which accounted for its distinctive features. It expressed the ambition and fears of an anglo-Jewish elite in 1872 and in later years provided a nucleus for the settlement of assimilated Jewish families in the southern suburbs" (Williams, 1976, p. 319). Given that Jacob's two eldest sons actively participated in the affairs of the Orthodox Jewish community, it would appear quite unlikely that their father would simultaneously be going in the direction of assimilation whether in Freiberg or in the predominantly Jewish section of Vienna where they lived, the Leopoldstadt.

Jacob Freud's Hebrew Inscriptions

The most direct evidence of Jacob Freud's knowledge of Hebrew and his commitment to the traditions and beliefs of Orthodox Judaism is found in his inscriptions in the family Bible. There are three Hebrew inscriptions in all. The first two, written in 1856 within a few months of each other, are the announcement of the death of Jacob's father, Solomon (Shlomo in Hebrew), and the birth of Sigmund. Jacob gave his newborn son the Hebrew name 'Shlomo,' naming him after his own father, and immediately followed it with an equivalent secular name, in Hebrew characters, 'Sigismund.' 'Sigismund' was to be changed in adolescence, presumably by Freud himself, to the more acceptable (in Vienna, at least) 'Sigmund'.

The third inscription, an original composition rich in Talmudic and Biblical learning, laden with a complex significance that addresses Jacob Freud's own complicated connection to Judaism as well as his son Sigmund's, will be examined in greater detail in Chapters 6 and 7. Certain aspects of that document will be examined in this chapter. The death and birth announcements, more straightforward in their composition, present a more direct sort of evidence that further validates the elder Freud's Jewish background and his commitment to tradition.

The translation presented here is new and is based on the clarified text. The written script has been transposed into Hebrew print so that comparison can be made and the accuracy of the translation evaluated. The footnotes in the Hebrew print refer to the Biblical and Talmudic sources of the Hebrew words. The numbers that are listed below that precede each Hebrew quote and its translation into English are identical to the numbers of the footnotes in Figures 5, 6, 8, 9.

I. Announcement of the Death of Solomon Freud (Fig. 4-6)

1. 'Artzot shamayim'—'Land of heaven'
These two words literally mean 'the land of the heavens or sky' and they may derive from a phrase that is found in at least three different psalms.

> *Psalm* 27:13
> Had I not the assurance
> that I would enjoy the goodness of the Lord
> in the land of the living . . .

> *Psalm* 52:7
> So God will tear you down for good,
> will break you and pluck you from your tent,
> and root you out of the land of the living.

Psalm 116:9
I shall walk before the Lord
in the lands of the living.

The 'land of the living' has traditionally referred to this world as opposed to the straits of the netherworld, or *Sheol*. 'Land of the living' appears to be equated with the 'Land of heaven' and thus may be a pseudonym for the 'Land of eternal life'. A Jewish cemetery is referred to as *Bet Olam*, i.e. , 'The house of eternity'.

2. 'Uvah limnuḥatoh'—'And came to his resting place'
The word *limnuḥato* is derived from Isaiah 11:10: And it shall come to pass in that day, that the root of Jesse, that standeth for an ensign of the peoples, upon him shall the nations seek; and his resting-place shall be glorious.

3. 'Al mishkavoh'—'His resting place'
The words *ahl mishkavoh* literally mean 'on his bed'. The words *limnuḥatoh* and *mishkavoh* mean 'his resting place' and 'on his bed' respectively and are here used synonymously and repetitively in a poetic fashion by both the prophet Isaiah and Jacob Freud. The concept of a 'bed' being an eternal resting place can be found in the concluding sentence of the Memorial Prayer, *Ayl Mohleh Raḥamim* ("O Lord, Who art full of compassion") the specific phrase being, *Veyanuḥoh ahl mishkevotam beshalom* which literally means "And may they repose in their resting places in peace". These words can also be translated as 'may he rest in peace'.

4. 'Yanuaḥ al mishkavoh holeykh nekhoḥo'—'He who walked a straight course shall have peace on his resting place'
This phrase is an almost direct quotation, in the Hebrew, from Isaiah 57:2:

Yet he shall come to peace,
He shall have rest on his couch
Who walked straightforward.
The word 'couch', in this verse, is a euphemism for 'grave'.

5. 'Ad eit kaitz'—'Until the time of the end'
This phrase is derived from the Book of Daniel 11:35 and 12:4:

11:35
Some of the knowledgeable will fall, that they
may be refined and purged and whitened
until the time of the end, for an
interval still remains until the appointed time.

12:4
"But you, Daniel, keep the words secret, and
seal the book until the time of the end.
Many will range far and wide and knowledge
will increase."

6. **'Lishainai afahr hakitzu'—'To those who sleep in dust'**
   This phrase is derived from the Book of Daniel 12:2:

> Many of those that sleep in the dust of the
> earth will awake, some to eternal life,
> others to reproaches, to everlasting abhorrence.

II. Announcement of the Birth of Sigmund Freud (Fig. 4-6)

Like the death announcement, the birth announcement is written in the Hebrew of one versed in traditional sources. Only in three minor instances are Yiddish or German words, though written in Hebrew characters, substituted for Hebrew words. They are not difficult words, and it is hard to explain why someone capable of producing Hebrew so well would stumble at these places, for they are words that are found with great frequency in the Bible and the prayers. The three words are *uhr* (hour), *nakhmittag* (afternoon), and *pathen* (godparents). The same applies to the last line of the birth announcement, in which three German words, *am* (on), *becom* (received) and *tzena* (teeth). The bracketed question mark on the last line of the Commemorative Page (Fig. 6) stands for a partly legible word which definitely refers to the month in which his first three teeth appeared. It could be either October, November, or December which are within the normal time frame of the emergence of the first teeth.

It is noteworthy that the secular calendar year on the *Gedenkblatt* is written without the number 'one', e.g., 848 on the top of the page and 856 in both the death and birth announcements. Orthodox Jews, especially of Eastern European origin, have never formally recognized the existence of a calendar based on Christianity. Even today, Orthodox Jews throughout the world use B.C.E. or C.E. (Before the Common Era and Common Era) instead of B.C. and A. D. (Before Christ and Anno Domini).[1] The inclusion of 'one', as in 1848 and 1856, would thus have implied a recognition of Christianity, as the counting of the calender begins in the year of Christ's birth. This piece of seemingly innocent behavior on the part of Jacob Freud adds a greater degree of plausibility that, at least as late as 1856, at forty-two years of age, he was indeed an Orthodox, rather than a Reform or an assimilated Jew.

To add further validation to his being Orthodox at the time, the reader should note the word in the first and last line of Figures 4-6 (the *Gedenkblatt* and the transposition into Hebrew print of the birth announcement), *sheyihye*, i.e. 'may he live a long life'. The last Hebrew letter *heh*, which is the English equivalent of the letter 'H', is missing and its absence is noted by an apostrophe after the Hebrew letter *yod*. The same holds for the word in the third line, *hayah*, where the last letter *heh* is omitted. This practice has existed for more than 2,000 years because the union of the two letters *yod* and *heh* come to represent the first two letters of the Tetragrammaton *YAWEH* which is one of the several biblical references to God. Since God's name cannot be written except on a Torah parchment scroll, it is incumbent upon the writer to leave out the *heh* and substitute an apostrophe whenever the two occur together at the end of a word. Again, only an Orthodox Jew would have maintained this practice. This is as true today as it was in 1856.

Despite the lessening of religious ritual observance in the Freud family that occurred over time, Jacob Freud again demonstrated this practice when he wrote a Hebrew dedication in honor of his son Sigmund's thirty-fifth birthday in 1891 (Fig. 7-9). On the second line he shortened the Tetragrammaton and on the last line omitted the number '1' from (1)891. These were certainly not practices that could be attributed to a completely assimilated Jew.[2]

The manner of signature at the end of the birthday benediction is also of revealing interest. It is signed 'Jacob son of Reb. Sh. Freud'. Only a Jew who still identified himself in some way with the Orthodox tradition would have signed it this way. If Jacob were as assimilated as has been thought, he would have just signed it 'Jacob Freud'.

As noted at the beginning of this study, Ernst Freud stated that the first translation into English of Jacob Freud's Hebrew dedication to his son Sigmund on the occasion of his thirty-fifth birthday "was made by one of Jacob's sons from his first marriage, both of whom settled in Manchester." The Bible was not taken out of Vienna until 1938, so that the translation must have been made during a visit that either Emanuel or Philipp made to Vienna not long after the dedication was inscribed (Philipp died in 1911 and Emanuel in 1914). The following is the first translation (Figure 13):

My dear son!

It was in the seventh year of your age that the spirit of God began to move you to learning. I would say the spirit of God speaketh to you — "make thee up and read in my book, there will be opened to thee the sources of sciences and of intellect." It is the book of the books, it is the well that wise men have digged and lawgivers have drawn the water of their knowledge.

Thou hast seen / in this book / the vision of the Allmighty, thou hast heard willingly, thou hast done and hast tried to fly high upon the wings of the holy spirit. From this time I have taken this book — the same Bible — to

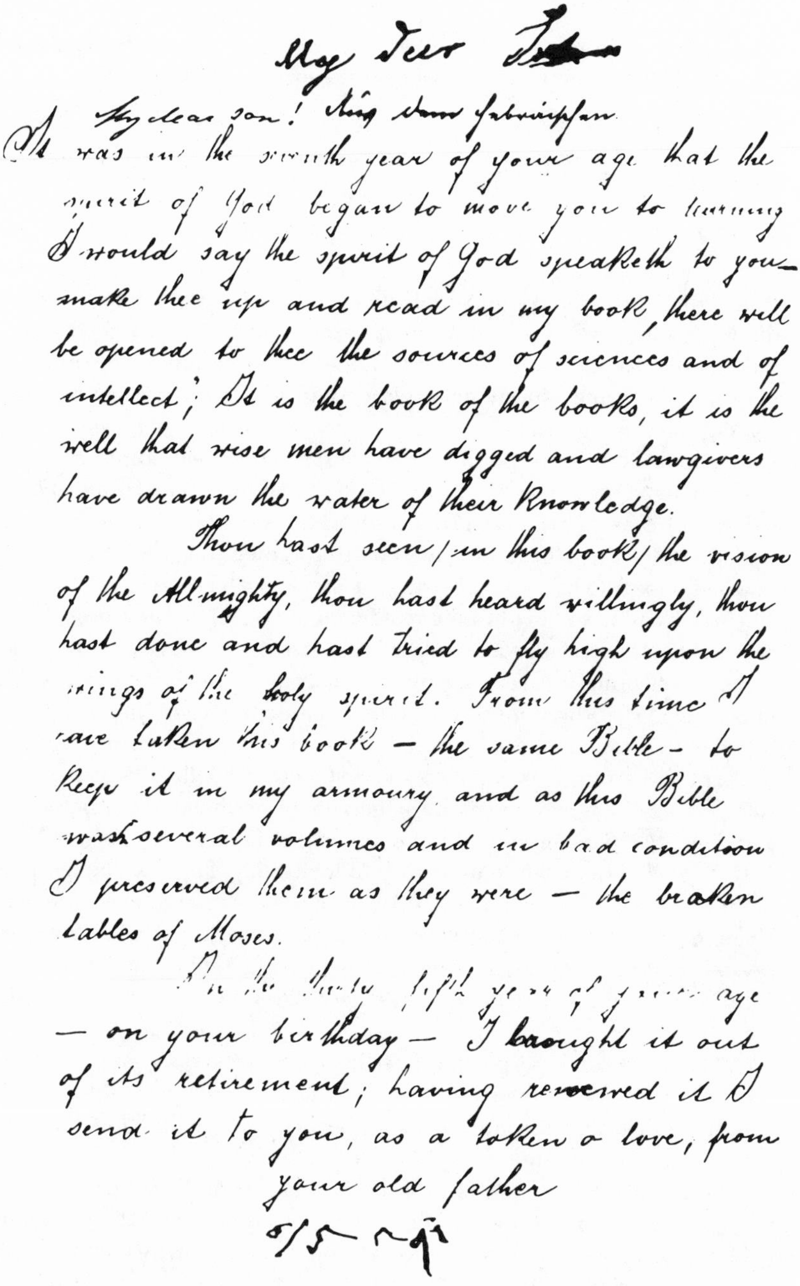

My Dear ~~Father~~

My dear son! ~~Mein lieber Sohn~~

It was in the seventh year of your age that the
spirit of God began to move you to learning
I would say the spirit of God speaketh to you
make thee up and read in my book, there will
be opened to thee the sources of sciences and of
intellect; It is the book of the books, it is the
well that wise men have digged and lawgivers
have drawn the water of their knowledge.

Thou hast seen / in this book / the vision
of the All-mighty, thou hast heard willingly, thou
hast done and hast tried to fly high upon the
wings of the holy spirit. From this time I
have taken this book — the same Bible — to
keep it in my armoury, and as this Bible
was several volumes and in bad condition
I preserved them as they were — the broken
tables of Moses.

In the thirty fifth year of your age
— on your birthday — I brought it out
of its retirement; having revised it I
send it to you, as a token o love, from
your old father

Figure 13. Translation of dedication by Emanuel and/or Philipp Freud. Courtesy of the Freud Museum London.

keep it in my armoury, and as this Bible was in several volumes and in bad condition I preserved them as they were—the broken tables of Moses.

In the thirty-fifth year of your age—on your birthday—I brought it out of its retirement; having renewed it I send it to you, as a token of love, from

Your old father

When this translation is compared with the one in Figure 9, done by scholars in Hebrew liturgy and literature, it appears to reflect a fairly good grasp of the Hebrew language. It would thus appear that Emanuel and/or Philipp may have had some educational experience in a *Yeshiva* in Tysmenitz prior to coming to Freiberg in 1852.

A look at this translation (Figure 13) will reveal some interesting phenomena. The top line is Jacob Freud's attempt at translation where he writes, in his own hand, *My dear son.* Immediately beneath it are the words *Auf dem hebraischen,* 'from the Hebrew'. It is written in a German script that does not appear to be the handwriting of either Jacob Freud or the translator. The handwriting of the phrase immediately to the left of the words *Auf dem hebraischen, My dear son!,* does not look like that of the translator either. So it appears that four different people had a hand in it. What is of striking interest is the handwriting on the bottom of the translation. In Jacob Freud's own handwriting it appears to be the date of the translation which also is the birthday of Sigmund Freud, May 6th. First there is *6/5* (the European custom is to put the day before the month), then the upper half of the number *eight* and then *91.* This suggests that there was a large family gathering on May 6, 1891 in celebration of Sigmund's thirty-fifth birthday. The Manchester branch of the family apparently thought enough of the occasion to make the trip to Vienna. Much attention must have been paid to the old father's Hebrew poem at this birthday party. Note the absence of the numeral '1' before '891'. This would indicate that as late as 1891 Jacob Freud was not a wholly assimilated Jew.

There are some perplexing questions about this document. First, why was it translated into English? A more obvious language would have been German or Yiddish. Secondly, why did Jacob Freud try his hand at English? Answers to these questions are not available.

From the evidence presented thus far there is ample justification to cast serious doubt on what appears to be the consensus of Freud's biographers (with the exception of Jones [1953] as noted earlier in this study) on the assimilated religious status of Jacob and Amalia Freud and their children. Jacob Freud's mastery of the Bible, Talmud and Hebrew language and the religious nature and content of the Hebrew writings themselves; his handling, according to the highest Orthodox Jewish tradition, of the Tetragrammaton and the elimination of the number 'l' in the writing of the calender year; Emanuel and Philipp's knowledge of the Hebrew language and their continued affiliation with the Orthodox Jewish community in Manchester, England; the observance of the religious festivals and the distinct possibility of the observance of the laws of *Kashruth* (i.e., kosher food and kitchen)—all point to a significantly less than enthusiastic adherence to assimilationism and the Reform Jewish movement. In fact, a continued, though somewhat weakened, Orthodoxy may well have been the true situation for the Freud family.

CHAPTER 6

The Biblical Sources of the Hebrew Dedication

The most commanding aspects of the birthday dedication have yet to be explored. To do so properly requires knowledge not only of the Freud family but of the Bible itself. The following data indicates that there was a shared fantasy between Jacob and Sigmund Freud that had as a motivating source the biblical story of Jacob and Joseph. The uncanny parallels between their respective family structures and experiences appear to have contributed to the formation and adhesiveness of this fantasy.

In the biblical story, Jacob was the third and last of the Patriarchs in direct descendency. He was supposed to have married his beloved Rachel but a deceptive trick was played upon him by Rachel's father, Laban, who, at the last moment, substituted his older daughter, Leah. Jacob had to work another seven years for his father-in-law so that he could also marry Rachel. He also acquired two concubines, named Zilpah and Bilah. With these four women Jacob fathered thirteen children, twelve sons and one daughter. Joseph was the first-born son of Rachel, and the eleventh of Jacob's twelve sons. He soon became the most beloved of all by Jacob. Joseph's behavior throughout his father's life appeared to justify the esteem and love that the father had for him. As is well known, the sibling rivalry and jealousy was intense.

Freud's identification with Joseph, the first biblical interpreter of dreams, is clear. In a footnote to his comments about his own dream which involved his close friend and benefactor Josef Paneth (S.E. V:484) he states,

> It will be noticed that the name Josef plays a great part in my dreams (cf. the dream about my uncle). My own ego finds it very easy to hide behind people of that name, since Joseph was the name of a man famous in the Bible as an interpreter of dreams.

The Josef here referred to was the brother of Jacob Freud. In his last written reference to the biblical Joseph, Freud wrote,

If one is the declared favorite of the dreaded father, one need not be surprised at the jealousy of one's brothers and sisters, and the Jewish legend of Joseph and his brethren shows very well where this jealousy can lead. (S.E. XXIII:106)

For our purposes it is what happened at the end of the Patriarch Jacob's life that is of significance. The scenario has served as a paradigm of father-son relationships down through the millenia. The impending loss of a beloved parent is movingly rendered, as is the transitional process from the old to the new generation.

The drama begins in Genesis 47:28:

47:28
Jacob lived seventeen years in the land of Egypt, so that the span of Jacob's life came to one hundred and forty-seven years.

47:29
And when the time approached for Israel to die, he summoned his son Joseph and said to him, "If you would please me, place your hand under my thigh as a pledge of your steadfast loyalty: pray do not bury me in Egypt.

47:30
When I lie down with my fathers, take me up from Egypt and bury me in their burial-place." And he said, "I will do as you have spoken."

47:31
And he said, "Swear to me." And he swore to him. Then Israel bowed at the head of the bed.

Shortly thereafter Joseph learns that his father is about to die. He quickly takes his two sons, Manasseh and Ephraim, into Jacob's bedroom for his father's blessing. Joseph sits down with Manasseh on his right side and Ephraim on his left, both between his knees. He then places them between Jacob's knees. Following the birth order, it is expected that Jacob, in blessing the children, will put his right hand on the head of Manasseh and his left on that of Ephraim. Instead, Jacob crosses his hands and put his right hand on the head of Ephraim, thus endowing him with the favored status of a first born, which he is not. Jacob puts his left hand on Manasseh. Joseph, disturbed by what he sees, tries to remove Jacob's right hand from Ephraim's head and put it on that of Manasseh, all the while protesting that Manasseh is the first-born son. Jacob, however, refuses and proclaims that though Manasseh and his descendants will be great, Ephraim and his progeny will be even greater and that "*his offspring shall be plentiful enough for nations*".[1] Jacob then issues the following blessing (48:20):

> So he blessed them that day, saying, "By you shall Israel invoke bless-
> ings, saying: God make you like Ephraim and Manasseh." Thus he put
> Ephraim before Manasseh.

Jacob then gives Joseph an extra portion of land *"more than to your brothers."*
This blessing has since become commonplace in many Orthodox Jewish
homes where, on the Sabbath eve, the father puts his hand on his children
and blesses them with the words: *God make you like Ephraim and Manasseh.*
(This scene of Jacob blessing his grandchildren has been painted by Rembrandt,
Figure 14.)

Figure 10 is a photograph of a page of the Book of Genesis, 48:19-22,
taken from the Freud family Bible. There are three words that were underlined
in red pencil, possibly by Sigmund Freud, as noted earlier. The first word of
verse 19, *vayimaeyn* means 'But his father [i.e., Jacob] objected', refusing to
change the position of his hands. The second word in the middle of verse 19
is *veoolam*, meaning 'yet'. The entire verse 19 is written as following:

> But his father objected, saying, "I know, my son, I know. He too shall
> become a people, and he too shall be great. Yet his younger brother shall be
> greater than he, and his offspring shall be plentiful enough for nations."

In verse 21 Jacob begins to bless Joseph:

> Then Israel said to Joseph, "I am about to die; but God will be with you
> and bring you back to the land of your fathers."[2]

In verse 22 the word underlined is *shekhem*. The entire sentence is as follows:

> "And now, I give one portion more than to your brothers, which I
> wrested from the Amorites with my sword and bow."

The partiality that Jacob demonstrates for Joseph is here made quite explicit,
i.e., he shall have more than his brothers for his inheritance.[3]

Jacob then calls in his other sons and gives them what might be described
as a 'mixed blessing'. He justifies his ambivalent blessing by citing both their
good and bad deeds. His most loving comments are reserved for Joseph,
who united that which was best and noblest in his older brothers, Reuben
and Judah. As one modern biblical commentator states *(Soncino Bible, 1936):*
*"He is the man of vision, the man of dreams, but to this he joins moral and spiritual
strength in all the vicissitudes of life. He is the ideal son, the ideal brother, the ideal
servant, the ideal administrator."* The blessing to Joseph is expressed in the following five sentences (Genesis 49:22-26):

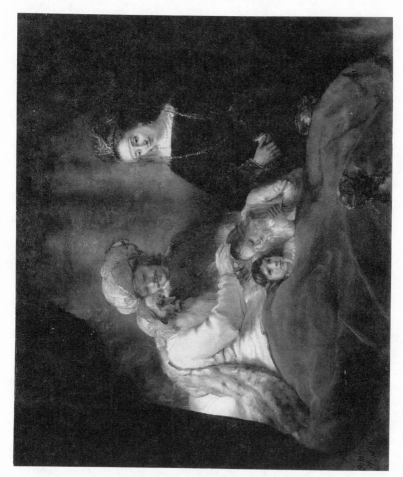

Figure 14. Painting by Rembrandt of Jacob blessing Ephraim and Manasseh. Courtesy of the Staatliche Kunstsammlungen Kassel.

22. Joseph is a wild ass,
      A wild ass by a spring
      — Wild colts on a hillside.
(Others translate this verse as follows)
      Joseph is a fruitful bough
      A fruitful bough by a spring,
      Its branches run over a wall.

23. Arches bitterly assailed him;
      They shot at him and harried him.

24. Yet his bow stayed taut,
      And his arms were made firm
      By the hands of the Mighty One of Jacob—
      There, the Shepherd, the Rock of Israel—

25. The God of your father who helps you,
      And Shaddai who blesses you
      With blessings of heaven above,
      Blessings of the deep that couches below,
      Blessings of the breast and womb.

26. The blessings of your father
      Surpass the blessings of my ancestors,
      To the utmost bounds of the eternal hills.
      May they rest on the head of Joseph,
      On the brow of the elect of his brothers.

These biblical verses beautifully and succinctly describe the kind of man Sigmund Freud was to become. Jacob Freud knew well the entire story of his biblical namesake and his most favored son. In retrospect, it appears as a prescient glance into his future—the worldwide fame and the spread of his ideas and discoveries, an inner emotional strength, the aroused opposition of his colleagues and his perseverence despite all adversity, in essence, a latter-day Joseph.

CHAPTER 7

The Latent Content of the Birthday Benediction

Just as a dream, a neurotic symptom, or, for that matter, any product of the mind, cannot be adequately understood without the individual's verbalized associations to it, so it is with Jacob Freud's Hebrew inscriptions. We obviously have no further comment from the author of the benediction but we do know exactly from where he mined the thoughts which he used to 'clothe' his feelings. The biblical sources and the stories behind them constitute part of the latent content for the manifest expression of the benediction. There is no doubt that Jacob Freud knew these sources well. As with many other Jews like him, they were an intrinsic component of his thoughts and his verbal and written productions, so thoroughly ingrained in him since birth that they became everpresent and immediately available for recall. This is why in this work the exegetical, as well as an approximate associative, approach is used to enhance understanding of the powerful feelings that were present in this father-son relationship. When the contents of all the sources are joined together we will obtain an almost living portrait of the ambivalence that bound father and son together, of tender and loving feelings as well as anger and disappointment. In sum, feelings that are intrinsic to every parent-child relationship.

(The numbers that follow refer to the numbered footnotes in the printed Hebrew version of the benediction [Figure 8])

1. **"Beyn yakir li"—"My precious son"**
    This phrase appears in the prayers in the *Musaph*, i.e., morning, services for the High Holy Days. The sentence for which this is the opening is taken from the Book of Jeremiah (31:20):[1]

> Truly, Ephraim is a dear son to Me,
> A child that is dandled!
> Whenever I have turned against him,

My thoughts would dwell on him still.
That is why My heart yearns for him;
I will receive him back in love
          —declares the Lord.

In the first line of this verse Ephraim is the symbol of the Israelites who were not exemplary in their behavior, that is, their devotion and allegiance to the God of Israel was inconsistent and their attitude, at times, hostile. In their rebelliousness they worshipped other gods. 'A child that is dandled' is one in whom the parents take great pride and delight.

It would appear that in Jacob Freud's mind there is an association between Ephraim and Sigmund. However, Sigmund Freud seems to have identified with Manasseh, the firstborn of the two brothers. In *The Interpretation of Dreams* (pp. 197-8), Freud relates an experience at the age of ten or twelve when he took a walk with his father who told him of an episode that took place when he was a young man. He was walking one Saturday in the streets of Freiberg. He was wearing a new fur cap when a young man came by, knocked the hat off his head and shouted, "Jew! Get off the pavement!" When young Sigmund asked what he did in response to this unprovoked attack, Jacob quietly replied, "I went into the roadway and picked up my cap!" Sigmund was upset by the unheroic conduct of his father and he contrasted this situation with that of Hannibal, the Carthaginian general. Hannibal's father made his son swear that he would some day take vengeance on the Romans. Since that episode in Sigmund's childhood, Hannibal became one of his heroes. Freud goes further back in his childhood when he had another hero, Napoleon's marshall, Massena. Freud states, "and at that time my declared favorite was already Massena (or to give the name its Jewish form, Manasseh.)" In a sentence added in 1914 he states, "No doubt this preference was also partly to be explained by the fact that my birthday fell on the same day as his exactly one hundred years later." In a footnote that Freud added in 1930 he writes, "Incidentally, doubts have been thrown on the marshall's Jewish origin." The identification of Freud with Massena is quite clear.

An analysis of this paragraph indicates that there was neither a logical nor a relevant need to insert the comment about Manasseh or of its being the Jewish form of Massena. Freud wanted very much for Massena to be Jewish so as to flesh out the identification. It would not have been necessary to even mention Manasseh, the older of the two Biblical brothers, unless he identified with him too. There is no evidence that Massena was Jewish or, for that matter, that the name derives from Manasseh. It was Freud's need to identify and the similar sounds of the consonants of the two names facilitated a connection between them. In this instance, Freud was, like Hannibal, intent on vengence for his father's humiliation so he chose Massena, an historical military figure who was closer to him in time and, in fantasy, religion. That the biblical Manasseh was less favored by his grandfather Jacob is therefore irrelevant to the sequence.

It is important to note that Sigmund Freud's youngest sibling and only surviving brother (after Julius who died in 1858), born on April 19, 1866, was named Alexander Gotthold *Ephraim* Freud. As noted earlier, he was, in part, named after Jacob Freud's paternal grandfather, Ephraim Freud, and, in all probability, after his maternal grandfather as well. Thus, we have a re-creation of the Biblical family unit on two simultaneous levels: first there is Jacob (Freud) and Joseph (i.e., Sigmund); then there is Manasseh (i.e., Sigmund) and Ephraim (i.e., Alexander).

In this same paragraph from *The Interpretation of Dreams*, Freud goes on to trace the development of this martial ideal to his childhood when at the age of three he had an adversarial relationship with his nephew John, who was a year older than he. John was the firstborn son of his half-brother Emanuel and the first grandson of Jacob. Did the insertion of Manasseh and John into the association sequence reflect an expression of the Biblical story of Ephraim (in this instance, associated with John) and Manasseh?

Much is revealed by Jacob Freud referring to his new fur cap that he wore on Saturday. As noted above, Jacob came from an Orthodox Ḥasidic background and, as a young man, still retained the observance of religious ritual and Ḥasidic customs. The Ḥasidim traditionally wear ordinary black hats during the week but on the Sabbath (and, in all probability, Jacob referred to the day as the 'Sabbath' rather than 'Saturday') married men wear the circular fur hat called the *shtreimel*. This hat would have made him immediately recognizable as a Jew. The contrast between the aggressive behavior of the Patriarch Jacob in retaking by force that portion of land known as *Shekhem* and Freud's father's behavior as the passive victim of the Gentile boy's attack is an interesting one. It was, after all, a piece of property that was legally purchased and owned by the Patriarch and then seized illegally by its prior owners.[2]

2. "Kisheva bimay shnai ḥayekhah"—"In the seventh of the years of your life"

This phrase translated literally would be 'In the seventh of the day of the years of your life'. It has its source in Genesis 47:28:

> Jacob lived seventeen years in the land of Egypt, so that the span of Jacob's life came to one hundred and forty-seven years.

The choice of the phrase, 'In the seventh of the years' has resulted in some interesting speculation. Jones (Volume I:15) notes that "Freud's continuous memories began at the age of seven." Schur (1972:p.466) states, "We know

that Freud began to read the Old Testament at the age of seven." But he gave
no source for this information. The number seven has mystical significance
as it is an oft used number among Jews (Roback, 1957), though there does
not appear to be any Biblical or Talmudic attribution to the importance of
this age. The choice of the thirty-fifth birthday for the dedication has some
cultural and realistic foundations. In Central Europe the thirty-fifth year
marks the transition from youth to middle age (Roback, 1957); by 1891 Freud
had already published the results of some of his neurophysiological research
and his first book, *On Aphasia*, was published that year. The only reference in
Freud's works that has something to do with the seventh year of his life is the
dream he had at that age:

> It is dozens of years since I myself had a true anxiety-dream. But I remember
> one from my seventh or eighth year, which I submitted to interpretation
> some thirty years later. It was a very vivid one, and in it I saw *my beloved
> mother, with a peculiarly peaceful, sleeping expression on her features, being carried
> into the room by two (or three) people with birds' beaks and laid upon the bed. I
> awoke in tears and screaming, and interrupted my parents' sleep. The strangely
> draped and unnaturally tall figures with birds' beaks were derived from the illustrations
> to Philippson's Bible. I fancy they must have been gods and falcons' heads from an
> ancient Egyptian funerary relief* ... (S.E. V:583, italics Freud's)

Woodcuts in the Philippson Bible

Figures 15 and 16, taken from the Philippson Bible, may have been the
woodcuts that served as part of the day residue for Freud's dream that night.
Figure 15. This woodcut appears in chapter 4 of Deuteronomy (p. 871 of
the Philippson Bible). There are Egyptian gods with falcon heads, human
face and bird combinations as well as other idols. The Biblical text refers to
Moses telling the Israelites about how they travelled through the wilderness,
how God protected them and helped them vanquish their enemies. He refers
to the Ten Commandments and warns them not to fashion or worship any
graven images, i.e., idols, but only the one invisible and non-representational
God that has always been on their side. Dire punishment is predicted if they
disobey God's commandments. The Israelite tribes would be broken up and
spread among other groups of people.

> There you will serve man-made gods of wood and stone, that cannot see or
> hear or eat or smell. (Deuteronomy 4:28)

In Philippson's comments on this section he refers to the different Egyptian
gods exemplified in the woodcut, and discusses idolatry, polytheism and

monotheism. He points out that Moses had to condemn the presence and worship of any concrete or visible representation of the godhead. Since the central focus of this section is the Ten Commandments, which are about to be announced in the next chapter, and all their moral implications, Grinstein (1968) postulates that Freud as a seven-year-old perceived a message that any expression or gratification of oedipal wishes are strictly forbidden. However, the rebelliousness implicit in idol worship may also have affected Freud.

Figure 16: This woodcut is entitled '*Bier. From a Bas Relief in Thebes*'. It is associated in the Philippson Bible (p. 394) with II Samuel 3:31-35. It would appear that it is most relevant to the dream. The bier looks like a bed on the back of an animal with a sphinx-like face. On this bed lies the body of a man. There is a female figure on each side ('*two or three people*') watching over the bier ('*unnaturally tall and strangely draped*'). There is a bird on top of each column and a bird with an extended, draping wing in the center of the canopy.

In his commentary on this illustration Philippson states that the bier looks very much like a bed. The quality and appearance of a particular bier were functions of the status of the deceased in society. The greater the wealth, the more luxurious the bier. He discusses the elaborate Roman funerals of antiquity and also the professional 'wailers', women who practiced their craft at the funerals of the Israelites.

In a most perceptive interpretation, McGrath (1986) suggests that the biblical Rachel, the most beloved wife of Jacob and the mother of her firstborn son Joseph, was identified in Freud's mind with his own mother. He notes that in a discussion of the Joseph story in Genesis 35, Philippson refers to the location of the grave of Rachel by citing I Samuel 10:2, where Samuel informs Saul, after his annointment as the first king of Israel,

> When you leave me today, you will meet two men near the tomb of Rachel in the territory of Benjamin, at Zelzah, and they will tell you that the asses you set out to look for have been found, and that your father has stopped being concerned about the asses and is worrying about you, saying: 'What shall I do about my son?'

3. Hayḥayl ruaḥ H' liphamekhah"—"The spirit of the Lord first moved you"
One possible source for these words is in the Book of Judges 13:25, which states,

> The spirit of the Lord first moved him in the encampment of Dan, between Zorah and Eshtaol.

One Biblical commentator (in the Soncino edition of the Bible) defines 'the spirit of the Lord' as an irresistable impulse accompanied by unusual physical strength.

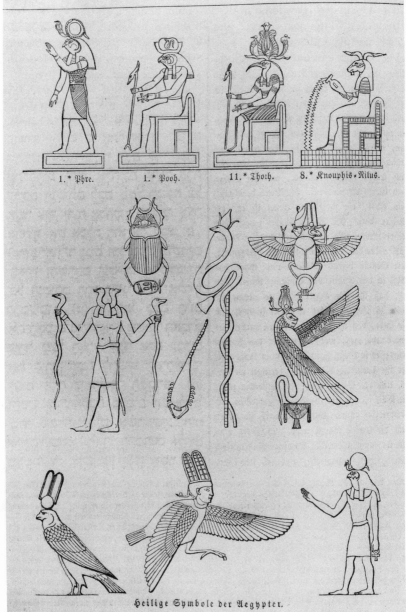

1.* Phre.   1.* Pooh.   11.* Thoth.   8.* Knouphis=Nilus.

Heilige Symbole der Aegypter.

Figure 15. Egyptian idols.

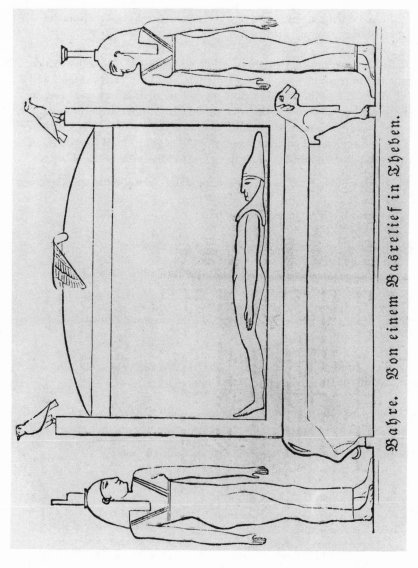

Bahre. Von einem Basrelief in Theben.

Figure 16. Egyptian bier.

4. **"Besifri asher katavti"—"In My book which I have written"**
This is derived from Exodus 32:32:

> And yet, if You would only forgive their sin! If not, erase me from the record which You have written!

This sentence appears in the portion of the Book of Exodus which pertains to the rebelliousness of the Israelites who have rejected God and turned to worship of the golden calf. Upon seeing their behavior Moses, in anger, breaks the two tablets which God had given him on the mountain. When the rebellion is over Moses asks them to atone for their sins. He then asks God to forgive their sin of making gods out of gold, and if God does not see fit to do so, He should then blot the name of Moses out of the Bible.

5. **"Vahyivakeuh likhah maainot"—"And fountains . . . will burst open before you"**
These words derive from Genesis 7:11:

> In the six hundredth year of Noah's life, in the second month, on the seventeenth day of the month, on that day
> All the fountains of the great deep burst apart,
> And the flood-gates of the sky broke open.

6. **"Binah deiah vehaskail"—"Knowledge, discernment and wisdom"**
This derives from Jeremiah 3:15:

> And I will give you shepherds after My own heart, who will pasture you with knowledge and skill.

The 'shepherds' refer to secular rulers. It also appears in the fourth of the eighteen silent blessings which are recited everyday during prayers.

7. **"Biairoh ḥafru ḥakhamim"—"The well unearthed by sages"**
This derives from Numbers 21:18:

> The well which the chieftians dug,
> Which the nobles of the people started
> With maces, with their own staffs.
> And from Midbar to Mattanah.

The 'nobles' refer to Moses and Aaron. The Septuagint, the first Greek translation of the Bible, translates the word 'midbar' as 'the well'.

This verse, *The Song of The Well*, appears to be a fragment of a poem that may be Moabite in origin but rewritten so as to refer to Israel.

This song, although we have only the opening lines, is among the oldest in the Hebrew Bible, along with the oracles of Balaam in Chapters 23-24. Its setting and meaning are clarified by an understanding of the nature of the soil in the wilderness. In low-lying areas of Transjordan and in the valleys of the Negeb, one comes suddenly upon damp land in very dry surroundings, at times marked by clumps of vegetation. Such a place is known to the Arabs as a Temilah. The earth can be dug easily and water is found at a shallow depth. This is the kind of well dug by the ancients with their sticks. (Cornfeld and Freedman, 1976, p. 57)

8. "Umeḥokikim"—"From which our rulers"

This word may have been derived from Numbers 21:18 where the word used is *bimḥokeyk* which means 'with the sceptre'. The root of the verb *ḥokeyk* means 'to engrave'. The noun can also refer to rulers, nobility or legislators.

9. "Maḥazeh Shadai ḥazitah"—"A vision of the Almighty have you beheld"

This derives from Numbers 24:4:

> Words of him who hears God's speech,
> Who beholds visions from the Almighty,
> Prostrate, but with eyes unveiled.

This sentence is part of what is called *The Book of Balaam*, a story that is contained within the Book of Numbers. It is about a man named Balaam, who initially is an enemy of the Israelites. He was a man of inherent contradictions or ambivalences, being represented in the Bible as, at times, a heathen sorcerer who wants to destroy Israel and, at others, a true prophet. His contradictions are reflected in the Jewish traditional views of him. Some see him as being wicked and deceitful while others see him as a prophet on a level with Moses.

Balaam was known as a soothsayer and sorcerer whose power to curse could not be defeated. When the Moabites perceived a threat of invasion by the Israelites they came to Balaam and pleaded with him to render a curse of destruction on them. Balaam had never met the Israelites and did not know anything about them. God appears to him and tells him that the Israelites are a blessed people and that he should really bless and not curse them. Balaam then hesitates and the princes of Moab raise the reward; they will give him all the honor, as well as all the silver and gold that he desires, if he will render his unbeatable curse. Balaam appears to be seduced by the Moabites but his greed and professional inclinations are then matched by the stubbornness of his ass, who refuses to take him to the place where he can see the Israelites and cause their destruction. God then opens the mouth of the ass and words of criticism of Balaam issue forth from it. When Balaam finally arrives at a point near the Israelite encampment and sees the tribes of Israel, he undergoes a dramatic emotional and ecstatic experience. The Bible describes it as 'the spirit of God coming unto him'. His eyes are now opened and he can see the vision of the Almighty, which represents the height of emotional and intellectual insight. The following verse, 24:5, which begins in the following way, "*How fair are your tents, O Jacob*", expresses his realization and appreciation of the value of the Israelites. (Is Jacob Freud unconsciously equating his son with Balaam? Did he wish that Sigmund would have the same vision and discard his antipathy towards Judaism?)

10. **"Verabot asitah"—"Many things have you heard and accomplished."**
    These words derive from Psalm 40:6:

> You, O Lord my God, have done many things;
> the wonders You have devised for us
> cannot be set before You;
> I would rehearse the tale of them,
> but they are more than can be told.

11. **"Vatehdeh al kanfai haruaḥ"—Gliding on the wings of wind (or spirit)"**
    These words are derived from Psalms 18:11:

> He mounted a cherub and flew,
> gliding on the wings of the wind.

(The King James version of the Bible uses 'spirit' while the more recent Jewish Publication Society version uses 'wind'.)

12. **"Min az hayah hasefer kamus"—"Since that time has the Book been sealed up!"**
    These words are derived from Deuteronomy 32:34:

> Lo, I have it all put away,
> Sealed up in My storehouses.

It is puzzling (but then again, maybe not) why Jacob Freud chose this verse. Consciously, he is referring to the Bible in which he is writing the dedication to his son. However, in the Biblical verse, 34, the object that is stored is symbolically its diametric opposite. The preceding verse, 33, states:

> Their wine is the venom of asps,
> The pitiless poison of vipers.

What is stored, therefore, is the symbolic poisonous wine which God can then use, if necessary, to punish the rebellious Israelites.

Chapter 32:1-44, known as the *Song of Moses*, is a farewell song stated in poetic form. Moses is now on the banks of Jordan, in view of the Promised Land which he himself is destined not to enter. He speaks as if it were a time long after his death. Moses looks back in time and reviews the relationship between God and Israel. God is described as a loving, caring and faithful father while Israel is depicted as rebellious and ungrateful. The disasters that befell Israel are considered merited. However, in the end, God will always intervene to save Israel.

13. "Beshivrai luḥot beahron imahdi"—"Like the broken tablets in the Ark"
These words are derived from Deuteronomy 10:1-3:

> 10:1. Thereupon the Lord said to me, "Carve out two tablets of stone like the first, and come up to Me on the mountain; and make an ark of wood.
> 10:2. I will inscribe on the tablets the commandments that were on the first tablets which you smashed, and you shall deposit them in the ark."
> 10:3. I made an ark of acacia wood and carved out two tablets of stone like the first; and taking those two tablets, I went up the mountain.

God then wrote ten words on the tablets just as He did the first time on the mount out of the midst of fire. He then gave the tablets to Moses and when he descended from the mount he put the tablets into the wooden ark.

In his use of 'Tables of the Law', Jacob Freud relies on the Rabbinic tradition (Babylonian Talmud, Tractate Menaḥot 99a) which in turn is derived from Exodus 32, Deuteronomy 10:1-2, and I Kings 8:9. The first set of tablets (Exodus 32) were broken by Moses in a rage at the rebellious and idol-worshipping Israelites. He then, according to this tradition, put the broken fragments away in the Ark of the Covenant for safekeeping.

14. "Mikhseh ohr ḥadash"—"Have I covered it with new leather"
These words are derived from Numbers 4:10:

> They shall put it and all its furnishings into a covering of dolphin skin, which they shall then place on a carrying frame.

In a clever use of metaphor, Jacob Freud compares the vicissitudes of the Tables of the Law to the covers and binding of the Bible, i.e., the two tablets are equated with the two covers. Both through use and age, the covers and binding of the Bible have fragmented and on the occasion of his son's thirty-fifth birthday he has had the Bible rebound. It is a matter of conjecture if Jacob unconsciously equated the Israelites' ambivalent reaction to the Tables of the Law to Sigmund's attitude toward the Bible and what it represented.

15. **"Ali beayr anu lah"—"Spring up, O well; greet it with song!"**
    These words are derived from Numbers 21:17:

> Then Israel sang this song:
> Spring up, O well—sing to it.

16. **"Ahavat olam"—"Who loves you with love eternal"**
    These words are derived from Jeremiah 31:3:[3]

> The LORD revealed Himself to me of old.
> Eternal love I conceived for you then;
> Therefore I continue My grace to you.

Several themes emerge from a study of the biblical sources of the Hebrew dedication. Overtly, Jacob expresses profound love and admiration for his brilliant son. He reminds him of the roots of his scholarly and scientific quests. Jacob's world is a theocentric one based on the Bible. Sigmund's first exposure to learning was through the Bible and his father earnestly entreats him not to forget it. Though based in the past, the 'Book of Books' will inspire him to the greatest achievements in the future.

The poem begins with the biblical Patriarch Jacob and his favorite son Joseph for whom he had made that special coat of many colors. That specialness was to have its real-life counterpart in the lives of Jacob and Sigmund. It was very shortly after the old man's death in 1896 that Freud began what he referred to as his 'self-analysis' which was to lead to the discoveries described in *The Interpretation of Dreams*. The poem ends with the theme of Moses and his experiences with the rebellious Israelites. It is indeed a most interesting coincidence that Sigmund's last major work was *Moses and Monotheism*.

The latent content, as seen in an examination of the biblical sources of the dedication, is revealing of the father's ambivalent feelings towards his son and the son's relationship to the Jewish religion. Jacob appears critical and yet forgiving of his son's rebellious attitude towards religion. He is reminded of the time in childhood when the Bible had much meaning for him and when it served as the impetus for his scholarly interests. References to Moses and the rebellious, idol-worshipping Israelites are numerous. In retrieving and rebinding the Bible, Jacob indicates how he would like his son to renew the tie to the Jewish tradition that he had forsaken. It may also reflect feelings that pertain to Jacob himself who, towards the end of his life, uses his son's birthday as a vehicle for return to his own religious roots. The dedication may have been meant for the father as much as it was for the son.

CHAPTER 8

Jacob Freud, Leopold Breuer, and Isaac Bernays—
Divergent Approaches to the 'Haskalah'

It is worth examining briefly the quality of Jewish thought and culture in Eastern Europe in the nineteenth century, for we will need to answer the question: Was Jacob Freud heir to an Enlightenment philosophy by which he abandoned the trappings of traditional Jewish faith, or did he in fact retain a good deal of his Jewish outlook and even aspects of Jewish practice, going as far as the regular study of the Talmud? It seems necessary to show that the Jewish Enlightenment itself was far more complicated than Freud biographers often assume and not at all synonymous with mere seculariization. Even at its most rebellious, the movement reflected an ambivalence toward traditional Judaism that many of its children carried with them throughout life.

Much has been made of Jacob Freud's being a member of the Haskalah, the Enlightenment movement that swept through European Jewish culture and religion in the nineteenth century (Aron, 1957; Halevy, 1958-9; Bergmann, 1982; Ostow, 1982). The evidence cited is his relative lack of ritual observance, the celebration of the major Jewish holidays, but no observance of dietary laws or synagogue attendance, and the writing style and content of the Hebrew dedication composed in honor of his son's thirty-fifth birthday.[1]

The Haskalah is the Jewish counterpart to the European post-Renaissance Enlightenment, which represented a departure from the rigid Aristotelian and Thomistic modes of thought and a drastic change in the metaphysical foundations of scientific thought, all of which led to the modern era of inductive reasoning and empiricism. Major political changes were required in Western Europe before the Enlightenment could effectively begin and somewhat more time was needed for the winds of change to blow eastward toward Austria-Hungary, Poland and Russia. Restrictive ghetto conditions helped insulate Jews against its influence for awhile, but the wall of the ghetto eventually yielded to these powerful ideas, though not without much opposition.

The Haskalah movement was resisted intensely by the Orthodox Jewish establishment, who viewed it as a very serious threat to their continued existence, and, in a sense, they were right. Most of the proponents of the movement did shed their Orthodoxy and often became quite militant against it.[2] However, these revolutionary ideas did not at first lead to assimilation and conversion to the Christian faith. A 'new' religion, within an elaborated framework of the 'old', took its place. The devotion and intensity of feeling that were previously channelled into the traditional Orthodox way of life were now invested in a new nationalistic and cultural system of thought and behavior.

The primary goal of the Haskalah was to create the conditions that would bring about the adjustment of Jewish life to the modern world. Once this was accomplished, it was felt, the social and political emancipation of the ghetto Jew would automatically follow. The Haskalah was not a monolithic entity and there is no consensus on how it can be defined. It is properly viewed as a spectrum of opinions, holding in common the goals of acquiring secular knowledge, gaining equality of opportunity and achieving physical and spiritual emancipation from the ghetto. This rebellion followed no set pattern and the decision to retain or abandon aspects of one's religious roots was a highly individual matter.

> In short, Haskalah aspired to reform Jewish life socially, religiously and aesthetically, to regenerate Hebrew literature by injecting into it the serum of reality . . . The Haskalah movement was the outgrowth of an idea. But ideas have a way of releasing strange forces, unforeseen by those with whom the ideas are original. Thus Haskalah, which aimed to teach the modern Jew to observe the world about him, eventually led the thinking Jew to look more deeply into his own world. (Bavli, 1949)

In Eastern Europe, the Maskilim (proponents of the Haskalah) were split between those who felt that the Yiddish language should be the vehicle of expression and communication of these new ideas and those who felt that Hebrew should serve this function. This resulted in an outburst of literary creativity in both Yiddish and Hebrew. The Yiddishists of the Haskalah wrote tracts propagating their ideas and polemics criticizing the ghetto life style and culture. The Hebraicists,

> in their quest for humanism and classic beauty, rediscovered the Bible as a source of poetic inspiration, as an instrument of cultural and social progress. (Bavli, 1949, p. 571)

What was conspicuously absent from the Enlightenment agenda was any mention of a positive role for the Talmud. On the contrary, the Talmud became the *bete noir*, for it symbolized to the Maskilim all that was responsible for the persistence of the ghetto mentality down through the ages and thus constituted a major obstacle that had to be overcome before the desired entry into Western European culture could be secured.

This charge ignored certain historical circumstances. With the possible exception of pre-inquisition Spain (1492), Jews were forbidden by law to participate in any way in mainstream activities of the countries in which they resided. They could not enter the schools or universities and their choices of occupation and movement were severely limited. For example, prior to 1848 Jews in the Austrian Empire were restricted to specific villages and needed special permits to leave them. Jacob Freud and his grandfather had to renew their permits to travel to and from Tysmenitz and were allowed to stay in Freiberg for no more than six months at a time. They were typical of the *Wanderjuden* (Traveling) Jews and 'Tolerated' Jews who bore the opprobrium of second- (or even lower) class citizens. Jews set up their own schools, the *Ḥeder* and the *Yeshiva*, in which the curriculum was limited to reading and writing Hebrew, Bible, Talmud and the ritual and law codes derived from them, and the Midrash (homiletic commentaries). However, the isolation from the influence of the Enlightenment was not the fault of the Talmud *per se*; it was the uses that were made of it that could justifiably be faulted. Indeed, some of the most outstanding Talmudic scholars on the faculties of German and American rabbinical seminaries in the nineteenth and early twentieth centuries were, as their contemporaries are to this day in the American and British seminaries, erudite in Western culture and tradition in all its manifold aspects. Many professors of Talmud are in the possession of a Doctor of Philosophy degree from an eminent university.

Lack of access to public institutions of learning was not the only factor that militated against the "enlightenment" or westernization of the East European Jew. The Orthodox Jewish community was basically a closed society and, as in any such group, tight controls had to be exerted against any secular influence that might threaten the unity, stability and cohesiveness of the long-established theological and ritualistic system of thought and activity. During the course of the nineteenth century, as the ideas of the Enlightenment made their way not only into the villages and cities of Eastern Europe but also into the *Yeshivot* (plural of *Yeshiva*), students were forbidden to read any secular literature that could be perceived as posing the remotest threat to their beliefs. Those who would not abide by this rule had to leave the *Yeshiva*. Young men who tasted of the fruits of Enlightenment and were influenced by it were left in a desperate situation. If they went public and rebelled, they risked rejection and ostracism while they did not have the option of becoming part of the Gentile majority. This gave rise to the phenomenon of the *bein hashmashot* Jew—one who lived in the 'twilight' between the 'darkness' of limited access to knowledge as exemplified by the closed society and the 'Enlightenment', between the Jewish and non-Jewish worlds (not that the latter were necessarily 'enlightened'). An enhanced understanding of this background will help the reader better appreciate and understand Leopold Breuer's reaction when he left the *Yeshiva* in Pressburg and went to Prague (as described by his son, Josef Breuer, later in this book).

Attitudes toward the Talmud within the Orthodox communities varied along a continuum from the Ḥasidim, who underplayed study of the Talmud and gave priority to piety, prayer, emotional expression and adherence to sanctified leadership, to the Misnagdim, the opponents of the Ḥasidim, who put an almost exclusive focus on the intellectual aspects of Judaism, i.e., the study of the Talmud. The *Yeshivot* were the major centers for such Talmudic study.

If the father of the house was a Talmudic scholar, able to study the Talmud without the frequent participation of a cohort, then this raised the intellectual level of the family unit far above that of Jews who were not similarly inclined. It created an attitude, a tone and an ambience in the family in which the pursuit of learning had the highest priority. For this to be sustained, the mother had to provide consistent reinforcement.

In his autobiography the philosopher Morris Raphael Cohen, who was born in a village in Russia and emigrated to the Lower East Side of New York City at the age of twelve in 1892, recalled his childhood educational experiences:

> ... my predominant feeling was of gratitude to the *rebbeh* for enabling
> me to obtain what I had desired in vain for several years—an opportunity
> to study Gemara [Talmud]. We had an old Talmudic scholar teach several of
> us the Tractate Baba Kama, while others were taught Russian by a young
> man. After the Passover my mother hired a young Talmudic scholar who
> was living in a nearby synagogue and waiting for a call to serve as a *rov*
> [Rabbi] to help me continue my Talmudic studies. I enjoyed that im-
> mensely, but probably more from pride at attaining the heights of pious study
> rather than because of any inherent interest in the minutiae of the Law of
> Divorce. (1949)

An aristocratic flavor was attributed to such a scholarly family. The father's Talmudic interests projected a powerful beam of intellectual curiosity and learning that affected the entire household, especially its male members.[3] As has been noted earlier, unfortunately scholarship in Eastern Europe was limited to the Talmud and related texts. The intrusion of secular knowledge was perceived as a threat to religious belief and the cohesiveness and unity of the social fabric. The systematic study of the cultural, legal and linguistic influences on the Talmud from the Greek, Roman and Arabic cultures and civilizations did not begin until the nineteenth century, when Jewish scholars in Germany had the requisite secular education and the freedom to pursue these interests. From the Orthodox perspective the exclusion of Western secular ideas was justified not only to inhibit any potentially heretical approaches but also by the thoroughly ingrained belief that the Talmud was of Divine origin and therefore immune to such critical scrutiny. The Bible was considered *Torah shebicsav*, the written word of God, and the Talmud was considered *Torah shebalpeh*, the word of God that was transmitted orally over a period of centuries through the Rabbis and only subsequently written down by their students. This activity continued until the end of the Talmudic period in the seventh century C.E. The divine origins of both the Bible and the Talmud, in the mind of the Orthodox Jew, rendered them immune to the critical scrutiny that could threaten their unity and integrity.

Jacob Freud and the Talmud

Questions have been raised about Jacob Freud's attachment to Orthodox tradition and his attitudes toward the Talmud. In 'Discussion Regarding Sigmund Freud's Ancestry' (1958-9) Mayer Halevy states that while living in Tysmenitz, Jacob Freud had already expressed interest in the Haskalah through his friendship with the major spokesman for it in that city, Zevi Menachem Pineles, who published a critique of the Talmud in 1861. Halevy states that in 1928, while visiting with the son of Pineles, he himself discovered two or three letters written to the elder Pineles by Jacob Freud. (These letters have not been seen again nor mentioned by anyone else. It is difficult to reconcile this view of Jacob Freud with the man who wrote Hebrew inscriptions in the family bible and who studied the Talmud into his last years as described by his granddaughter, Judith Bernays Heller (1956).

In any event, this scholarly attitude toward the Talmud must have pervaded the Freud household and must have had some influence on Sigmund's choice of an academic and scholarly pathway in his intellectual and emotional development. This same 'beam' of Talmudic scholarship projected by the father, when subjected to the prism of the enlightened attitude of Vienna, resulted in a fairly wide spectrum of scholarly and cultural interests.

As with any inquiry, the unearthing of existing clues, which either may not have been noticed or, if noticed, not given adequate attention, leads to the unraveling of the hidden picture, in this case that of the intellectual and emotional development of Sigmund Freud. Jacob Freud's granddaughter Judith Bernays Heller (daughter of Sigmund's oldest sister, Anna), lived with her maternal grandparents in 1892-93. In 1956 she wrote an account of her experiences with them. Relevant to this discussion are these comments:

I cannot say who really supported this establishment. I do know that my grandfather was no longer working, but divided his time between reading the Talmud (in the original) at home, sitting in a coffee house, and walking in the parks. Occasionally, he took me with him, when the others were too busy to occupy themselves with me ... It seems to me, as I look back now, that Freud's father lived somewhat aloof from the others in his family, reading a great deal—German and Hebrew (not Yiddish)—and seeing his own friends away from home. He would come home for meals, but took no real part in the general talk of the others. It was not a pious household, but I do remember one Seder at which I, as the youngest at the table, had to make the responses to the reading of the song about the sacrifice of the kid; I was greatly impressed by the way my grandfather recited the ritual, and the fact that he knew it by heart amazed me.

Jacob Freud's study of the Talmud reveals much about the Freud family and their attitude toward scholarship. Most significant to this discussion is the statement that he "read the Talmud (in the original) at home." Before carrying this piece of revealing information further it might be helpful to give a brief description of the contents and style of the Talmud. It is known as the Babylonian Talmud because it was composed during the exile of the Jews in Babylon following the destruction of the Second Temple by the Romans in the first century of the Common Era. Academies of higher learning were set up by the exiles. (The phrase 'higher learning' must be kept in perspective, considering the state of general knowledge at the time.)

Historically, the creation of the polity of the Jewish people began with the Bible, which was considered to be divinely revealed to Moses. With the passage of time the Bible was found insufficient to cover the needs of the growing communities. New laws were needed and the Bible became the equivalent of the United States Constitution, all subsequent laws being derived from it. The discussions and decisions were then incorporated in the 'Mishnah' which was written in Hebrew.[4] The Mishnah, too, eventually became insufficient, so the rabbis in Babylon, like the judges in America with regard to the Constitution, used the Mishnah as a basic framework of established principles and precedents in the formulation of new laws. The Talmud consists of 63 Tractates which were finally bound into 20 volumes and are roughly grouped according to subject matter, though the same subject may also be discussed in different Tractates.

In a typical page (Figures 17-18) the specific text of the Mishnah occupies the center of the page. Each topic under discussion begins with a quote from the Mishnah followed by discussions of the rabbis, written down by students at the academies. These seemingly rambling discussions are, essentially, the Talmud. The transcribed discussions are as close to the free association system of the psychoanalytic situation as any piece of literature can be. The language

זה בורר פרק שלישי סנהדרין כט

תורה אור

קרובים ונתרחקו הוו אתו לקמיה לדינא אמר להו פסילנא לכו לדינא אמרו ליה מאי דעתיך כר' יהודה אנן *מייתינן איגרתא ממערבא דאין הלכה כרבי יהודה אמר להו אטו בקבא דקירא אידבקנא בכו דלא קאמינא פסילנא לכו לדינא אלא משום דלא צייתיתו דינא : אוהב זה שושבינו וכו': וכמה אמר ר' אבא אמר רבי ירמיה אמר רב כל שבעת ימי המשתה ורבנן משמיה דרבא אמרי אפילו מיום ראשון ואילך : השונא כל שלא דבר כו': ת"ר והוא לא אויב לו יעידנו ולא מבקש רעתו ידיננו אשכחן שונא אוהב מנלן קרי ביה הכי והוא לא אויב לו ולא אוהב לו יעידנו ולא מבקש רעתו ולא טובתו ידיננו מידי אוהב כתיב אלא סברא הוא אויב מאי טעמא משום דמרחקא דעתיה אוהב נמי מקרבא דעתיה ורבנן האי לא אויב לו ולא מבקש רעתו מאי דרשי ביה חד *לדיין אידך כדתניא אמר רבי יוסי ברבי יהודה והוא לא אויב לו ולא מבקש רעתו מכאן לשני תלמידי חכמים ששונאין זה את זה שאין יושבין בדין כאחד: מתני' כיצד בודקים את העדים היו מכניסין אותן לחדר ומאיימין עליהן ומוציאין *את כל האדם לחוץ ומשיירין את הגדול שבהן ואומרים לו אמור היאך אתה יודע שזה חייב לזה *אם אמר הוא אמר *לי שאני חייב לו איש פלוני אמר לי שהוא חייב לו לא אמר כלום עד שיאמר בפנינו הודה לו שהוא חייב לו מאתים זוז ואחר כך מכניסין את השני ובודקין אותו אם נמצאו דבריהן מכוונין נושאין ונותנין בדבר *שנים אומרים זכאי ואחד אומר חייב זכאי שנים אומרים חייב ואחד אומר זכאי חייב אחד אומר חייב ואחד אומר זכאי *אפילו שנים מזכין או שנים מחייבין ואחד אומר איני יודע יוסיפו הדיינין *גמרו את הדבר היו מכניסין אותן הגדול שבדיינין אומר איש פלוני אתה זכאי איש פלוני אתה חייב ומניין *לכשיצא לא יאמר אני מזכה וחבירי מחייבים אבל מה אעשה שחבירי רבו עלי על זה נאמר (לא תלך רכיל בעמך ואומר)[א] הולך רכיל מגלה סוד : גמ' היכי אמרי להו אמר רב יהודה הכי אמרינן להו נשיאים ורוח וגשם אין איש מתהלל במתת שקר אמר (*ליה) רבא יכלי למימר שב שני הוה כפנא ואבבא אומנא לא חליף אלא אמר רבא אמרינן להו מפיץ* וחרב וחץ שנון איש עונה ברעהו עד שקר אמר (*ליה) רב אשי יכלי למימר שב שני הוה מותנא ואיניש בלא שניה לא שכיב אלא אמר רב אשי אמר לי נתן בר מר זוטרא אמרינן להו סהדי שקרי אאוגרייהו זילי דכתיב והושיבו שנים אנשים בני בליעל נגדו ויעידוהו לאמר ברכת אלהים ומלך : אם אמר הוא אמר לי כו' עד שיאמרו בפנינו הודה לו שהוא חייב לו מאתים זוז : מסייע ליה לרב יהודה דאמר רב יהודה אמר רב צריך שיאמר אתם עדיי איתמר נמי א"ר חייא בר אבא א"ר יוחנן *(מנה לי בידך אמר לו הן למחר אמר לו תנהו לי אמר משטה אני בך פטור) תניא נמי הכי מנה לי בידך אמר לו הן למחר אמר לו תנהו לי אמר לו משטה אני בך פטור ולא עוד אלא אפילו הכמין לו עדים אחורי גדר ואמר לו מנה לי בידך אמר לו הן רצונך שתודה בפני פלוני ופלוני אמר לו מתיירא אני שמא תכפיני לדין למחר אמר לו תנהו לי אמר לו משטה אני בך פטור ואין טוענין למסית מסית כאן דבר שמיה חסורי מיחסרא והכי קתני אם לא טען אין טוענין לו בדיני נפשות אע"ג דלא טען טוענין לו ואין טוענין למסית מאי שנא מסית אמר ר' חמא בר חנינא מפירקיה דרבי חייא בר אבא שמיע לי שאני מסית *דרחמנא אמר לא תחמול ולא תכסה עליו אמר רבי שמואל בר נחמן אמר רבי יונתן מניין שאין טוענין למסית מנחש הקדמוני דא"ר שמלאי הרבה טענות היה לו לנחש לטעון ולא טען ומפני מה לא טען לו הקב"ה לפי שלא טען הוא מאי הוה ליה למימר דברי *הרב ודברי התלמיד דברי מי שומעין דברי הרב שומעין אמר חזקיה מניין שכל המוסיף גורע שנאמר אמר אלהים לא תאכלו ממנו ולא תגעו בו רב משרשיא אמר מהכא אמתים וחצי ארכו רב אשי אמר מהכא עשתי עשרה יריעות אמר אביי לא שנו אלא דאמר משטה אני בך אבל אמר

לא

Figure 17. Specimen page from Babylonian Talmud

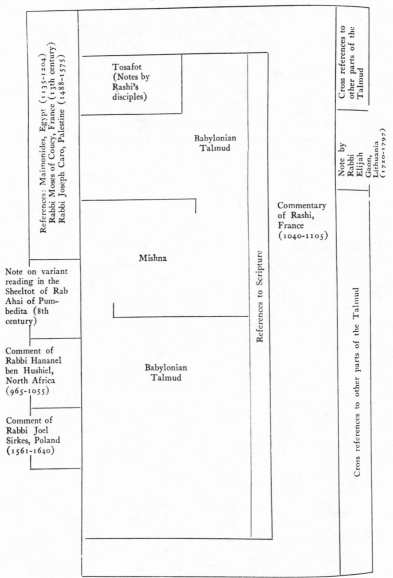

A PAGE FROM THE BABYLONIAN TALMUD
Treatise Sanhedrin, 29a
Romm edition, Vilna, 1895

A discussion of methods of examining witnesses and
ascertaining the validity of their evidence

Cross references to other parts of the Talmud

References: Maimonides, Egypt (1135-1204)
Rabbi Moses of Coucy, France (13th century)
Rabbi Joseph Caro, Palestine (1488-1575)

Tosafot
(Notes by
Rashi's
disciples)

Babylonian
Talmud

Note by
Rabbi
Elijah
Gaon,
Lithuania
(1720-1797)

Commentary
of Rashi,
France
(1040-1105)

Mishna

References to Scripture

Note on variant
reading in the
Sheeltot of Rab
Ahai of Pum-
bedita (8th
century)

Comment of
Rabbi Hananel
ben Hushiel,
North Africa
(965-1055)

Babylonian
Talmud

Cross references to other parts of the Talmud

Comment of
Rabbi Joel
Sirkes, Poland
(1561-1640)

Figure 18. Explanation in English of specimen page from Babylonian Talmud. Figure from *THE JEWS* by Louis Finkelstein. Copyright 1949, 1955, 1960 by Louis Finkelstein. Reprinted by permission of Harper & Row, Publishers, Inc.

is that which was spoken by Jews in ancient Israel and Babylon, i.e., Aramaic, but it is written in Hebrew characters.[5] There are no capital letters, punctuation, or vowels. The comments are syntactically structured, that is, based on what was considered its own syntax at the time of their composition and transcription, but flow into each other. Discussion of legalities (called *Halakhah*) is interlaced with stories (called *Aggadah*), sometimes to make a point and at other times just for the sake of telling an interesting story. The entire Talmud contains five centuries of such discussions and arguments. On the right side of the page are commentaries in Hebrew by the twelfth century French scholar Rashi. On the left side are commentaries from scholars prior, and subsequent, to Rashi. The Talmudic discussions reflect a distinctive mode of logic and thought as well as the proverbial hairsplitting discussions that have pejoratively characterized the Talmud through the centuries. (Amid the Freud-Jung controversy over the latter's penchant for mystical thought, Karl Abraham wrote to Freud, "After all, our Talmudic mode of thought cannot disappear just like that." [Freud-Abraham letters, p. 34].)[6]

The laws that are found in all the sacred scriptures, from the Bible through the Talmud, are based on casuistic formulations of the law. In addition, there is also an apodictic-style set of laws, e.g., the Ten Commandments, among many others, which are considered to have been stated by God in the form of categorical imperatives, the fulfillment or violation of which were met either with Divine blessing or punishment.[7] Hypothetical situations, drawn by the rabbis in the Talmud from real life as well as from the realm of the improbable if not impossible, are described and then the legal ramifications and consequences are derived from them.[8] The Talmud is very difficult. The absence of punctuation in an ancient and unspoken language like Aramaic increases the obstacles already presented by abstruse arguments of what are often insoluble dilemmas.

The Talmud cannot be 'read'; it has to be studied very intently. It was not taught in the *Ḥeder* in the early years of childhood and was briefly touched on in the latency years. It was studied only in the *Yeshiva* in adolescence and adulthood. The rare exceptions were when a private tutor was engaged or when the parent was a Talmudic scholar himself, but it would nevertheless require a great deal of study for mastery to be acquired. In the *Yeshiva*, the Dean (*Rosh Hayeshiva*) would give a lecture once or twice a week and the rest of the time the students would study in pairs for many hours a day, everyday. This sequence and schedule for the study of the Talmud is as true today as it was in nineteenth century Eastern Europe.

For Jacob Freud to be able to study the Talmud alone implies that he must have spent many years as a student in a *Yeshiva* in Tysmenitz and continued the practice of such study for many years thereafter. Some anecdotal verification for this hypothesis was provided by Henry Bondi who was told by his uncle Samuel Bondi, who knew Jacob Freud well, that Jacob was always referred to fondly by family and friends as the *Yeshiva Boher*, the Hebrew expression for 'a young yeshiva student totally immersed in his studies', because he had studied as a youth in the *Yeshiva* in Tysmenitz and was always found studying the Talmud to the very end of his life in 1896. Unless they had studied for many years in a *Yeshiva*, most Hasidic Jews, for example, do not know how to study the Talmud, certainly not without help from a cohort. Such voluntary studies by Jacob Freud also indicate that he could not have been much of a *Maskil*, a committed adherent to the Haskalah movement, for with the *Maskil* the study of the Talmud received little or no priority.

There were exceptions, however, to the relationship between the Talmud and the *Maskil* as described above. For some former students of the *Yeshiva* who had rebelled and shed their Orthodoxy, be they Lithuanian or Galician, the devotion to and study of the Talmud persisted to the very end of their lives. For them, study of the Talmud was completely independent of a religious frame of reference; it was studied for its own sake. For one who has mastered the Hebrew and Aramaic languages, as well as the Talmudic mode of reasoning, the study of the Talmud can be an exciting intellectual and emotional experience.

Jacob Freud's ability to study the Talmud alone, and at home, strongly implies that he owned a complete set of the Talmud (*Shas* as it is referred to by Orthodox Jews). Not many Jewish families, then or now, have a complete set in their private libraries. Jacob Freud may well have been a *Maskil* but such an individual would certainly not be thought of as assimilated. He was deeply anchored in both the Jewish religious and scholastic traditions and though the tether was lengthened during his lifetime it was never severed.

A most interesting and significant discovery was made recently at the Freud Museum in London. The curators found the complete, twelve volume, German translation of the Babylonian Talmud in Freud's library. The curators provided a copy of the face-sheet of Freud's copy (Figure 19), along with a copy of a face-sheet of an as yet unidentified book, one of four volumes, presumably 'unidentified' because it was in Hebrew characters (Figure 20). It was immediately identified by me as the Babylonian Talmud in the original Aramaic language. *Freud possessed not only the German translation but also the complete four-volume set of the Babylonian Talmud in the original Aramaic. This four volume edition was printed in Berlin in 1928.*[9] It is an exact replica of the classic 20 volume set of the Vilna Edition of the Babylonian Talmud. (The city of Vilna [Vilnius], in Lithuania, was for centuries one of the main centers for Talmudic scholarship.)

There are no written annotations in the margins of these volumes of the Talmud so that it is not known how thoroughly Freud read them, if at all. If Freud admitted that he could not read Hebrew and certainly not Aramaic, then why did he possess a complete set of the Talmud? Was the influence of

Jacob Freud's intense interest in the Talmud a factor? Were they gifts of some admiring friend or did Freud acquire them on his own? The four-volume set of the Talmud that was in Freud's possession was printed in 1928 (Figure 20) and the German translation in 1929 and 1930 (Figure 19). Freud thus acquired these volumes at a time late in his life when his interest in his religious roots was undergoing revival. Their acquisition may have been a reflection of his return journey to the Judaism of his father. It came at a time when he was beginning, or was heavily involved in, his research on the Biblical and historical character of Moses. The question then could also be asked why did Freud, in making the selection of those books from his library in Vienna which he felt he had to take with him to London, include both sets of the Talmud?

Leopold Breuer—From Mattesdorf to Vienna

To highlight the varied approaches to the Haskalah, it might be helpful to discuss two other first-generation Jews of the Enlightenment, Leopold Breuer, the father of Josef Breuer, and Rabbi Isaac Bernays, the paternal grandfather of Martha Freud.

Leopold Breuer was born in 1791 in Mattesdorf, Hungary. When he was thirteen, he entered the *Yeshiva* at Pressburg. His teacher was one of the greatest Talmudic scholars of the early nineteenth century, Rabbi Moses Schreiber, also known as the *Ḥatam Sofer*.[10] At the age of sixteen, Leopold Breuer hitchhiked to Prague, where, as his son Josef wrote in his autobiography:

> ... the metamorphosis of the student of the Talmud into a man of the nineteenth century began. Leopold Breuer, as the date of his birth indicates, belonged to that generation of Jews who were the first to emerge from the intellectual ghetto into the free atmosphere of Western civilization. This occurred in Austro-Hungary later than in Berlin, in which city the impetus originated. I think that one cannot estimate too highly the intellectual energy which was contributed by that generation. The most reverent honour from their sons and grandsons, for whom all paths have been made easy, is due to those pathfinders. They replaced Jewish jargon by literate German and the slovenliness of the ghetto by the cultured custom of the Western world, to win for themselves a place in the literature, poetry, and philosophy of the German people. All this required the highest degree of mental effort in observation of the environment, in a sympathetic striving for union with it, and in study which received almost no encouragement. (Autobiography of Josef Breuer)[11]

In 1835 Leopold Breuer was appointed as director of the school of religion of the IKG. He wrote the textbook that was used by Freud and for

תלמוד בבלי

DER BABYLONISCHE TALMUD

NACH DER ERSTEN ZENSURFREIEN AUSGABE UNTER
BERÜCKSICHTIGUNG DER NEUEREN AUSGABEN UND
HANDSCHRIFTLICHEN MATERIALS NEU ÜBERTRAGEN
DURCH

LAZARUS GOLDSCHMIDT

ERSTER BAND

BERLIN

VERLAG BIBLION

1929

Figure 19. Face-sheet of Sigmund Freud's copy of German translation of the Babylonian Talmud. Courtesy of the Freud Museum, London.

מסכת

ראש השנה
מן

תלמוד בבלי

עם פירוש רש־י ותוספות ופסקי תוספות
ופירוש המשניות להרמב־ם ועם
מסירת הש־ס ועין משפט נר מצוה
ותורה אור והגהות גדולי האחרונים

ונלוה עליה

תוספתא ראש השנה

Figure 20. Face-sheet of Sigmund Freud's copy of the Babylonian Talmud in the original Aramaic
language. Courtesy of the Freud Museum, London.

many years in German-speaking countries (*Leitfaden beim Religions-unterrichte der israelitischen Jugen*, Vienna: Klopfsen und Eurich, 1855). He also established a library for the IKG which was to become one of the longest-lived and most valuable of its kind (Grunwald, 1936). He was a classical representative of the very bright young Jew who, driven to emancipate himself from the ghetto and all it represented, had to rely on his own inner resources in order to succeed in his intellectual and emotional journey to Western civilization and all that that implies. Despite financial impoverishment, limited opportunity to enter the government educational system and persistant discouragement in the pursuit of secular knowledge, he became a supreme exemplar of that phenomenon of rebellious nineteenth-century Jewish youth: the autodidact. The secular knowledge he acquired appears to have been all at his own initiative. He was able to affect the personal compromise that inevitably occurs within the first generation that has tasted of the old and the new without having to resort to assimilation.

Rabbi Isaac Bernays—Paradigm of Orthodox Judaism in Germany

An example of someone at the Orthodox end of the Enlightenment continuum is the paternal grandfather of Martha Bernays Freud, Rabbi Isaac Bernays (1792-1849). He was the fourth of ten children born to Jacob (1747-1817) and Martha Welsch Bernays (1761-?) of Mainz. The Orthodox Jewish community of Hamburg, threatened by the inroads of Reform Judaism, selected as its leader a man who was comfortable in both the secular and religious worlds. Isaac Bernays was a graduate of both the University of Wurzberg and the *Yeshiva* headed by Rabbi Abraham Bing, by whom he was ordained. He was appointed Chief Rabbi of Hamburg in 1821 but not until the community leaders agreed to three nonnegotiable conditions:

1. That he have complete control over the parochial schools.

2. That he receive a fixed salary rather than have to depend on contributions, gifts, or fees for the performance of religious rites such as marriages and funerals.

3. That he be called Ḥakham, rather than the customary *Moreh Zedek* ('Righteous', or 'Holy Teacher') or Rabbi, Ḥakham being considered more prestigious since it was the title that the Sephardic Jews used for such an exalted position (The Jewish Encyclopedia, 1906, Vol. III, p. 90).[12]

According to Henry Bondi, the Bernays were not a 'rabbinical' family in the classical sense. Ḥakham Bernays was the first, and only, rabbi in the family. The family came originally from Mainz, Germany where their name was Behrmann. While he and his brother Adolphus (1794-1864) were students at the University of Wurzburg they changed their name to Bernays (though it is possible that the name change occurred somewhat earlier).[13] Adolphus, in addition, converted to Christianity and after graduation emigrated to England, where he became a scholar of some prominence. He was Professor of Modern Languages at King's College, London. His descendants became prominent Conservative Party politicians, scientists and bankers.[14]

Examination of the Bernays family tree[15] confirms Bondi's comment that the only rabbi in the Bernays family was the Ḥakham. The family tree dates back to the eighteenth century. The family name listed is Bernays but the one who compiled the lengthy family tree may not have been aware that the prior name may possibly have been Behrmann. The Ḥakham's paternal uncle had six children and two of the sons were named Pious (who was born in 1779 and appears to have married a first-cousin, Hanna Bernays, born 1797, who was a sister of the Ḥakham) and Christian (born 1786) not typical Jewish names, to say the least.

Isaac's emotional conflicts in terms of personal identity and self-esteem did not end with the change of name and his appointment as Chief Rabbi. In the early part of the nineteenth century in Hamburg, only Jews of Portuguese and Spanish descent (i.e., Sephardim), who had been longtime residents there, were permitted to live in Hamburg proper. They were the major merchant bankers and shipping magnates. Ashkenazi Jews (those other than Spanish and Portuguese, but basically referring to the German Jews) had to be out of the city by dusk. The Sephardim had their own synagogue in Hamburg, which obviously had no Ashkenazi members or worshippers.[16]

Isaac Bernays was a supreme orator and was the first Orthodox rabbi to preach in German and to attempt to adapt religious Orthodoxy to Enlightenment times. In 1822 he set about to change the curriculum of the *Talmud Torah* (which was the equivalent to the private religious *Volksschule* in Vienna). Originally only Hebrew and some arithmetic were taught but he added German, natural science, geography and history. He was so successful in this endeavor that by 1827 what was once only a religious school had become an excellent primary school whose graduates could go on to the *Gymnasium*. One of his students was Samson Raphael Hirsch, who went on to become the most prominent and influential Orthodox rabbi in nineteenth-century Germany.

Jacob Freud, Leopold Breuer and Isaac Bernays can be considered, for purposes of our discussion, as first generation heirs of Orthodox Judaism. It is interesting to see how the second generation not only adapted to the pathways followed by their fathers, but also how it affected their individual compromises in regard to their Jewish religious tradition.

The Children of Ḥakham Isaac Bernays

The Ḥakham had seven children, four sons and three daughters. Biographical data could be found for only three of the sons: Jacob (1824-1881), Berman (1826-1879), and Michael (1834-1897). Basically, Jacob kept the faith but his religious adjustment and compromise were slightly more modern than that of his father in the sense that he was affiliated with a rabbinical seminary that was not the complete equivalent of a traditional Orthodox one. In 1849 he was appointed an instructor in philology at the University of Breslau. He was one of the founders, in 1854, of The Jewish Theological Seminary of Breslau (the forerunner of The Jewish Theological Seminary of America, founded at the end of the nineteenth century, as the center for the new movement of Conservative Judaism, the centrist group on the Orthodox-Reform continuum). He was a Classical and Hebrew scholar with extensive university experience but yet remained intensely Jewish in his thoughts, feelings and life style. He was strictly observant of all the Jewish rituals and was a prominent member of the faculty of the seminary. In 1868 he was appointed Assistant Professor and Librarian at The University of Bonn. Among the subjects he taught were Greek, Latin, history of German literature and philosophy of religion.

Berman Bernays, the father of Martha Freud, became the secretary to the economist Lorenz von Stein in Vienna. Both he and his wife, Emmeline, were Orthodox Jews as we know from Freud's difficulties with Martha during their long courtship (e.g., she was forbidden to write to him on the Sabbath but finally affected a secret compromise by using a pencil rather than a pen; she refused to give up fasting on Yom Kippur, etc.).

Michael Bernays (1834-1897) was fourteen years old when his father died. Whether because of this traumatic loss at an early age or other factors, his adjustment was radically different from his two brothers. He rebelled against the family tradition and in 1856 was baptised a Christian, as his uncle Adolphus had been. As a result, he became completely estranged from his family. Jones (1953, I:101) notes that Jacob Bernays 'sat Shiva', i.e., undertook seven days of mourning for his brother as a result of this act; the apostate was treated as one who was legally, in Jewish tradition, dead. Jones points out that conversion was an indispensable requirement for appointment to full professorship at a German university. (As the Jewish poet Heinrich Heine put it, conversion was his own ticket of entry to European culture and society; so it was with the composer Gustav Mahler who converted to further his career, one of his rewards being the appointment as conductor of the Vienna Symphony Orchestra.) Michael became a well-known historian of literature at the University of Bonn, then at the University of Leipzig and in 1874, at the University of Munich, where he was among the most popular teachers and socialized with the rich and famous, including King Ludwig II of Bavaria.

Josef Breuer

Josef Breuer (1842-1925) was born in Vienna, the elder of two sons. His father did not marry till 1840, at the age of forty-nine, and his young wife died at the birth of their second son, when Josef was two years of age. His maternal grandmother moved into the house and assumed the role of mother. In his brief autobiography (1953) Josef wrote:

> I did not attend public school, but did the same work at home without any difficulty under the excellent instruction of my father. I was able to read perfectly at the age of four. When I was eight years old, I entered the Akademische Gymnasium (located on Universitatsplatz) which was conducted according to the Bonitz-Exner plan of instruction, probably the first of its kind.

In 1848, by Imperial decree, the Emperor granted permission for Jewish students to attend the *Gymnasium* without having to obtain consent from the local government. His father, unlike Jacob Freud, was obviously quite capable of teaching him at home. Leopold Breuer instructed his son not only in secular subjects but also in Hebrew, Bible and Talmud.

Breuer was graduated from the *Gymnasium* in 1858 and wanted to start medical studies immediately, but his father persuaded him to spend a year enhancing his education in the liberal arts. He did not consider it a fruitful year, but the teacher that most impressed him was the Economics professor, Lorenz von Stein, the man who subsequently became Berman Bernays' employer. Breuer distinguished himself in medical school and stayed on after graduation to conduct research on the relationship of the vagus nerve to respiration under the guidance of the physiologist E. Hering. In 1868, Hering read the paper on their presumably (there has been some question as to the degree of Hering's input into the research project) joint findings. The discovery of this new reflex mechanism pertains to the automatic central nervous system regulation of the respiratory process of inhalation and exhalation which became known as the Hering-Breuer Reflex.

Breuer became the favorite of the chief of the medical clinic, Oppolzer, and upon graduation in 1867 was appointed his assistant. In 1871 he became a *Privatdozent*.[17] He was on his way to an academic career but the demise of Oppolzer shortly thereafter forced a change in plans. The new chief, Bamberger, took away the *Privatdozent* appointment and with it went the ward beds that were indispensable to Breuer for clinical teaching and research. Billroth [see Appendix I] came to the rescue with an offer to propose Breuer to the Faculty Senate for the honorary position of Professor Extraordianius but Breuer declined the offer, severed all academic ties to the medical school and went into private practice, becoming the most sought-after and successful internist in Vienna. Nevertheless, he continued laboratory research in a part of his own apartment.

In 1880 he treated a young woman who was suffering from severe hysteria accompanied by numerous conversion symptoms, such as transient paralysis of hands and legs, abnormal body movements, persistent cough, occasional trance, etc. This was Bertha Pappenheim, the famous "Anna O." whose case is described in Breuer's joint study with Freud, *Studies on Hysteria* (1895, S.E. II). The concept of emotional catharsis (Breuer's term) received its first clinical application here. Anna O. referred to this process as the 'talking cure' and 'chimney sweeping', the early forerunner of the 'free association' technique later elaborated by Freud.

Breuer's attitude toward his Jewishness was, on balance, quite positive. His relationship with his father was a close one. Throughout his life Josef Breuer was positively identified with the Jewish community and participated actively in it. An item of revealing interest was his membership in the *Hevra Kadushah*, Hebrew for 'Holy Congregation or Fellowship' from 1873 until his death in 1925. Only the most Orthodox of Jews were permitted to serve on this committee. Their duties involved washing the deceased, putting on the shrouds and prayer shawl, and covering the eyes and mouth prior to burial. Such activities were believed to fulfill the noblest and most holy commandment a Jew could fulfill. There was a male committee and a female counterpart. Once a year, the entire community or congregation would give a party specifically to honor the members of this committee.

This evidence can only lead to the inevitable conclusion that Breuer was an Orthodox Jew. However, it appears that the Jewish community of Vienna had a different conception of the *Hevra Kadushah* as the following demonstrates (Grunwald, 1936, p. 384):

> In 1763, a group of young people founded a society which they called 'Hevra Kadushah Shel Bahure Hemed be-Vina' (The Holy Society of Choice Young Men of Vienna) Its purposes were the following:
>
> 1. to conduct lectures on Halakha and Aggadah every Saturday, instead of spending the day in amusement;
>
> 2. to support the poor in a manner not humiliating to them;
>
> 3. to provide for poor brides;

4. to clothe the needy;

5. to visit the sick, provide them with medical treatment, pray for their restoration to health, and, in case of death, to arrange for the recital of the kaddish by a relative or an orphan of a neighboring community.

The young founders of the society hoped by their example to encourage the older generation to engage in similar work. Every member undertook to devote some time daily to the study of the Talmud, privately or with a teacher. In view of the fact that communal worship was prohibited in Vienna, it was arranged that on every eve of Rosh Hodesh (the New Moon or first day of the Hebrew month) six members should take their turn in fasting. Offerings were made for the building of a synagogue, for the poor in Palestine, for the redemption of captives from pirates, and so on. When a member became ill, ten of his associates read the Psalms in his behalf daily and studied a chapter of the Mishna. As in other cases, anyone who was unable to perform his duties contributed money to the treasury of the organization or provided a substitute for himself.

When Breuer was first inducted into the *Hevra Kadushah* in 1873, he and the other new members were told by a member of the Executive Committee (Klein, 1985, p. 58):

Intimacy and brotherhood are very deep and inalienable elements of the Jewish heritage; intimacy and brotherhood are also the bases of *Hevra Kadusha.*

The degree and extent of Breuer's participation in the activities of this organization are not known. Whether it was a reflection of his ambivalence toward his religious background or of his liberal, enlightened beliefs, Breuer's choice of cremation after his death is certainly a convincing indication that the Viennese *Hevra Kadushah* was just a fellowship since cremation is absolutely forbidden by Orthodox Judaism.

Breuer was eulogized by a close friend, Hans Horst Meyer, at a memorial service in 1925. The first sentence, seemingly perfunctory, may contain a clue to Breuer's Jewishness.

On June 23 1925, the cremation of the late Dr. Josef Breuer took place— according to his last will—quietly and without pomp, nevertheless with un- usually large and serious participation by all strata of the citizenry of Vienna.

The statement, 'according to his Last Will' is surprising. If Breuer had been a longstanding member of the liberal Jewish establishment then why was it even necessary to mention his desire for cremation? Cremation was, and still is, not an unusual practice among liberal Jews and it would have been not worthy of mention in a eulogy. Does this imply that in the years prior to the making of his last will he inclined toward a traditional Jewish life style and then underwent a radical change in the last years of his life?

The degree of Breuer's religious commitment and ritual observance is not known with certainty. Kathe Breuer, his daughter-in-law, sent Ellenberger (1970, p. 424) a copy of a letter from Breuer to Kadimah, the student Zionist society at the university, in 1894 regarding its hypersensitivity to anti-Semitism:

> Our epidermis has almost become too sensitive, and I would wish that we Jews had a firm consciousness of our own value, quiet and half indifferent to the judgement of the others, rather than this wavering, easily insulted, hypersensitive *point d'honneur*. Be that as it may, that *point d'honneur* is certainly a product of the 'Assimilation'.

He signed it *'Josef Breuer, Stirpe Judeus, Natione Germanus'* ('Jew by Origin, German by Nationality'). For reasons that are not clear, it appears that Breuer had to make himself oblivious to, or not allow himself to be affected by, the obvious presence and prevalence of anti-Semitism. As noted above in regard to his comments about his father's East European background, Breuer placed a very high premium on his 'German' identification.

There is another part of this letter which was not published, in which Breuer states that he had *departed* (italics mine) from Orthodox Judaism and adopted the views of so-called liberal Judaism.

Ellenberger (1970) compares Breuer's attitudes with those of Freud:

> No doubt there were many among Freud's Jewish contemporaries whose lives and careers followed a similar pattern (without, however, gaining world fame). A comparison of Freud and Breuer may be instructive: Breuer, who had been the victim of intrigues and who had missed the opportunity of a brilliant career, never attributed any of his setbacks to anti-Semitism, and declared that he was perfectly content with the life he had; whereas Freud repeatedly referred to the hostile attitude of anti-Semitic colleagues and officials. Speaking of his father, Breuer emphasized how wonderful it had been for a man of his generation to be free from the ghetto and able to enter the wider world; Freud's only reference to his father's youth was the story of the affront he suffered from a Gentile. Breuer devoted half of his autobiography to a eulogy of his father, in contrast to Freud who had no compunction against expressing hostile feelings toward his father. Breuer criticized the hypersensitivity of the Jew to the slightest anti-Semitic touch, and ascribed it to imperfect assimilation; from the beginning Freud felt he belonged to a persecuted minority and attributed his creativeness partly to the fact that he had been compelled to think differently from the majority. Benedikt, in his autobiography, gave a long list of complaints about many of

his contemporaries, but never accused them of anti-Semitism. Thus, to be a Jew in Vienna could lead one to adopt different attitudes toward Judaism and the Gentile world, and it was no obstacle to feeling thoroughly Viennese at the same time.

The relationship between Freud and Breuer was indeed a rather complex one and yet was typical of the 'sturm und drang' of Freud's intense ties to other men whom he initially perceived as his superiors. The ambivalence of his friendship with Fliess is well known; that with Breuer is much more difficult to understand. Here was a man, fourteen years his senior, who provided extensive emotional, financial and professional support for many years, whose normality, basic humanity and decency were consistently acclaimed by all who knew him, suddenly becoming an arch enemy.[18] It was all Freud's doing, without any reciprocal animosity from Breuer. Their personal estrangement has been attributed to purely scientific differences (Jones, I:253; Sulloway, 1983, p. 99) but I find such explanations unsatisfactory.

In a letter to Fliess on January 22, 1898 Freud wrote:

> My anger at Breuer is constantly being refueled. Recently I was disturbed to hear from a patient that mutual acquaintances had said that Breuer severed his relationship with me because he dissaproved of the way in which I conduct my life and money matters—a man who earns so much money must save some of it and think of the future. This last remark they have from Breuer himself, who is their family physician. If you want to understand the full extent of his neurotic dishonesty, put the above together with the remark in his letter that he thought my debt to him had already been paid. Did he really think I would start saving money *before* I had paid back my old debts for my education? In all of this, one may always assume that one hears only a small part of the rumors that are being spread about.

There is a pathetic element in this stormy relationship. In the early 1920s, Breuer's daughter Hannah related that she and her elderly father were out for a stroll when they saw Freud walking in the opposite direction. Breuer opened his arms to greet him but Freud ignored him and continued to walk on at a quickened pace.

Freud's personal animosity towards Breuer was obviously unrequited. When Breuer died, Freud sent a condolence letter to the family. In response the eldest son, Robert Breuer, stated "that his late father had always watched Freud's development and success with pleasure and pride." Freud was touched and pleased (Gay, 1988, pp. 482-483). Breuer was indeed a true friend, gentleman and humanitarian to the very end of his life.

A year before he died Breuer wrote in his curriculum vitae:

If I can add to this outline of my life that I have been and am happy in my own house, that my beloved wife has presented me with five excellent children, that I have lost none and none ever caused me serious sorrow, then I may well confess to be one of the happy ones. If there is anything that can avert the jealousy of the gods, it is my deep conviction that I have been made happy beyond merit.

CHAPTER 9

'One Must Close the Eyes'

Unlike Breuer, whose rebellion against his religious origins was less extreme than Freud's and seems to have caused him less pain, Freud was far more complicated in his approach to Judaism. So too was Freud's approach to death and dying.

Using the presumably predictive numerology of his friend Wilhelm Fliess, Freud was constantly prognosticating the year of his own death. There is no clear explanation why a man so devoted to rational thought and science would resort to so mystical a practice. It is easy to say that Freud was perpetuating an aspect of his Ḥasidic heritage by indulging in *gematria*, the branch of Jewish mysticism devoted to numerology. He most certainly was not. But it may be true that the spiritual concerns so long suppressed by Freud the avowed atheist found expression, ironically, in the realm of pure superstition.[1]

Freud was frequently in dread of an untimely death and especially fearful that it would precede that of his parents. The varied coping mechanisms that he utilized in dealing with the funerals of his parents is revealing not only of his attitude towards death but his ambivalent feelings towards them.

In the light of what appears to be a shared unconscious fantasy between Jacob and Sigmund Freud based on the Biblical Jacob and Joseph story, it is now possible to amplify the interpretation of one of Freud's dreams, first described in his letter to Fliess on November 2, 1896. Jacob Freud died on October 23, 1896, and the dream occurred, according to the letter, on the night after the funeral.

> I must tell you about a nice dream I had the night after the funeral. I was in a place where I read a sign:
>
> > you are requested
> > to close the eyes.

I immediately recognized the location as the barbershop I visit every day. On the day of the funeral I was kept waiting and therefore arrived a little late at the house of mourning. At that time my family was displeased with me because I had arranged for the funeral to be quiet and simple, which they later agreed was quite justified. They were also somewhat offended by my lateness. The sentence on the sign has a double meaning: one should do one's duty to the dead (an apology as though I had not done it and were in need of leniency) and the actual duty itself. The dream thus stems from the inclination to self-reproach that regularly sets in among the survivors.

In describing the same dream in *The Interpretation of Dreams* (1900, p. 317f.) Freud makes several changes. The first involves a change in the time of occurrence of the dream, from the night *after* the funeral to the night *before*. In the Fliess letter he found himself in a shop to which he associated the barbershop. In *The Interpretation of Dreams* the notice reminds him of a notice in a railway waiting room that forbids smoking. He also adds uncertainty as to whether the notice stated that he should close one eye or both eyes.

It can be assumed justifiably that the version described in the Fliess letter is the correct one as it is the closer in time to its occurrence and was written with the freedom of a man who never thought the letter would be published. It is not certain whether Freud was being completely candid about the events surrounding the funeral and his role and behavior in it. There is also the question of whether the textual changes in the later version were consciously or unconsciously motivated. He associates to the barber and arriving late to the funeral. He also expresses some guilt over having arranged for a funeral service that was simpler than the family would have wanted. In *The Interpretation of Dreams* he adds that the simplest possible ritual would have been in accordance with his father's known views on such ceremonies. (The analysis of Jacob Freud's Hebrew inscriptions would indicate that he may have overestimated his father's 'liberal' views on such matters.)

It is difficult to imagine what Freud meant in regard to simplifying the religious ritual. An Orthodox funeral service would take no longer than three minutes if one adhered to the barest essentials. My impression is that the reference to Freud's dream may well have concerned an indispensable ritual that occurs prior to the funeral service, the cleansing of the body by the *Hevra Kedusha*, the burial committee. Did Freud modify or even dispense with this ritual? There is a possibility that the guilt over not doing 'one's duty to the dead' may also refer to his having violated the religious injunction against the bereaved cutting his hair for thirty days after the death of a parent.

There is an intriguing question about whether Freud recited the mourner's *Kaddish* prayer at the burial site, as is required of the sons of a deceased parent. It is possible that he did so even though this would have contravened his own beliefs, but evidence is lacking. The family and peer pressure to recite the prayer at such a time would have been enormous, but then again Freud might have been rebellious enough not to carry out this ritual. He certainly did not recite it daily for one year afterwards in the synagogue, as is the ritual requirement.

There is another indispensable ritual whose elimination would better explain this dream, one that was certainly known to Jacob and most probably to Sigmund since its practice is not limited to Jews. It is incumbent on the son to gently close the eyes and mouth of the deceased father prior to the funeral. If the son is not present this is done by the *Hevra Kedusha*. This ritual is based on Genesis 46:4 where God tells Jacob,

> "I Myself will go down with you to Egypt,
> and I Myself will also bring you back;
> and Joseph's hand shall close your eyes."

Jacob was thus assured by God that Joseph would fulfill this commandment of closing his father's eyes just after he dies.

On September 12, 1930 Amalia Freud passed away at the age of ninety-five. On September 15, 1930 he wrote to Jones (1957, p. 152):

> I will not disguise the fact that my reaction to this event has because of special circumstances been a curious one. Assuredly, there is no saying, what effects such an experience may produce in deeper layers, but on the surface I can detect only two things: an increase in personal freedom, since it was always a terrifying thought that she might come to hear of my death; and secondly, the satisfaction that at last she has achieved the deliverance for which she had earned a right after such a long life. No grief otherwise, such as my ten years younger brother is painfully experiencing. I was not at the funeral; again Anna represented me as at Frankfort. Her value to me can hardly be heightened.

On September 16, 1930 Freud wrote to Ferenczi:

> Above all my warm thanks for your beautiful words about the death of my mother. It has affected me in a peculiar way, this great event. No pain, no grief, which probably can be explained by the special circumstances — her great age, my pity for her helplessness toward the end; at the same time a feeling of liberation, of release, which I think I also understand. I was not free to die as long as she was alive, and now I am. The values of life will somehow have changed noticeably in the deeper layers. I did not go to the funeral; Anna represented me there, too. (Letters, 1960, p. 400)

Only two weeks prior to Amalia's death, Freud sent his daughter Anna to Frankfurt to accept the Goethe Prize for Literature on his behalf. He could not make the journey because of the poor state of his health. But how do we explain his absence from his mother's funeral which was held in Vienna? As far as is known, he was not bedridden at the time. One can only speculate. Did he feel too weakened by his debilitating cancer of the jaw for which he was still being treated? Was he fearful of experiencing the same intensity of grief as that of his brother Alexander? Was he expressing his hostile feelings towards her? Was it the idea of a funeral service itself that deterred him? Was it the religious component of the service? In apologetically explaining his absence from the funeral to his brother Alexander, he said that he was not as well as people thought and, in addition, did not particularly care for ceremonies (Gay, 1988, p. 573). The entire family, with the notable exception of Freud, presumably did attend the funeral, so why did he even have to make the point that he was sending Anna as his representative? He was certainly well represented by Martha, his other children and grandchildren.

Freud's conflict about his mother expressed itself in a parapraxis not hitherto noticed or mentioned. On September 12, 1930 he wrote to his nephew in Manchester, Samuel Freud:

> Mother died peacefully this morning in her bedroom in Vienna. The funeral may be on Saturday. At 95 she well deserved to be relieved. (As quoted in Clark, 1980, p. 482)

September 12th fell on a Friday and the funeral, according to Jewish law, had to have taken place on either Friday or Sunday. Funerals and burials are never permitted on the Sabbath. This was obviously also true in Vienna among the entire spectrum of Jews, from Orthodox to Reform.[2] Amalia Freud was buried alongside her husband in the principal Jewish cemetery which was under the control of the IKG. Freud certainly must have known that no Jew could be buried on the Sabbath. One can only speculate about the psychodynamic meaning of this most interesting slip of the pen. Adding further to this mystery is the fact that he went to great lengths to make certain that she had a strictly Orthodox funeral and burial.[3]

CHAPTER 10

Sigmund Freud — Theism vs. Atheism

It has been shown thus far that the departure from the religion of one's childhood is a most difficult task. It is one that is rarely, if ever, fully completed. True, one-time believers have become atheists but the end result is all too often a self-deceptive one. Intense scrutiny will reveal sufficient residue, however much disguised, of what was seemingly left behind.[1]

In 1987, Peter Gay published a study on Freud and religion entitled *A Godless Jew.*[2] In it, Gay focuses on Freud's religious faith rather than on his religious identity or, for lack of a better word, his ethnicity. Freud's Jewishness did not lie on the surface of his life but at its core and to reach that core one must resort to psychoanalytic methods among others. Gay's acceptance of the traditional view of Freud's biographers that his parents were Reform Jews runs counter to the evidence. He posits that Freud was a direct philosophical and ideological descendant of the eighteenth century philosophers, Voltaire and Diderot, the nineteenth century philosopher Feuerbach and the biologist Darwin.[3] This intellectual heritage was complemented by the important influence of his mentors who were arch representatives of nineteenth-century physical science — the physicist Hermann Helmholtz; the physiologist Ernst Brucke; the psychiatrist and brain anatomist Theodore Meynert and the internist Herman Nothnagel. All had the same scientific orientation — positivistic, atheistic and deterministic. There was absolutely no room for teleology in their frame of reference, no place for 'purpose', 'intention' and 'aim' in nature. According to Jones (I:45), and Gay is in agreement, Freud's mentors would have been shocked at his re-adoption of these rejected concepts of pre-nineteenth century science for use in psychoanalytic theory. True, Freud was a thoroughgoing determinist but, despite his implicit protestations, and Jones statement to the contrary, ripples of teleology do permeate his work. His postulate of the life and death instincts are but one notable example. Freud was not immune to syncretistic ideas and tendencies, whether in religion or science.

Freud was not brought up in, nor did he live only, in the rarefied atmosphere of enlightenment ideas. His early East European cultural and religious bases, as represented by his parents and extended family, were only thinly covered over by his subsequent exposure to enlightenment forces. They certainly did not disappear but lingered, unavoidably, to influence him to the very end of his life.

The subject of Freud's atheism lends itself to much discussion. There is no question that he was consciously an avowed atheist. It is not clear exactly when he became aware of a godless universe, or more precisely, when it became an issue of vital concern. Other than the Freud-Silberstein correspondence we have no evidence that would reveal Freud's religious views in childhood and adolescence. The Freud-Fluss correspondence cited earlier focuses on his feelings pertaining to Jewish ethnicity. When he was a student at the University of Vienna he took a course with the philosopher Franz Brentano, a former priest who believed in both God and Darwin. As revealed in his letters to his friend Silberstein, Freud admired him greatly. In Gay's words, "he wrestled with Brentano's seductive theism", but obviously atheism eventually won out. Given Freud's feelings toward father figures, one would have to wonder whether it was due to the attraction to the theistic ideas *per se* or to the bearer of them, what Brentano transferentially represented to him.

In a letter to his friend Eduard Silberstein, dated November 8, 1874, when Freud was eighteen years of age, he wrote, after complaining that Silberstein had left him in the dark about his 'inner spiritual (or intellectual) life' (for which Freud used that difficult-to-translate word *geisteges*):

> I should be sorry, for instance, if you, the lawyer, were to neglect philosophy altogether, while I, the godless physician and empiricist, am attending two courses in philosophy and reading Feuerbach in Paneth's company. One of the courses — listen and marvel! — deals with the existence of God, and Prof. Brentano, who gives the lectures, is a splendid man, a scholar and a philosopher, even though he deems it necessary to support God's airy existence with his own expositions. I shall let you know just as soon as one of his arguments gets to the point (we have not yet progressed beyond the preliminary problems), lest your path to salvation in the faith be cut off.[4]

The process of the development of an individual's theistic and/or atheistic orientation has its roots in childhood, if not earlier. One can never completely shed certain ideas inculcated in childhood, especially when they are so intimately bound with feelings toward the most significant figures of one's life, one's parents.[5] Though one can obviously arrive intellectually, and with all sincerity, at an atheistic view of the universe, this hard-won position often turns out to be a cover and defense against an equally, if not more convincing, perception of a theistic one. It simply resides, in Spinoza's words, 'in the nature of things'. As long as a father and mother are required to bring us into this world, whether it be due to a need that is built into our genetic makeup, or to the crucial interpersonal relationship of infancy and childhood, a Supreme Deity in some form, shape, or manner, will be postulated to exist and thence become the object of adoring and hateful worship. If one denies the existence of the Deity, then this denial will be in need of continued and repetitive reinforcement, as was the case with Freud. This is by no means an argument for Theism. Every individual has to resolve this conflict in his own way based on his own needs and background. Just as no two siblings have the exact, identical, perception of their parent, so no two people have the same perception or concept of God. There are as many Supreme Deities in this world as there are people.[6]

The theistic-atheistic conflict does not begin to emerge until early adolescence, a stormy period in life when one begins to emotionally and physically disengage from the comforts of home, parents and siblings. It is also a time of intense physiological change, when one's own sexual and individual identities are being solidified. The emergence, development and conceptualization of religious belief and its contents appear to be, among other factors, inextricably connected to, and reflective of, the vicissitudes of instinctual drive development. No evidence for atheism, suddenly discovered, is enough to propel an overnight conversion that will last until death. More is needed — an emotional readiness, a predisposition that permits the gradual conviction to take root. Atheism is like every other product of the mind, a compromise formation, a unique resultant of the many conflicting, reconciling, gratifying and punitive unconscious forces. If atheism is discovered much later in life, then the maintenance of that position has, of necessity, to be a militant one in order to guard against the possible and fearful re-emergence of a theistic orientation and the ambivalent feelings that are associated with it. With such individuals, it becomes almost an obsession as with any late-blooming, born-again phenomenon. The same would apply to any systematized ideological outlook — religious, political, or otherwise — which emerges in adolescence, regardless of the merits of the inevitable choice, especially when a degree of passion and commitment is attached to it.

Conversely, there is the phenomenon of a reverse rebellion where an adolescent coming from a completely non, or minimally, religious home, suddenly finds God and takes to religion with passionate intensity, and, at times, with a vengeful quality. In Jewish families, they often inform their parents that henceforth the home must be made kosher or they will not eat in it. There is usually some extra-familial father figure who has stimulated this reaction for which the adolescent was quite ready.

Examples abound of the difficulty in fully surrendering theistic views that were thoroughly inculcated in childhood. Spinoza (1949), often referred to as 'God intoxicated', in his 'Pantheism' or 'Intellectual Love of God' (the attainment of the highest form and level of knowledge), or Mordecai Kaplan (1949) with his redefinition of God as an impersonal 'Power that makes for righteousness', appear to have brought God even closer to earth, for all their rebellion against the supernatural. True, it is not a personal God but it is, nevertheless, a force in nature that fulfills a personally desired function, a force for which there is obviously no empirical proof. (Some may interpret Spinoza's and Kaplan's concepts as metaphors, rather than descriptive, but the style and force of their respective author's expression does not make it feel that way.) The philosopher and psychologist William James, in his own pragmatic way, tried to reconcile religion, philosophy and psychology, though not with much success.

The philosopher and arch-naturalist (in philosophic orientation), Morris Raphael Cohen, provides an example of the overnight adolescent conversion that is deceptively simple. He suddenly discovered that he was an atheist at the age of twelve and began a process of cessation of all ritual observance. He even remembered the exact moment that it had occurred.

> A more important factor, however, in my drift from religious Orthodoxy, was provided by a conversation which I overheard between my father and a certain Mr. Tunick, in the fall of 1892. Mr Tunick's brother had been a neighbor of ours in Minsk, and my father had helped him to come to this country. Our visitor challenged my father to prove that there was a personal God who would be influenced by human prayers or deeds, or that the Jewish religion had any more evidence in favor of its truth than other religions. To this challenge my father could only answer, "I am a believer." This did not satisfy my own mind. And after some reflection I concluded that in all my studies no such evidence was available. After that I saw no reason for prayer or the specifically Jewish religious observances. But there was no use arguing with my father. He insisted that so long as I was in his house I must say my prayers regularly whether I believed in them or not. Such is the Orthodox conception. I had to conform to it until I was in a position to refuse to obey and tell my father I would leave his house if he insisted. This occurred in the fall of 1899. (Cohen, 1949, pp.69-70)

This statement by Cohen is most intriguing. Recall the crucial episode in Freud's childhood, when he was ten or twelve years old, where his father told him of that humiliating experience at the hands of the Gentile, on a Sabbath in Freiberg, who knocked his hat off his head. Without responding, Jacob Freud meekly picked up his hat from the street and walked away. The common element in these stories, though Cohen was a direct witness to the event while Freud was only told about it and then held onto the memory of the telling with tenacity, was a revelation of weakness, humiliation and surrender in the previously powerful father. The elder Cohen did not care to do battle with his friend, as was the case with the elder Freud and his attacker. The father is now vulnerable to the ambivalent feelings of the son. What is then attacked is not the personna of the father but an object that is of considerable importance to the patriarch, i.e., his religion —more specifically, his God.

This series of events, i.e., emergent adolescence and detection of weakness and vulnerability in the father, may well be the first step in the awareness and adoption of an atheistic position. The unconscious feeling of disillusionment must be enormous. The disbelief is then projected onto the supernatural realm. One could speculate further, and it is pure speculation without the corroborating data of a patient in treatment, that the need for an omnipotent and omniscient Father Figure to replace the fallen one is all the more imperative. This, however, has to be denied for the emergent powerful, erotic and aggressive drives of adolescence, coupled with conflicts pertaining to feelings of submission and defiance and unconsciously perceived threats to the stability of one's sexual identity, would then be directed toward this Deity. To deny the existence of this Deity is, therefore, to deny these frightening impulses and the fantasies attached to them.

Cohen eventually arrived at an agnostic position without ever fully giving up a theistic component. His daughter, Leonora Cohen Rosenfeld (1962), relates how he dealt with the problem.

> Cohen adhered to agnosticism all of his life. I never knew him to attend religious services. He definitely did not belong to that brand of philosophers who, in the words of his friend Professor C.J. Ducasse, act like public-relations officers for God, handing out press releases from cosmic headquarters. Nor did he consider himself on such intimate relations with the Almighty as did his old Harvard masters. The story is told that Cohen's younger son as a small boy asked his father one day: "Daddy, what has God been doing since He created the world?" To which the father replied, "Of late, Willie, He's been busy sitting for His portrait by [William] James and [Josiah] Royce."

Atheism, however, was not to Cohen's liking. "Those who called themselves atheists," he once wrote, "seemed to be singularly blind, as a rule, to the limitations of our knowledge and to the infinite possibilities beyond us."

> In two instances worthy of recall, Cohen used the word "God" with positive effect, the first in his letter to Mary Ryshpan, when he implored her to "Take me and inspire me further to my life's ideals—ideals that

are at one with your own—and together we will reach up to God." Later,
he defined God as "not only an existent power but an ideal of holiness,
which enables us to distinguish between the good and the evil in men.
(p. 208)

There is obviously no question that Freud and Cohen were avowed atheists
in that neither believed in a personal God. Yet they could not rid themselves
of the need to use the concept and word of God. In 1887 Freud wrote his
sister-in-law Minna Bernays about the status of his practice. Gay (1989) writes:

> Several weeks before, Freud had notified Minna Bernays with sham piety
> that 'since January 1, a fresh wind is blowing through my practice.' True,
> 'since then two patients have left me, but God now performs a miracle every
> day so that we are earning a few Gulden, and it would be very nice of him if
> he continued to act this way.' There is a malicious point to Freud's mockery:
> Frau Bernays, Minna's mother, to whom most of these letters were also
> addressed, was as devout a Jew as Freud was an aggressive atheist.

Freud's 'aggressive atheism', a phrase Gay repeatedly uses when discuss-
ing Freud's views on religion, is really not as aggressive as Gay portrays it to be.
In a corner of his mind Freud still retained, however consciously repudiated,
some kind of belief in the Deity. Gay does not cite any evidence of a malicious or mocking intent towards Frau Bernays in this letter. Obviously, Freud
was consciously referring to God in a metaphorical, not literal, way but the
choice of the word reveals the everpresent conflicts pertaining to the subject.

An essential point of this work is that, in contrast to Gay's views (1987,
pp. 31, 37, 41), the ultimate conscious adoption of an atheistic position, as
in Freud's case, does not, in the long run, result in an inherently marked
change in oneself or in one's attitudes. The same set of unconscious wishes
and conflicts that revolve around theism and then result in the conscious
adoption of atheism, are often displaced to another object or set of ideas
with an intensity that is really contradictory to the scientific spirit. The
object and/or set of ideas which receive these feelings then become 'reli-
gionized', so to speak. This is true of politics, ethics, or even a presumed
scientific position which is retained after convincing evidence to the contrary is discovered. Karl Marx condemned religion as an 'opiate of the masses' but then put in its place an 'opiate' of his own manufacture. His ideas,
valid or invalid, ultimately took on the dimensions of a full-scale religion,
though the 'divinities' were kept in the natural realm. Erich Fromm (1950),
who came from an Orthodox German Jewish background, tried to serve all
his masters by combining psychoanalysis with religion and Marxism but the
end result was a lovely piece of poetic inspiration that had little to do with
real life.

Despite his intense opposition to religion, Freud was not of one mind on the subject. Gay quotes a sentence from an unpublished letter that Freud wrote in 1927 to the psychoanalyst Max Eitingon,[7] who was probably the most overtly Jewish of his disciples:

> It remains to be considered whether analysis *in itself* must really lead to the giving up of religion. (p. 12)

In 1928 he wrote to another disciple, Marie Bonaparte:

> You are right: one is in danger of overestimating the frequency of an irreligious attitude among intellectuals. I get convinced of that just now on observing the reactions to my [*Future of An*] *Illusion*. That comes from the most varied drinks being offered under the name of 'religion', with a minimal percentage of alcohol—really non-alcoholic; but they still get drunk on it. The old drinkers were after all a respectable body, but to get tipsy on pomerit (apple-juice) is really ridiculous. (Jones III:447)

It would appear that despite Freud's intense wish for the riddance of religion, there is another part, not too far beneath the surface, which yearns for its retention in its original Orthodox form. If that is so he must have been thinking, on a pre- or unconscious level to be sure, of the partly repudiated Orthodox Judaism of his father as the basic model. His acquisition of a complete set of the Babylonian Talmud shortly after these letters were written may well express an identification with his father.

Gay (1987) is correct when he writes:

> But it was as the last of the philosophes that Freud denigrated the religious way—any religious way—of understanding the world as wholly incompatible with the scientific way. (p. 42)

And there is no question that Freud would have seen himself in this light and, that he was himself profoundly uncomfortable with notions of "spirit."[8] However, Gay (1987) is off-target when he categorically states that a residue of religious belief would have kept Freud from his pioneering work:

> With their robust prose, honest self-exploration, psychological penetration, and trusting surrender to higher powers, William James's writings on religion form a backdrop against which Freud's unbelief stands out sharply. It is impossible to conjecture what kind of psychology James would have developed if he had been an atheist like Freud, but it is certain—and I am devoting the rest of this book to demonstrating this argument—that if Freud had been a believer like James, he would not have developed psychoanalysis. (p. 30)

In and of itself a belief in the existence of a Supreme Deity initially would not have interfered with the discovery of psychoanalysis. However, further development of this discovery would necessitate a radical change in philosophical and scientific orientation, from a supernatural frame of reference to a completely natural one. In 1918, in a letter to Oskar Pfister who was Swiss, a professional pastor and lay analyst, Freud asked:

> Quite by the way, why did none of the devout create psychoanalysis? Why did one have to wait for a completely godless Jew? (as quoted in Gay, 1987, p. 37)

If Freud had heard such an emphatic 'completely' from a patient, he would have seriously questioned how 'complete' it was.

The reader should not be left with the impression that a fully successful psychoanalysis, if there be such, will automatically result in the patient's becoming an avowed atheist. This is attributing a power to psychoanalysis which it does not have. It is a known fact that a patient will go only so far therapeutically as his own and the psychoanalyst's unconscious resistances will permit. Each human being has the ultimate responsibility of developing his own world view, religious and secular. It cannot be imposed on anybody without their own, very willing, consent. The same obviously holds true with any vital choice in life, such as the choice of mate or profession.

The Supreme Deity, if one is to believe in such an entity, does not necessarily have to be viewed as, on one extreme, a forever-giving, limitlessly indulgent, and wish fulfilling Santa Claus (in whatever denominational version), or on the other, as an unforgiving, punitive, vengeful, ungiving demon. After all, the underlying conflicts that have led, since the dawn of history, to a need to believe in a transcendent, powerful deity of some sort are of the very same stuff that enters into the making of transference, one of Freud's great discoveries, without the proper analysis of which, meaningful and lasting therapeutic improvement, or cure, could not take place. One could say, without questioning the validity of the actual existence or non-existence of the Supreme Deity, that God, in whatever form, is a transference figure that is subject to the same kind of scrutiny and analysis as any other such figure. It will reveal more about the figurer than the figure.

Knowledge of the physical world, the world of ideas, and of one's inner self will certainly result in a change of formerly cherished beliefs.

> Francis Bacon once made the remark that "a little philosophy inclineth man's mind to atheism, but depth in philosophy bringeth men's minds

about to religion." George Santayana wisely comments that Bacon "forgot to add that the God to whom depth in philosophy brings men's minds is far from being the same [God] from whom a little philosophy estranges them." (Rice, 1953)

The question then logically arises—onto which objects did Freud displace his theistic conflicts? Freud's idealization of Science, without necessarily meaning to do so on a conscious level, may be an example of such displacement. The thrill of scientific discovery certainly does have seductive aspects which blind one to its inherent limitations. The tendency to extend the significance of a discovery is too often carried beyond a point that is justified by the verifiable data. His repeated return to the subject of religion, while an obvious necessity in any meaningful attempt to understand the vicissitudes of thought and behavior, appears to have been motivated more by underlying psychic conflicts related to his father than by the exigencies of psychoanalytic investigation. His relationship with Franz Brentano, Samuel Hammerschlag, Wilhelm Fliess, Carl Gustav Jung and Oskar Pfister, among others, might have provided theaters for his theistic conflicts. So may have his fascination with numerology and parapsychology, which are not the hallmark of a positivistic and empirical man of science. The intense interest in Greek and Roman antiquities, archeology and biblical characters is another manifestation which may have served as vehicles for his ambivalent feelings. Freud was not a mystic in the classical sense, and was certainly not part of, nor influenced by, the Jewish mystical tradition. Bakan (1958) attempted to demonstate that Freud was the heir of this tradition but his arguments, though attractive, are not persuasive.[9]

Though Freud repeatedly stressed the supremacy of science, his application of scientific criteria was not always consistent and, where applied, at times idiosyncratically interpreted and utilized. Obviously, the compromised scientific methodology that he did use resulted in the discovery of something new and remarkable despite the protests and negativism of other scientists and philosophers. Freud's creativity involved more than a scrupulous adherence to a methodology derived from a hard science and applied to a soft one like psychoanalysis. The softer the science, the stricter must be the adherence to a scientific attitude. This leads one to wonder if Freud would have made his discoveries if he had been as strict in his application of positivistic and empirical methodology as his mentors at medical school.

Contrary to her husband's aggressive atheism and all that it implies, Martha had views of her own as evidenced by the following episodes.

[Freud's] conviction [of the supremacy of scientific truth] governed his life, always. On a Friday afternoon in the summer of 1938, in London, not long after Freud had been rescued from Nazified Vienna, a young Oxford philosopher came to call. They talked of psychoanalysis in Britain, of Freud's recent adventures in Austria after the Anschluss. As it came to be around five in the afternoon, Martha Freud joined them and said to the visitor, "You must know that on Friday evenings good Jewish women light candles for the approach of the Sabbath. But this monster— *Unmensch*—will not allow this, because he says that religion is a superstition." Freud gravely nodded and agreed: "Yes," he said, "it is a superstition," to which the Frau Professor, addressing her visitor, rejoined: "You see?" In retrospect, their guest, perceptive but generous, thought the indignation humorous, mingled with obvious affection, a standing joke, repeated for half a century for the benefit of sympathetic visitors. (Private communication to the author [Gay], May 8, 1984.) (Gay, 1987, pp. 152-153)

The performance of certain religious rituals and the celebration of the Sabbath and other religious holidays may have meant more to Martha Freud than is revealed by this 'humorous' encounter. One of Martha's cousins wrote: "I remember very well her telling me how not being allowed to light the Sabbath lights on the first Friday night after her marriage was one of the more upsetting experiences of her life." (as quoted in Clark, 1980, p. 89)

Young-Bruehl (1988, p. 89, with further elaboration in a personal communication to the author) notes that after her husband's death Martha became more observant as exemplified in a resumption of some of her earlier, pre-Sigmund Freud, religious practices. She celebrated the Passover Seder in which she was joined by her family and many visitors, which included some of the women who worked at Anna Freud's wartime nursery. In 1945 she wrote a Jewish New Year's greeting, in the form of a poem, to an old Viennese friend who was living in the then Palestine:

Zu Roschhaschonoh!

Es war der Brauch in alten Zeiten,
an Feiertagen sich Freud zu bereiten,
so will denn heute auch ich es wagen,
den schonen Brauch aus alten Tagen
in unsre Zeit zu ubertragen.
Dieser kleine alte Becher,
einst bestimmt zum Kiddusch sagen
weck Erinnerung aus Jugendtagen!
Und wenn's auch nicht grade rother Wein
so schenken Sie was andres drein
und denken manchmal in Liebe mein!

Ihre alte Freundin
Marta Freud

(Translation)

To Rosh Hashanah!

It was the custom in olden days,
to give joy on Holidays,
so I will try to transfer the custom
from the olden days to our time.
This small old goblet,
was intended to be used with the reciting of the Kiddush
but it awakened memories of the days of our youth!
If you do not want to fill it with red wine
you can fill it with whatever you wish
and then sometimes think of me with love!

Your old friend
Marta Freud[10]

Further evidence, though at present of an anecdotal nature, was obtained from the widow of Wily Aron, the author of an historical study of the Jewish community of Hamburg. Aron had maintained an extensive correspondence with Martha Freud as well as other members of the Freud and Bernays families after World War II in preparation for his book. Aron had told his wife, who cannot read German, that in one of Martha's letters she had closed it with the comment that "it is now *Erev Shabbos* and I must stop writing." *Erev Shabbos* is a Hebrew phrase which means, roughly, 'just prior to the beginning of the Sabbath' and, in this instance, refers to the prohibition against the act of writing on the Sabbath.[11] I went through Martha Freud's correspondence with Aron but I could not find this letter. Nevertheless, Mrs. Aron insisted that her late husband made numerous references to this letter and that he had shown it to her. This calls into question Peter Gay's (1988), assertion that:

> Freud's rigorous secularism did not permit the slightest trace of religious observance to survive in his domestic life. The Freuds studiously ignored even the companionable Jewish family holidays, like Passover, which Freud's parents had continued to celebrate despite their emancipation from tradition. Ruthlessly, Freud swept aside his wife's youthful orthodoxy, much to her pain and regret. "Our festivals," Freud's son Martin recalled, "were Christmas, with presents under a candle-lit tree, and Easter, with gaily painted Easter eggs. I had never been in a synagogue, nor to my knowledge had my brothers or sisters. (p. 600)

The celebration of Christmas and Easter by the Freud family would thus reveal an inconsistency on the part of Sigmund whose religious orientation was felicitously described by Gay (1987) as a 'longstanding pugilistic atheism'. One would assume that his opposition to the celebration of any practice or ceremony that is related to organized religion would contravene such behavior. It now appears that this assumption may well be a correct one. Paul Roazen, Professor of Political Science at York University in Canada and a Freud biographer, interviewed a Gentile neighbor of the Freuds at 19 Bergasse, a Mrs. Oschner.[12] She told Roazen that members of the Freud family would come upstairs to her apartment to see the Christmas tree because Sigmund and Martha Freud did not have a tree.

Martin Freud's comment that his siblings had never been in a synagogue is also not quite accurate. His sister Anna, as a child, attended classes at the Reform synagogue on Sabbath mornings. In a letter to Herman de Levie, dated March 9, 1968, Anna Freud wrote:

> We were taught the Hebrew letters on one side of the page, the German text on the other. Knowing the letters of the alphabet enabled us to 'read' the Hebrew text. But we were not taught the meaning of the words, and knowledge of the letters disappeared, of course, very quickly after the school years were over . . . Neither I nor any of my classmates were able to read and translate even a simple Hebrew sentence. (as quoted in Young-Bruehl, 1988, p. 49)

Attendance at Sabbath School, most certainly, must have involved some attendance at synagogue service. Martin Freud's comment is even more puzzling when one considers the fact that religious instruction, which included Hebrew, was compulsory for all Jewish children and adolescents.

CHAPTER 11

Freud and Moses—The Long Journey Home

The Moses of Michelangelo

In that very important document, the dedication written in Hebrew by Jacob Freud on the occasion of his son's thirty-fifth birthday, we can see, in retrospect, the nuclei of specific factors that had played, and were subsequently to play, a significant role in Sigmund Freud's life. The dedication begins with hidden references to the biblical figures Jacob and Joseph and Joseph's children and ends with an explicit reference to Moses ('Since that time has the Book been sealed up with me like the broken Tablets in the Ark'). It is not clear whether it was the empathic fine tuning of sensitivity between father and son that facilitated the sharing of thoughts and interests, or whether the dedication itself served as a stimulus that reoriented Freud's psychic conflicts in specific, goal oriented, patterned formation. However, for the remainder of his life, Sigmund Freud displayed an abiding involvement not only with the subject of religion in general but also in his own idiosyncratic way, with Judaism in particular.

In 1935 Freud wrote a 'Postscript' for the American edition of his work *An Autobiographical Study* (S.E. XX:71-72) in which he reveals the emotional undercurrents that were, in part, the motivation for his creative activity. It should be noted that this was written while he was in the process of working on *Moses and Monotheism*, the first draft of which was completed in the summer of 1934.

> Two themes run through these pages: the story of my life and the history of psychoanalysis. They are intimately interwoven ... Shortly before I wrote the study it seemed as though my life would soon be brought to an end by the recurrence of a malignant disease; but surgical skill saved me in 1923 and I was able to continue my life and work, though no longer in freedom from pain. In the period of more than ten years that has passed since then, I

123

have never ceased my analytic work nor my writing—as is proved by the completion of the twelfth volume of the German edition of my collected works. But I myself find that a significant change has come about. Threads which in the course of my development had become intertangled have now begun to separate; interests which I had acquired in the later part of my life have receded, while the older and original ones become prominent once more. It is true that in this last decade I have carried out some important pieces of analytic work ... What I have written on the subject since then [1923] has been either unessential or would soon have been supplied by someone else. This circumstance is connected with an alteration in myself, with what might be described as a phase of regressive development. My interest, after making a lifelong detour through the natural sciences, medicine and psychotherapy, returned to the cultural problems which had fascinated me long before, when I was a youth scarcely old enough for thinking ... I perceived ever more clearly that the events of human history, the interactions between human nature, cultural development and the precipitates of primeval experiences (the most prominent example of which is religion) are no more than a reflection of the dynamic conflicts between the ego, the id and the super-ego, which psychoanalysis studies in the individual—are the very same processes repeated upon a wider stage.

The biblical figure of Moses had fascinated Freud for a long time, starting with his early childhood involvement with the Bible. As Jones (II: 364-5) points out, Moses was both a formidable father-image and an object of identification. On January 6, 1935 Freud wrote to Lou Andreas-Salome that the figure of Moses had haunted him all his life (Gay, 1988, p. 605). In his adult years Freud became almost entranced by the famous sculpture by Michelangelo which depicts Moses seated after having come down from the mountain with the Tables of the Law. On his first visit to Rome in 1901 he paid daily visits to the church where the statue was located. This statue was originally commissioned by Pope Julius II to be installed at the entrance of the tomb that was to be built for him after his death. (Whether Freud's emotional investment in this work of art had something to do with the death of his own sibling Julius, who died in infancy when Sigmund was less than two years old, is a matter of some conjecture.) In 1933, Freud wrote to the Italian translator of his book:

> My feeling for this piece of work is rather like that towards a love-child. For three lonely September weeks in 1913 I stood every day in the church in front of the statue, studied it, measured it, sketched it, until I captured the understanding of it which I ventured to express in the essay only anonymously. Only much later did I legitimatize this non-analytical child (Jones 1955, II: 367)

For reasons that are not clear, the study was published anonymously in 1914 and its authorship was not revealed until 1924 when it was included in the first German edition of Freud's collected writings. Though the immediate motivation for the writing of *The Moses of Michelangelo* (SE: XIII) may have been due to the rebellion of his disciples Alfred Adler and Carl Gustav Jung, the deeper issues pertain to his life-long struggle with his father and what he represented. Freud's initial fascination with the biblical character of Moses was the manifest forerunner of his latent interest in the historical character of Moses which did not emerge into consciousness (as far as we know) until the last years of his life when he wrote *Moses and Monotheism*.

In both works on Moses, Freud went counter to the prevailing interpretation of the biblical and historical Moses. It is important to note that any mental production, be it dream, waking fantasy or organized abstract, is the result of various conflicting forces—wishful, regulating and punitive—contending in the mind. These products of the mind are what we refer to as 'compromise formations' and they are what make for the uniqueness of thought and personality. They are basically approximations of reality and their truthfulness is a function of the distance from the ultimate reality that is being perceived or described. An identity of the two obviously makes for perfect, literal, truth, if such can ever be attained. (As Freud points out in *Moses and Monotheism*, mental productions are really closer to psychological or historical truth than to material reality, but more on this later.) If the distance is greater, what we may see is more a product of the inner psychological reality of the perceiver than that of external reality. So that in Freud's case, especially when his views on the subject were so different from that of experts in the field, we would have to assume that they bear the imprint of projection and identification; that they represent the manifest expression, in disguise, of his own deep inner emotional conflicts and fantasies.

The Bible is explicit as to what happened on Mount Sinai. After receiving the words which God inscribed on the two Tablets of stone, Moses started to make his way down the mountain. What he then saw horrified and infuriated him. The Israelites had regressed to idol-worship; they were now dancing wildly around the Golden Calf. Moses, in disillusionment and anger, cast the Tablets away and they were broken.

Michelangelo, according to most art critics and historians, depicted the moment of calm before the storm, capturing Moses as he was about to cast the Tablets away. Freud saw the scene quite differently. He felt that Michelangelo froze the moment in time just *after* Moses was seized by the impulse to break the Tablets, but *before* he cast them away. Supposedly, this was to highlight the strength of character and purpose in Moses who was intent, despite all adversity, on controlling his rage and *preserving* the tablets.

What we see before us is not the inception of a violent action but the remains of a movement that has already taken place. In his first transport of fury, Moses desired to act, to spring up and take vengeance and forget the Tablets; but he has overcome the temptation, and he will now remain seated and still, in his frozen wrath and in his pain mingled with contempt. Nor will he throw away the Tablets so that they will break on the stones, for it is on their especial account that he has controlled his anger; it was to preserve them that he kept his passion in check. (S.E. XIII: 229)

This passage highlights the significant themes, the overcoming of the temptation to break the Tablets, as well as the phrase, 'Moses desired to act, to *spring up* (italics mine) and take vengeance and forget the Tablets.' Let us now return to Figure 9, Jacob Freud's dedication on the occasion of Sigmund's thirty-fifth birthday, and re-read the following phrases:

Since that time has the Book been sealed up with me like the broken Tablets in the Ark

For the day on which your years amount to thirty five

Have I covered it with new leather,

Calling it: "*Spring up*, O well; greet it with song!"

And offering it to you as a remembrance,

A reminder of love   From your father

When we compare Jacob Freud's dedication with the above passage in *The Moses of Michelangelo* we find a striking identity of words (e.g., 'Spring up') and themes. No doubt Freud's conflicts over his own rage at his rebellious disciples, Jung and Adler, informed an aspect of his interpretation; on a deeper level he is also identifying with his father in his attempt to overcome the disillusionment and fury and preserve the Tablets for posterity because of the message they bring to the world. This very same conflict appears again in *Moses and Monotheism* where Freud first attempts to destroy one facet of the Jewish religion but ends up in an earnest but confused plea for preservation of another facet, but more on this shortly.

It is of striking significance that the words 'spring up' do not appear in the English translation rendered by Freud's half-brothers (Figure 13). There were no other English translations of Jacob Freud's Hebrew dedication extant at the time he wrote the piece on Michelangelo. Are the identities of words pure coincidence or did Freud know the precise meaning of the Hebrew phrase in the dedication?[1]

In a later passage in his monograph, Freud observes Michelangelo's reworking of the scriptures to suit his sculpture. More than that, he notes— and applauds—the sculptor's recasting of the very character of Moses:

> More important than his infidelity to the text of the Scriptures is the alteration which Michelangelo has, in our supposition, made in the character of Moses. The Moses of legend and tradition had a hasty temper and was subject to fits of passion. It was in a transport of divine wrath of this kind that he slew an Egyptian who was maltreating an Israelite, and had to flee out of the land into the wilderness; and it was in a similar passion that he broke the Tablets of the Law, inscribed by God Himself. Tradition, in recording such a characteristic, is unbiased, and preserves the impression of a great personality who once lived. But Michelangelo has placed a different Moses on the tomb of the Pope, one superior to the historical or traditional Moses. He has modified the theme of the broken Tablets; he does not let Moses break them in his wrath, but makes him be influenced by the danger that they will be broken and makes him calm that wrath, or at any rate prevent it from becoming an act. In this way he has added something new and more than human to the figure of Moses; so that the giant frame with its tremendous physical power becomes only a concrete expression of the highest mental achievement that is possible in a man, that of struggling successfully against an inward passion for the sake of a cause to which he has devoted himself. (S.E. XIII: 233)

The freedom Michelangelo took in making his statue is one Freud himself will claim when he becomes creator as much as interpreter of Moses thirty years later in *Moses and Monotheism*.

Moses and Monotheism

Moses and Monotheism is a work of genius and ingeniousness but it is highly flawed in data selection, methodology and validation. Though Freud repeatedly protests that it is a scientific work, it falls far short of what we would today, or even in Freud's day, consider a 'scientific' study. He readily admits that he selected data that supported his hypotheses and disregarded data that contradicted them. It is highly speculative, with too many conceptual structures built upon unverifiable hypotheses.

If one can tentatively accept Freud's premises, however, a journey of dazzling, intuitive and intellectual brilliance unfolds. It is not an easy book to read and as a matter of fact, it cannot be read as such, it has to be studied. Part of the problem lies in its structure. It was written and published in parts over a period of several years. In this sense, it is the most disorganized of

Freud's works. It has three prefaces, two at the beginning of the third section and another in the middle of it. There are many repetitions and recapitulations which, though occasionally helpful, often confuse. Jones (1957, III: 362) attributes this to upheavals that were occurring in Freud's life during its composition—the Nazi occupation of Vienna and the preparations for Freud's own exodus to England.

No doubt external factors did play a role, but the conflict-laden nature of the subject matter itself contributed to the book's seeming disorganization. While the thematic consistency is not evident in the structure of the work, the same cannot be said for Freud's thinking. Despite advancing age, illness and the mounting political crisis, *Moses and Monotheism* is on a par with his previous works. The difference is that, despite the intellectual and 'scholarly' tone of the work, it is fundamentally a personal document, second only to *The Interpretation of Dreams* in what it reveals. In contrast to the latter, Freud was probably not aware of what he was revealing of himself in *Moses and Monotheism*. This work was a continuation, and ultimately the culmination, of his quest for personal identity.

As in a classical psychoanalysis, Freud re-enacts, through the many mythical, biblical and historical figures who serve as transient transference objects, the underlying emotional conflicts that not only formed his character but also fed his creative and productive genius.

> Every novelty must have its preliminaries and preconditions in something earlier. (XXIII: 21)

Meissner (1984) perceptively notes that:

> It seems clear that Freud's religious views, perhaps more than any other aspect of his work and his psychology, reflect underlying and unresolved ambivalences and conflicts stemming from the earliest psychic strata. Behind the Freudian argument about religion stands Freud the man, and behind Freud the man, with his prejudices, beliefs, and convictions, lurks the shadow of Freud the child. A basic psychoanalytic insight says that the nature and content of any thinker or creative artist's work reflect essential aspects of the dynamic configurations and conflicts embedded in the individual's personality structure. Freud is no exception, and his religious thinking unveils these inner conflicts and unresolved ambivalences more tellingly than any other aspect of his work. A review and synthesis of Freud's inner psychic conflicts and the basic interplay of forces, defenses, fantasies, ideals, ambitions, and beliefs that played themselves out in his inner life form the essential backdrop for the ensuing discussion [of Freud and Religion]. (p. VII)

Given Freud's religious background and the nature of psychoanalysis it was only natural that he would eventually turn the focus of his unique brand of depth psychology to matters of religion. His first work on religion appeared in 1907 and was entitled *Obsessive Acts and Religious Practices* (S.E. IX), a perceptive study on the relationship between religious practices and obsessive-compulsive phenomena. In 1913, he published a most significant study on the primitive origins of religion, *Totem and Taboo*, in which the findings of certain ethnologists and anthropologists were scrutinized from a psychoanalytic perspective. The next major work on religion was *The Future of an Illusion*, published in 1927 (S.E. XXI) References to religion were scattered through his many other works. All of these concerned religion in general. In the very late 1920's he made his return journey to the Jewish religion.

In the Preface to the Hebrew translation of *Totem and Taboo*, Freud wrote:

> No reader of [the Hebrew version of] this book will find it easy to put himself in the emotional position of an author who is ignorant of the language of holy writ, who is completely estranged from the religion of his fathers—as well as from every other religion—and who cannot take a share in nationalist ideals, but who has yet never repudiated his people, who feels that he is in his essential nature a Jew and who has no desire to alter that nature. If the question were put to him: 'Since you have abandoned all these common characteristics of your countrymen, what is there left to you that is Jewish?' he would reply: 'A very great deal, and probably its very essence.' He could not now express that essence clearly in words; but some day, no doubt, it will become accessible to the scientific mind.
>
> Thus it is an experience of a quite special kind for such an author when a book of his is translated into the Hebrew language and put into the hands of readers for whom that historic idiom is a living tongue: a book, moreover, which deals with the origin of religion and morality, though it adopts no Jewish standpoint and makes no exceptions in favour of Jewry. The author hopes, however, that he will be at one with his readers in the conviction that unprejudiced science cannot remain a stranger to the spirit of the new Jewry.
>
> Vienna, December 1930

Freud's reply to his own question as to what was left of his Jewishness, 'A very great deal, and probably its very essence', may well have been the beginning of his quest for a renewed Jewish identity that was consistent with the changing beliefs and values that he had acquired over a lifetime. This attempt flowered into the work that focused specifically on the Jewish religion and it revolved around the central historical character of Moses.

In the letter to Yehudah Dvosis-Dvir (Figure 11), written on December 15, 1930 and which accompanied the above-quoted preface, his yearnings for the Judaism of his father are clearly expressed. He obviously felt some kind of emotional pressure to achieve a new compromise, a reconciliation, on his own terms and in his own way.

On September 30, 1934 he wrote to Arnold Zweig (Letters, ed. by Ernst Freud, 1960):

> ... You think you know why I haven't written to you for so long? No, you don't ... but the main reason was another one. For, in a time of relative freedom and at a loss to know what to do with my surplus leisure, I have written something myself; and this, contrary to my original intention, has taken such a hold of me that everything else has been left undone ... The starting point of my work is known to you; ... Faced with the renewed persecutions, one asks oneself again how the Jew came to be what he is and why he has drawn upon himself this undying hatred. I soon found the formula: Moses created the Jew. And my essay received the title: '*The Man Moses, A Historical Novel*' ... The material is divided into three parts; the first reads like an interesting novel; the second is laborious and lengthy, the third substantial and exciting. The enterprise foundered on the third section, for it contains a theory of religion which, although nothing new to me after *Totem and Taboo*, is nevertheless bound to be something fundamentally new and shattering to the uninitiated. Concern for these uninitiated compels me to keep the completed essay secret ... And in addition to all this there is the feeling that the essay doesn't seem to me too well substantiated, nor do I like it entirely ...

In his letter to Yehudah Dvosis-Dvir dated December 11, 1938 (Figure 12) we see a slightly disguised expression of his yearning for acceptance by his fellow Jews and an overt plea that *Moses and Monotheism*, though potentially injurious to Jewish sensitivity, be accepted on its scientific merits. Freud released his study despite requests from prominent members of the Jewish academic and religious communities to withhold publication of his work on Moses, given the deep meaning that the biblical and historical character had for the Jews, coupled with fear over the rise in anti-Semitism on the continent of Europe. He cited the responsibility of a scientist to pursue the truth and make it known. After all, wasn't this the essence of the prophetic tradition?

The Pharoah, Akhenaten, and Moses

Moses and Monotheism is a book of men. There are only three or four instances where women are mentioned. Reduced to its barest essentials, one can say that this is a story of father and son, indeed, a love story between father and son, dressed in aggressive garb, and with all the passionate ambivalence that that entails. In his attempt to write a biography of the Jewish people, Freud succeeded in writing a true autobiography.

Freud proposes a radical change in our conception of the history of the Jewish people and their religion. It begins not with the biblical patriarch Abraham but occurs much later in Egypt with Moses. Moses, according to Freud, was not a Hebrew but an Egyptian and a member of the royal entourage. He was influenced by the pharaoh Akhenaten who had obliterated all traces of the idol-worshipping religion of his ancestors and replaced it with a monotheistic one. Moses organized the Hebrews, became their leader and made the Egyptian monotheism the basis of the new Israelite religion. After the exodus, while wandering in the desert, the Egyptian Jews overthrew their leader Moses and slew him. The guilt resulting from this heinous crime was to play a major role in the future of the Israelites.

About one hundred years later the Egyptian Jews met another group of Jews who had never been to Egypt at a place called Kadesh. This group was led by a different Moses, a Midianite.[2] The two groups agreed to unite, provided certain conditions were met. The Egyptian contingent had brought the practice of circumcision with them and insisted on its indispensability. The Midianites had worshipped Yahweh, an invisible local volcano god, and were equally insistent on His place as the Supreme Being of the united, or more precisely, reunited, people. Thus the ethical monotheism of Moses was suppressed by the religion of Yahweh and was not to re-emerge until the days of the Hebrew prophets centuries later. Therefore, the ethical monotheism of today originated with the Egyptian Moses and not, as the Bible relates, with the patriarch Abraham.

Freud felt that the murder of Moses was a repetition of events that occurred in pre-historic times, many millenia prior to the genesis of human society. This was the murder of the Primal Father by his horde of rebellious sons, an event that was to be repeated many times over many millenia of time. The same phenomenon was to be repeated in historic times, twelve hundred years after the slaying of Moses, with the crucifixion of Jesus. The memory of the murder of Moses had been repressed, thereby resulting, on a conscious level, in an intense desire for the coming of a Messiah to relieve the burden of guilt that was a result of this act. Thus there is a continuous chain of events through time that lead from the murder of the Primal Father, Moses, to the murder of Jesus.

Moses and Monotheism focuses on, in part creates, the story, or stories, of Moses. First, briefly, the biblical version. Moses was born in Egypt to parents of the tribe of Levi. When the Pharoaoh issued an edict that all the male children born to the Israelites should be drowned, his mother hid him for three months. When she could no longer hide him she put him in an ark of bulrushes and let it float on the river. The daughter of Pharoaoh came along with her entourage, rescued the infant and raised him as her own child. Thus he became, by adoption, a member of Egyptian royalty. When he grew up he assumed the leadership of the Israelites. After God vanquished the Egyptians, Moses led the Exodus out of Egypt. The Israelites came to Mount Sinai where Moses spent forty days and nights on the mountain with God amid lightning, thunder, fire and clouds of smoke, received the Ten Commandments and, presumably, the rest of the Bible. The people wandered for forty years in the desert but Moses was not destined to reach the Promised Land. That was left to his chosen successor, Joshua.[3]

With the concept of 'Divine Revelation' removed, the story of Moses was looked upon by Bible critics, archeologists and ethnologists in natural, rather than supernatural, terms. Freud adapted many of their ideas to a psychoanalytic frame of reference and came up with a remarkably different story.

The story begins in the eighteenth Dynasty of Egypt, under which it became a world power. According to Freud (S.E. XXIII p. 65) the new vastness of the expanding Egyptian empire, under the leadership of powerful pharaohs, facilitated the emergence of the concept of an omnipotent unitary ruler both on an earthly and a cosmic level, with the former being a representative of the latter. It was the year 1375 B.C.E. and the leader was a young Pharaoh originally named Amenophis IV.[4] He instituted a new monotheistic religion which was contrary to the polytheism which had preceded him for many millenia. This movement was initially begun by his father, Amenophis III, who looked upon the Sun as the godhead and included himself somewhere in the 'Divine Family'. There also may have been political reasons involved as he felt that Amun, the god of Thebes, and his worshippers had become too powerful. Amenophis IV purified his father's concepts by postulating a Monotheism, with the sun being only one expression of an invisible, all-powerful, universal divine entity. He changed his name to Akhenaten, the suffix 'Aten' being the name that he gave to the geographic locale where he ruled. It became known as the 'Aten' religion, in contrast to the 'Amun' religion of Thebes. (It is important to remember this duality and polarity as they are repeated in many different guises and disguises throughout the rest of Freud's study.)

The rule of Akhenaten and his reforms lasted only seventeen years, until 1358 B.C.E., when he was overrun by a general from the previously defeated Amun worshippers, Haremhab, and killed. At this point Moses enters the picture. It had been thought by scholars that Moses was an Egyptian name. The suffix 'mose' in the Egyptian language (which was an early variant of Coptic) meant 'a child'; the final 's' was added later in the Septuagint, the Greek translation of the Old Testament. Freud now went a step further and posited that Moses was not a Jew but an Egyptian and a member of the aristocracy. With the death of Akhenaten, Moses decided to continue the new religion, and in order to do so, 'adopted' the persecuted Israelites in Egypt and imposed it upon them. Prior to this event they were presumably idol-worshippers like the Egyptians. (Curiously, Freud makes no mention of the religious beliefs and practices of the Egyptian Jews prior to Moses.) The monotheism of Moses, like that of his royal predecessor, was a highly ethical one. It was based on truth, order and justice; there was a contempt for the ceremonial aspects of religion, ritual and magic. There was a complete dematerialization of God and an enhancement of self-esteem by being the chosen one of God. The belief in an after-life, as exemplified in the worship of the god of the dead, Osiris, which was an element of supreme importance in the Amun religion, was nullified. The elevation of God to a higher degree of intellectuality and the renunciation of instincts and sensuality, enhanced the self-esteem of the believer and solidified the feeling of chosenness.

Central to this new religion was the insistence on circumcision, which was practiced only in Egypt and nowhere else. This is highly questionable. Freud attributes his knowledge of the subject to the historian Herodotus who lived in the fifth century, B.C.E. As far as we know today, with the exception of Philistia, circumcision was common practice throughout the entire Middle and Near East during Mosaic times. Freud did not mention the differences in age for circumcision. The Egyptians, as well as the others, carried out the ritual between the ages of six and twelve while, among Jews, with the exception of certain biblical characters, it is performed on the eighth day of life. Pubertal circumcision is common practice in Moslem countries.

The slaying of Moses

Freud held to the theory that somewhere between 1358 and 1350 B.C.E. the Exodus, under the leadership of Moses, took place. (Many scholars now believe that the Exodus took place early in the reign of the Pharaoh Rameses II [1304-1237 B.C.E.] and that the unified Israelites entered the land of Canaan no later than 1230 B.C.E.) In their travels in the desert the Israelites rebelled against their leader, and then murdered him. Here Freud introduces the core of his Primal Horde theory, which he developed in *Totem and Taboo*. Just as with the Primal Horde, where the sons rebelled against the father who had tyrannized them and taken all the women for himself, killing him and eating him raw, so the Israelites destroyed Moses. To describe the fate of Moses, Freud uses expressions such as, 'violent end' (p. 36), 'shamefully murdered' (p. 36), 'catastrophe' (p. 32). Surprisingly, Freud does not include the element of cannibalism in the Mosaic part of this sequence, but more on this omission later.

The fate of the Primal Father is central to Freud's conceptual frame of reference; this was the crime of eternity, the memory of which was never to disappear. It represented a paradigm of human behavior that had continued from the dawn of mankind. The murder of Moses was an inevitable, repetitive expression of this aspect of human 'fate'. The religion of Moses, with its emphasis on ethical monotheism, disappeared and the leaderless tribes regressed to their primitive, polytheistic idol worship.

About one hundred or so years later the Israelites came to a place called Kadesh where there was another group of Israelites who never had been to Egypt, who had another leader named Moses, a Midianite, and who worshipped a god called Yahweh, named after the volcano god in that area.[5] The two groups eventually banded together to form a unified Jewish people.[6]

From a behavioral and ethical perspective, Yahweh was conceived by Freud as the polar opposite of the Mosaic god. Freud refers to the 'demon' god Yahweh.

> ... he [Yahweh] was an uncanny, bloodthirsty demon who went about by night and shunned the light of day. (S.E. XXIII: 34)

He was a god who was more insistent on ritual and ceremony, who was crude, bloodthirsty, vindictive and unpredictable.

Since circumcision, according to Freud, was not part of the Yahweh religion but was crucial to the Egyptian Mosaic religion, as part of the compromise in forming a union of all tribes, the Yahwists made the practice obligatory for all males. Freud traces the origins and significance of circumcision further back into time.

> But the father's will was not only something which one might not touch, which one had to hold in high respect, but also something one trembled before, because it demanded a painful instinctual renunciation. When we hear that Moses made his people holy (Exodus 19:6) by introducing the custom of circumcision we now understand the deep meaning of that assertion. Circumcision is the symbolic substitute for the castration which the primal father once inflicted upon his sons in the plentitude of his absolute power, and whoever accepted that symbol was showing by it that he was prepared to submit to the father's will, even if it imposed the most painful sacrifice on him. (S.E. XXIII: 122)

Somehow the guilt from the heinous crime against Moses, the memory of which had been repressed in the group's unconscious, made itself felt over the succeeding centuries. Guilt led to atonement and penance, which in turn led to instinctual renunciation, intellectuality and morality. In the ensuing struggle between the Egyptian Mosaic and the Yahwistic religions, the former, after a period of several centuries, finally won out. This victory was in large measure due to the Prophets who, in essence, became the spokesmen for the Mosaic version of Judaism.

And here, it seems, I have reached the conclusion of my study, which was directed to the single aim of introducing the figure of an Egyptian Moses into the nexus of Jewish history. Our findings may be thus expressed in the most concise formula. Jewish history is familiar to us for its dualities: *two* groups of people who came together to form the nation, *two* kingdoms into which this nation fell apart, *two* gods' names in the documentary sources of the Bible. To these we add two fresh ones: the foundation of *two* religions— the first repressed by the second but nevertheless later emerging victoriously behind it, and *two* religious founders, who are both called by the same name of Moses and whose personalities we have to distinguish from each other. All of these dualities are the necessary consequences of the first one: the fact that one portion of the people had an experience which must be regarded as traumatic and which the other escaped. (S.E. XXIII: 52)[7]

Freud's 'Family Romance'

Let us now analyze Freud's view of the history of Judaism. In 1909 he published a most insightful essay entitled *The Family Romance*. Freud describes a fantasy which is common to all of us, that is, that the humble people said to be our parents are not our true biological parents but only adoptive ones; our real parents were the ones we had in childhood and they were members of the aristocracy and royalty. He attributes this to the child's initial perception of his parents as all-powerful giants and his difficulty, as he grows older, in accepting the ordinary mortal aspects of his parents. The 'humility' of the parents leads to an underlying contempt and hostility. For fear that the 'humbleness' will rub off on him, the adolescent and adult 'disowns' these parents and places himself in royal lineage. Of course, 'royalty' can be expressed in any one of many derivative terms—being famous, possessing much wealth, and, in some circles, being highly cultured and erudite.

A good example of this phenomenon is Freud's tracing his family tree to Cologne. There, in an effort to overcome his Eastern European origins, he posits an "aristocratic" German ancestry. In *Moses and Monotheism* he again returns to the subject in another context (but without referring to himself):

This applies, for instance, to the city of Cologne, to which the Jews came with the Romans, before it was occupied by the Germans. (S.E. XXIII: 90)

The city of Cologne was founded in the year 50 C.E. as a Roman colony. In the 1930s a Jewish cemetery was discovered that dated from the eleventh century. The Jews were expelled in 1384 and settlement was resumed in 1798. The Jews did, in fact, precede the Germans. This adds another wrinkle to Freud's family romance, for now the Jewish presence predates the German and becomes the true aristocracy. In either case, Freud's fantasy bears out a very apt quote from *Moses and Monotheism*,

> We have ... found that our intellect very easily goes astray without any
> warning, and that nothing is more easily believed by us than what, without
> reference to the truth, comes to meet our wishful illusions. (S.E. XXIII: 129)

In *Moses and Monotheism*, Freud reverses the traditional fantasy. The
real, not imagined, parents of Moses are royalty. He then becomes involved
and identified with ordinary mortals. The way Freud describes this descen-
dence reveals much about his own conflict.

> The deviation of the legend of Moses from all the others of its kind can be
> traced back to a special feature of its history. Whereas normally a hero, in
> the course of his life rises above his humble beginnings, the heroic life of the
> man Moses began with his stepping down from his exalted position and
> descending to the level of the children of Israel. (S.E. XXIII: 15)

A few pages later, Freud comments:

> But it is not easy to guess what could induce an aristocratic Egyptian—a
> prince, perhaps, or a priest or high official—to put himself at the head of a
> crowd of immigrant foreigners at a backward level of civilization and to
> leave his country with them. The well-known contempt felt by the Egyptians
> for foreign nationals makes such a proceeding particularly unlikely. (S.E.
> XXIII: 18)

Was Moses an Egyptian?

In regard to Freud's hypothesis that Moses was an Egyptian rather than
a Jewish Egyptian, Auerbach (1975) expresses surprise that Freud did not
quote the one sentence in the Bible that might have supported it. It is in
Exodus 2:19:

> They answered, "An Egyptian rescued us from the shepherds; he even drew
> water for us and watered the flock."

This sentence refers to Reuel (in the J document; in the E document he is
referred to as Jethro), the eventual father-in-law of Moses.[8] His daughters
had taken their flock to water but male shepherds would not allow them
access. Moses interceded for the women by somehow persuading the men to
allow them to water their flock. The Bible itself does not offer anything more
descriptive of Moses. However, commentators on the Bible, according to
Jewish tradition, have thought that Moses was really a Hebrew who on this
occasion was dressed as an Egyptian and spoke a Hebrew dialect that was
close to the dialect of the Midianites so as to be understood. Also of interest is

Freud's equation of name and nationality, i.e., since Moses was an Egyptian name he therefore must have been an Egyptian. Freud's interpretation of the name and the family romance pertaining to Moses' adoption by Egyptian royalty are the only bases for his positing the concept that Moses was an Egyptian. He may not have been aware of *Genesis* 41:45 where Pharaoah gave Joseph an Egyptian name:

> Pharaoh then gave Joseph the name of Zaphenath-paneah; and he gave him for a wife Asenath daughter of Poti-phera priest of On. Thus Joseph emerged in charge of the land of Egypt.

(The word Zaphenath-paneah is an Egyptian word that means 'God speaks; he lives', or 'creator of life'.)

Auerbach (1975) comments:

> A historian living 2,000 years hence who does not know the background, would surely think a man bearing the two thoroughly German names Sigmund Freud to be of German descent—to the detriment of the Jewish people, which is proud to reckon him among its own.

Without excessive imagination it is possible to see how Freud identifies with the Egyptians and equates them with middle- and upper-class Germans and Austrians. Their attitudes towards immigrant Jews appear to be identical—witness his phrase 'immigrant foreigners at a backward level of civilization,' and his reference to the Egyptian Jews as

> . . . savage Semites [who] took fate into their own hands and rid themselves of their tyrant [Moses]. (p.47)

Without reflecting on its validity, the concept of Moses as an aristocratic Egyptian and the stress on the superiority of Egyptian ethical monotheism would thus serve in the interest of Freud's 'Family Romance' fantasy and personal prejudice. Like George Clare, who never forgave his mother for having been born in Poland, Freud felt the same, though it was never overtly stated, about his parents and their native Galicia.

Freud's prejudices pertaining to upper and lower classes enter into his personal conception of the history of the united Israelites after their victorious entry into the land of Canaan, one not corroborated by any historian. Earlier conflicts presumably re-emerged between the cultured Egyptian and the nomadic, primitive Midianite Jews.[9] This resulted in a deep religious and geographical split, with the Egyptian component settling in the south to form the kingdom of Judah and the Midianites going to the north to form the kingdom of Israel. The Bible also refers to Israel as the land of Ephraim. It should be noted that the names of Jacob and Israel are used interchangeably in the Bible to refer to the same person and that these three names have some considerable significance for Freud. The inhabitants of Judah were religiously and culturally superior to their northern brethren. In describing the Levites, who, according to Freud, were the Egyptian descendants of the learned retinue surrounding Moses and who still retained their aristocratic position, he writes,

> At the time of the union with the disciples of Yahweh they formed an influential minority, culturally superior to the rest. (S.E. XXIII: 39)

Freud may well be partly correct in his intuitive presumption. The regressive pull to paganism was far stronger in the north throughout its entire history with the notable exception of the apostate King Manasseh of Judah who reigned from 697 to 640 B.C.E. The houses of David and Solomon and their subsequent dynasties were in Judah, and the relationship between the northern and southern kingdoms was consistently a rivalrous one, with the south trying to make the north subservient to it. Judah always retained a cultural and, contrary to Freud's hypothesis about the pacifist origins of the Egyptian Mosaic Judaism, military superiority.

But historical and biblical data dispute Freud's hypothesis about the Egyptian Mosaic contingent of Jews settling in the south. The descendents of the Mosaic priesthood resided in the northern kingdom of Israel while their priestly competitors were in the southern kingdom of Judah. Both groups were Levites but they delineated their ancestral parentage between the primal biblical figures of Moses and his brother Aaron. In addition, Moses successor, Joshua, was a northern hero, descended from the tribe of Ephraim.

The natural brotherhood of Moses and Aaron is open to question. In parts of the *Book of Exodus* it appears that Moses was the firstborn of his Israelite mother and in others he has an older brother named Aaron and a sister named Miriam. Accounts of the sibling rivalry between Moses on the one hand and Aaron and Miriam on the other are openly discussed in the Bible. Whether fraternity was there from the beginning of the story of the Jewish people, or created retrospectively by the documentary authors and editors centuries later, is an unresolved question.

Akhenaten and Egyptian Monotheism

There are also some serious doubts and inconsistencies about Freud's portrait of the reputed religious iconoclast, Akhenaten.[10] His exalted estimation of Akhenaten was derived from the works of the Egyptologist,

J.H. Breasted (1906, 1933). He quotes Breasted (1906, p. 356) when he refers to this pharaoh as 'the first individual in human history' (S.E. XXIII: 21). Freud elaborates further on this adulation when he states that

> Whatever we can learn about this remarkable and, indeed, unique personality is deserving of the highest interest (S.E. XXIII: 21)

Freud appears to have ignored other findings that might have contradicted his perception of this presumably great reformer of religion. The mummy of Akhenaten was discovered in 1907 lying in the tomb of his mother, Queen Teye. Examination of the remains suggested an age of between twenty-five and twenty-eight years at the time of death. Since he ruled for seventeen years he must have been eleven years of age, or even younger, at the time of his ascension to the throne. (He did not attain the acme of his power and influence, with the completed construction of his new capital, until the age of seventeen.) Just as he was depicted in the ancient artistic Egyptian renditions of him, the examining anatomist described him as having pathological malformations such as a peculiarly shaped and enlarged skull, a protruding abdomen, an abnormal pelvis and an almost feminine build (Albright, 1957, pp. 219-220).

The nobility of thought and spirit which Breasted and Freud ascribe to Akhenaten would not be in accord with his youthfulness. In all probability, he was the tool of power-brokers either through his mother who, according to the archaeological findings, was still alive in the eleventh year of his reign, or his wife Neferte, who may have been older that her husband, or others.

> Hence it was only the flattery of his courtiers which pictured him as the promulgator of a new 'teaching'. (Albright, 1957, p. 220)

The notion that the religion of Aten was representative of a true monotheism has been called into serious question (Meek, 1969; Wilson, 1969). In the ancient Egyptian texts (Amarna) Akhenaten's god is referred to as 'the sole god, like whom there is no other' but this statement is quite deceptive. The religious systems that prevailed during the second millenium, B.C.E., and for a time thereafter, would more appropriately be described as Monolatry, the focus on one god to the exclusion of other gods that are deemed to coexist with it, or Henotheism, which is the absorption of these other deities into the main one that is the object of worship. As Wilson (1969) stresses, for more than a thousand years before the Amarna, (Akhenaten's revolution), the Egyptian gods Amun-re and Har-Akhti were at different times referred to as 'the sole god'. Their monotheism never expressed the idea of the existence of the one and only God and, at the same time, the total and complete exclusion of all other gods. This was a concept, though beginning to emerge, that was still alien to the Egyptian mind.

Akhenaten, which Wilson (1969) translates as 'He-who-is-serviceable-to-the-Aten', stated that he was the physical son of the Aten. Thus there were two gods, not one. There are many scenes in the Amarna tombs which show Akhenaten serving the 'living sun-disk' while, at the same time, the Egyptian masses are bowing to the Pharaoh. The prayers of the masses were addressed to Akhenaten and not the Aten. In essence, Akhenaten was a god-king. The sun, which was either Aten himself, or part of his physical expression, was concerned with the creation and sustenance of life, while ethics and religion derived from Akhenaten. The Sun-god was pictured as, or represented by, a round disk with numerous rays protruding from it which ultimately end in human hands. Neither could Akhenaten rid himself of the influence of pagan religion. He saw no contradiction between Aten and the Mnevis-bull of Heliopolis which was considered an incarnation of the sun-god.

Meek (1969) and Rowley (1969) believe that the monotheism of Moses was basically a henotheistic one. Albright (1969), on the other hand, is of the opinion that the monotheism of Moses was uniquely his own creation and, for the most part, unrelated to Akhenaten's vision. However, many scholars agree that the final form of ethical monotheism as we know it did not achieve complete fruition until the writing of Deutero-Isaiah (also known as Second Isaiah) in the sixth century, B.C.E. Deutero-Isaiah, which consists of chapters 40 through 55 of the Book of Isaiah, is believed to have been written by a prophet many years later than the earlier Isaiah. The two books appear to have been joined by a later editor(s). Deutero-Isaiah marks the end-point in the evolutionary process of a unique religious system, beginning with the religion of Israel being that of a local tribal cult and culminating in an ethical monotheism that has universal dimension and application.[11]

Albright (1949) and Sarna (1986), among many others, have called into serious question the publicized 'ethics' of the Aten religion and its founder. The famous 'Hymn to Aten', presumably written by Akhenaten, is completely devoid of ethical content. If his own personal behavior is any indication, the 'ethics' of Aten would appear to be a retrospective projection of some nineteenth century, C.E. biblical archeologists onto their conception of this 'revolution' in man's religious and moral development. Sarna (1986) writes:

> It calls for no ethical discipline in the formation of character and evinces no interest in social justice or the welfare of society. Akhenaten's own sexual morality as exhibited in his marriages is repugnant to biblical standards. He married his twelve-year-old daughter in order to obtain a male heir, and later took to wife another daughter as well. Certainly, the religious revolution of Akhenaten in no wise constituted any advance upon traditional values in

the sphere of ethics and morality ... The religion of Akhenaten had been confined to members of the royal family and the new aristocracy that he created and had no impact on the Egyptian people. It is not impossible that its revolutionary ideas lingered on for a while, and enjoyed an underground existence among small groups. However, they did not advance the religion of Egypt in the direction of monotheism. True, Aten was not represented in material form, whether human or animal, but he was not an invisible god, being very much visible in his daily shining circuit across the sky. This religion showed no concern for the common man, and its ethical content was ambiguous at best. Its emergence was rooted in Egyptian political and religious history, and without the person of the pharaoh as the sole and indispensable intermediary between the god and the people, it was meaningless. There is no basis for a conclusion that Akhenaten's Atenism was the inspiration for Mosaic monotheism. (pp. 156-7)

The question remains why, if so much of the evidence is tenuous, did Freud select Moses as the basis for his book. Could it have been that the birthday dedication laid a foundation for Freud's later pursuit of the Biblical leader? Added to this is Freud's attraction, in later life, to what he called the "essence" of Judaism, impossible to define yet somehow connected to the view put forward by the Hebrew prophets. It is also plausible that to some degree Freud identified with these prophets, in particular with Moses, on a personal level. It is interesting to recall Freud's description of Michelangelo's Moses, who fights against primitive impulses to preserve the tables of the law. Freud calls this

> ... a concrete expression of the highest mental achievement that is possible in a man, that of struggling successfully against an inward passion for the sake of a cause to which he has devoted himself.

Freud saw himself in terms very much like this when he described his own battle against cancer in the postscript to his *An Autobiographical Study*:

> ... surgical skill saved me in 1923 and I was able to continue my life and work, though no longer in freedom from pain. In the period of more than twelve years that have passed since then I have never ceased in my analytic work.

It is precisely in that preface that Freud speaks of his return to earlier considerations of religion and culture.

From a therapeutic perspective, psychoanalysis can be viewed as a method to assist neurotically troubled patients who, in becoming aware of their primitive unconscious wishes through their derivatives in conscious thought and behavior and through such awareness and consequent understanding, reach a higher level of wisdom and maturity. For the Hebrew prophets, the attempt to attain the same goals, but obviously within a theological framework, was perceived as a battle against paganism. For Freud, primitive society was in a sense, the unconscious writ large. Pagan deities and symbols, and the rituals of worship pertaining to them, often operate like neurotic symptoms that express as well as conceal infantile longings and desires.

The very same constellation of impulses, fantasies and potential behavior that underlies paganism, is the sum and substance of the conflicts that are basic to neurotic illness and misery. The goal of psychoanalysis and psycho-analytically informed psychotherapy is to help the individual free himself from this primitive, regressive bind to achieve a higher level of emotional and intellectual maturity, and to enhance one's ability to attain a life of truth, justice and respect for one's fellow man. This is achieved by a very gradual, slow and embarrassingly painful process of conscious awareness of hitherto unconscious impulses, desires and fantasies, and their assimilation into the total unity of thought and feeling. In this secular sense, Freud was indeed a true prophet in the Jewish prophetic tradition.[12]

Albright (1969) perceptively describes the kind of primitive thinking that lay behind pagan religion. It is strikingly similar to the Primary Process mode of thought which Freud found characteristic of the infant and child and that is forever ready for activation in our unconscious as adults.

Proto-logical thinking is illustrated in ancient Near-Eastern literature by mythology, especially by the myths relating to gods of fertility, where sex and personality are fluid, changing from one to its opposite with the most disconcerting ease. A deity may be male and female at different times—or simultaneously. A goddess may be fruitful mother and virgin at the same time. Heaven may be a cow, a woman, or a sea; the moon may be a young bull, a jewelled tiara, a mother-womb—all in the same hymn. A god may be lord of and giver of fertility, healer and destroyer. The Canaanite Anath is both the loving mother of her people and the destroying avenger. Cuneiform magic vividly illustrates proto-logical thinking, since all its branches are based upon logically untenable causal relations of dynamistic origin. Thus we may have divination from the movement of drops of oil in a bowl of water, from the appearance of the liver of a sacrificial animal, from the movements of heavenly bodies, etc., etc. However, our oldest Babylonian magical texts already bear the imprint of the empirico-logical stage of thinking, as we shall presently see. (p. 26)

With primitive man it is, accordingly, empirical logic that governs almost everything he does. It is only when he leaves the world of everyday activity, controlled directly by the senses, that he enters the magical zone of proto-logical thought, a zone where the logical principles of identity and contradiction are flouted constantly, but a world in which man can rise above the petty limitations of his daily routine into a new and wonderful region of direct contact with the superhuman and divine. Without a proto-logical probation there would have been no poetry, no folk-tales—in short no imaginative literature. There would have been no science, since science arose from primitive magic. Above all, there would have been no religion to distinguish man from the beasts and to carry him into the presence of God. (p. 28)

Moses was the first of the great Hebrew prophets, the initiator of social, religious and ethical reforms. Akhenaten seemed to embody many of these attributes in the dress of the non-Jew. Freud's religious roots, deep in ethical monotheism, led him to Moses. His social training, the self-hate inflicted by Viennese Jewish society on itself and the assimilationist aspirations it taught, led him to Akhenaten.

Like the Biblical Joseph, with whom he so identified, Freud found refuge in an Egyptian court. And just as Joseph allowed his brothers to think him an Egyptian to punish their betrayal, so Freud enacts, in *Moses and Monotheism*, a kind of charade in Egyptian dress. Joseph ultimately sends for his father and reveals himself to his brothers. Freud, more ambivalent perhaps, nevertheless provides enough clues, even if unconsciously planted, to leave the encoded message that will reveal him to his brethren. The great interest he took in the book's Hebrew translation, the prefaces he wrote, and the hope he had of its acceptance among Jews, adds to this notion as if, after his long sojourn in Egypt, he wished to say, "It's really me, Joseph, the Jewish interpreter of dreams."

The Aggressivization of the Hero

And yet, just as the biblical Joseph required the submission of his father and his brothers as a precondition for reconciliation, so Freud seeks a kind of mastery over his origins and insists on playing the role of father as well as son. It must be remembered that even the biblical Joseph tricks Jacob when Joseph brings forth his children for a paternal blessing, just as Jacob had once tricked his own father, Isaac.

Freud's concept of the hero, as it develops in *Moses and Monotheism*, is a rather revealing one. On page 12 (S.E. XXIII), he writes,

A hero is someone who has had the courage to rebel against his father and has in the end victoriously overcome him.

On page 87 (S.E. XXIII), the definition is intensified,

But no matter whether what we have here is a fantasy or the return of a forgotten reality, in any case the origin of the concept of a hero is to be found at this point—the hero who always rebels against his father and kills him in some shape or other.

From the concept, "victoriously overcomes him," there is an increase in aggressiveness to: "and kills him in some shape or other." The shifting and alternating identifications between Moses, his father and himself may well be operative here. Jacob Freud, Judaism, Moses are all inseparable, but then again, so are Sigmund and Moses. The roles of hero and victim change to suit the need and circumstance.

Wallace (1978) has expressed similar ideas:

> Freud began this work with a revealing sentence: "To deny a people the man whom it praises as the greatest of its sons is not a deed to be taken light-heartedly." (S.E. XXIII:11). He was well aware of what he was meting out. His own father (by passive behavior toward an insulting Gentile, among other things) had broken Freud's image of the omnipotent father, and Freud never forgave his father for this weakness. A prime determinant of *Moses and Monotheism* was Freud's effort to recreate the old family romance (just as Moses tried to reinstitute the glory of Ikhnaton, previously effaced by priests of Amun); but he also wanted to gain a measure of revenge against Jacob Freud. The old man's Judaism would be dashed on the rocks of Freud's psychohistorical scholarship. "A hero is a man who stands up manfully against his father and in the end overcomes him." (S.E. XXIII: 18) . . . That Freud could accept as fact Sellin's weakly supported argument that Moses was murdered suggests that Freud's strong need to believe was related to two things: on the one hand Freud had identified Moses with his father, and Moses's murder was an expression of Freud's unconscious hostility; on the other hand, Freud identified himself with Moses and the murder was punishment for his parricidal wish and his success vis-a-vis the father.

Here one must move away from biblical paradigms to the darker, more primitive impulses Freud explored in *Totem and Taboo* and that inform his notion of rebellion.

The Primal Father and his Horde

In *Totem and Taboo*, Freud combined the theoretical ideas of Darwin and the ethnologists, Atkinson and Robertson-Smith with findings derived from the psychoanalysis of individuals. Darwin suggested that human beings originally lived in small hordes, each of which was led by a tyrant who took all the females to himself and castrated or killed the younger men, including his own sons. Atkinson carried this further by suggesting that such a system came to an end by the rebellion of the surviving sons who slew the father and devoured him. In sequential development, the father-horde was replaced by a totemic brother-clan. In order to have a peaceful society, the brothers decided to renounce the woman on whose account they had killed their father and instituted a system previously unknown, exogamy, which is marriage outside of the same kinship group. The families were temporarily organized as a matriarchy.

However, though the primal father was dead, the ambivalence toward him did not disappear. For the purpose of description Freud relates the sequence of the formation of the primal horde led by a primal father, the rebellion of the sons against this tyrannical father, his murder and canni-balization as though it all happened on a single occasion. However, in fact this connected series was repeated many times over a period of many millenia. The murdered father was replaced by the totem animal who was regarded as an ancestor, protective spirit and an object of worship. It could not be injured or killed except on one exceptional occasion. Once a year, all the males gathered for the totem feast; they tore the animal to pieces and ate it raw. Attendance at this meal was compulsory. In this ceremony the memory of the primal murder surfaced and was translated into action. Robertson-Smith theorized that social order, morality and religion owe their origins to this ritual and the memories behind it. Freud agrees with Robertson-Smith that the Christian Lord's [Last] Supper and the rite of Holy Communion, in which the believer incorporates the flesh and blood of his God in symbolic form, bear a striking resemblance to this ritual.[13]

Freud creates his own 'chain' of continuity in first postulating the commission in prehistoric times of the primal murder. He then posits the murder of Moses and the crucifixion of Jesus as events of equivalence in terms of their being the 'acting out' in contrast to conscious remembering; that is, a compelling repetition in action of the unconscious memory of the primal event and its effect on the course of history. Freud utilizes a psychoanalytic concept that can be experientially seen in clinical practice whereby the patient reinforces the defense against remembering infantile trauma by seeking a pathway through action without making a conscious connection between the forgotten trauma and the current action. The guilt pertaining to the murder of the Primal Father is reawakened and intensified with each succeeding event. This nucleus of the unconscious basis of this guilt is what Freud refers to as 'historical' truth in which an actual prehistoric or historic event has been repressed to the unconscious and has become the core determinant in the formation of the fantasy, symptom or myth. This is in contrast to the 'material' or literal truth which pertains to everyday reality and is confirmable by the senses. Is Freud here postulating a secular version of the discarded theological concept of the sins of the father being visited unto the third and fourth generations?

> From that time [i.e., 1912, in *Totem and Taboo*] I have never doubted that
> religious phenomena are only to be understood on the pattern of the
> individual neurotic symptoms familiar to us—as the return of long since
> forgotten, important events in the primeval history of the human family—
> and that they have to thank precisely this origin for their compulsive
> character and that, accordingly, they are effective on human beings by force
> of the historical truth of their content (S.E. XXIII: 58)

> That is to say, we do not believe that there is a single great god today, but
> that in primeval times there was a single person who was bound to appear
> huge at that time and who afterwards returned in men's memory elevated to
> divinity. (S.E. XXIII: 129)

Obviously the murder of the Primal Father did not dispense with the need
for a replacement figure who was larger than life. As noted, the totem animal
was the successor but not for long. The object of worship, the totem animal,
was eventually humanized but its animal origins were only thinly concealed.

> The father once more became the head of the family but was not by any
> means so absolute as the father of the primal horde had been. The totem
> animal was replaced by a god in a series of transitions which are still very
> plain. To begin with, the god in human form still bore an animal's head;
> later he turned himself by preference into that particular animal, and after-
> wards it became sacred to him and was his favorite attendant; or he killed
> the animal and himself bore its name as an epithet. (S.E. XXIII: 133)

In response to this hypothesis, let it be said first that few scholars in the
appropriate fields of study agree with the whole concept of the primal horde
(Baron, 1939). Secondly, the central weakness in the theory is Freud's seemingly
irrational dependence on Lamarck's (1744-1829) theory of inheritance of
acquired characteristics. Freud stubbornly adhered to the theories of the
process of evolution propagated by Lamarck despite the antagonism of his
colleagues and its rejection by nearly all biologists. Freud may have felt that
the discredited Lamarckian views were more appropriate for an explanation
of psychological phenomena than those of Darwin (Ritvo, 1965). Given the
original opposition from the biologists and physicists of his day to his theory
of natural selection, Darwin was subsequently compelled to acknowledge
Lamarckian mechanisms in his attempts to justify his radically new theory.
Ritvo (1965) offers other possible explanations for Freud's stubborn attitude.
To the end of his life Freud was caught in a conflict between biology and
psychology. The most significant, and highly debatable (Sulloway, 1983;
Masson, 1984) example of this conflict was seen in 1897 when Freud radically
modified his seduction theory in which he switched from an *actual* seduction
being the prime factor in the etiology of a neurosis to a *fantasied* seduction.

Thereafter, whenever there was a conflict between biological and psychological explanations, he would choose the psychological. In terms of the significance of evolution for psychology, Freud was more concerned with phylogenesis than with ontogenesis, phylogenesis being the cumulative experience of the race which was more important than what was innate in the individual.

Already in 1923 Freud was expressing ideas that he was to use in *Moses and Monotheism* when he postulated an evolutionary mechanism, in accordance with Lamarckian theory, that would help explain the transmission of repeated experiences to succeeding generations.

> Nevertheless it is not possible to speak of direct inheritance in the ego. It is here that the gulf between an actual individual and the concept of species becomes evident ... The experiences of the ego seem at first to be lost for inheritance; but when they have been repeated often enough and with sufficient strength in many individuals in successive generations, they transform themselves, so to say, into experiences of the id, the impressions of which are preserved by heredity. Thus in the id, which is capable of being inherited, are harboured residues of the existences of countless egos; and when the ego forms its super-ego out of the id, it may perhaps only be reviving shapes of former egos and be bringing them to resurrection. (S.E. XIX: 38)

It should be noted that when Freud speaks of acquired characteristics he is not referring to the physical aspects of the human organism but to the memory-traces of external events which, through repetition, become permanently embedded in the unconscious *id* through which, after a presumed saturation point is reached, is transmitted to subsequent generations. It is the *id* of the progenitor that is inherited by the offspring. The discovery of the gene as the basic unit and vehicle of hereditary transmission was not known to Freud.

With regard to Moses, Freud relates that the primal murder and the subsequent telling and retelling of the calamitous event over long periods of time left an imprint in the listener's unconscious, which then somehow got transmitted genetically to succeeding generations. If Freud had said that we find in every male evidence of the existence of such impulses and fantasies, and, in addition, that the psychological defense mechanism of identification may serve as a vehicle of transmission as his colleagues Hartmann, Kris, Erikson, and Jones felt (Ritvo, 196) he would have stood on firm empiric and scientific ground. However, to say that this collective wish and guilt are due to an actual episode, or repeated episodes, many millenia ago which, by force of this repetition became embedded in the constitutional makeup of each subsequent descendant, collectively and individually, is purely speculative. In doing psychoanalytically informed work with patients, it is not difficult to see the structural outlines of an incestuous, murderous, cannibalistic fantasy; it is obviously present in all of us. Observation of the stories children love to hear over and over again, the cartoons they watch and the story-books they read should be sufficiently convincing.

Freud, nevertheless, argues:

> We must finally make up our minds to adopt the hypothesis that the psychical precipitates of the primeval period became inherited property which, in each fresh generation, called not for acquisition but only for awakening. In this we have in mind the example of what is certainly the 'innate' symbolism which derives from the period of the development of speech, which is familiar to all children without their being instructed and which is the same among the peoples despite their different languages. What we may perhaps lack in certainty here is made good by other products of psychoanalytic research. We find that in a number of important relations our children react, not in a manner corresponding to their own experience, but instinctively, like the animal, in a manner that is only explicable as phylogenetic acquisition. (S.E. XXIII: 132)

Freud is here referring to the important concept of 'primal fantasies', or 'archaic heritage' which is part of our phylogenetic makeup and which is acquired over many aeons of time, transmitted genetically from parent to child. How these fantasies originate, imprint genetically and then transmit from generation to generation is still an unanswered question. Freud felt that the Lamarckian concept of an actual experience being imprinted and then remaining in the *id* forever, unless modified by subsequent experiences, was an answer to this very difficult problem of genetic makeup and transmission. However, projecting this process on to a group of people, wherein the group, qua group, transmits the characteristics acquired as a result of the group's experience, is a diminution of the significance of Freud's thoughts on the matter.

Ernst Sellin and his 'Scientific Discovery'

This leads us back to Moses. In 1922 and 1924, Ernst Sellin, the well-known biblical scholar, published studies of the prophet Hosea, who lived and wrote in the eighth century B.C.E., 500 years after the Exodus was supposed to have taken place. In Freud's words, Sellin *discovered*, or found *unmistakable signs*, in certain passages in Hosea that Moses was killed by the Israelites because of their desire to worship the local gods. According to Sellin, knowledge of the tradition of the murder of Moses was kept in the possession of the priests who, in turn, must have transmitted it to the prophets. The word 'discover' is used several times to describe Sellin's presumed finding. Chapter and verse are not given by Freud nor were they cited. What Sellin actually did was to re-interpret several verses. He did not find an older version of *Hosea*, or even a different one. To call this a 'scientific discovery' is indeed strange.

Freud was apparently unaware of another possible contradiction that was built into his hypotheses. As noted earlier, he postulated that the Egyptian Jews formed the southern kingdom of Judah. However, Hosea was a prophet of the northern kingdom of Israel and his concerns, though universal in value and scope, were limited to that area. In support of Freud's hypothesis we can say that there is a connection between Hosea and Moses in that the Levitic descendents of Moses were practicing their priestly craft in the northern kingdom. However, if the Egyptian contingent settled in the South, then the name of God should have been that of the one agreed to at the time of union in the desert, Yahweh. But that does not appear to be the case. Yahweh was the name of God in Israel in the North, while that of Elohim prevailed in the South in Judah. Freud, relying on Sellin's ideas, did not seem to be aware of the inherent contradiction when he hypothesized that the original Yahwists, those Hebrews who had lived in the desert, had never heard of the Egyptian Moses until years after the calamitous insurrection and certainly had nothing to do with his supposed violent demise, had settled in the North. Being a northerner, how could Hosea have been aware of, or even be so concerned about, the fate of Moses in the desert?

Freud used Sellin's 'discovery' and attached it to the primal horde theory. For personal reasons, this is what Freud wanted to hear. It was the stimulus that intensified and organized his own conflicts which were then expressed in a work of presumed scientific scholarship. When Freud was told by another biblical scholar in 1938 that he had heard that Sellin may have changed his mind, he responded, "It might be true all the same." (Jones 111:373) He was obviously heavily invested in it and such investment, or cathexis, to use a psychoanalytic term, implies the strong involvement of personal psychic conflicts.

One of the crucial supports for Freud's hypothesis, that the Egyptian Moses was murdered in the desert by rebellious, idol-worshipping Israelites was the work of Sellin. Yet Freud did not cite the specific chapters and verses involved and not a single biblical scholar had noticed this reference in *Hosea* or elsewhere, before or after Sellin.

The Prophet Hosea

Hosea lived and wrote circa 750 B.C.E. during the reign of Jeroboam II. He was from the Northern Kingdom of Israel, or Ephraim, as it was occasionally called, and aside from a few references to the Southern Kingdom of Judah, his prophecies (i.e., predictions, but mostly exhortations and excoriations) were limited to that area. He shared that touch of madness that appeared to be the essential ingredient for achieving that lofty professional status of Prophecy (Arlow, 1951). It is difficult to ascertain how a prophet was selected. Supernaturally tinged explanations are aplenty, but naturalistic ones are few or absent. It appears that in most cases the prophets were self-selected in that they claimed to have had a visionary experience with God resulting in a 'call' to devote their lives to the cause. They also had to be able to create poetry in Hebrew and that they did eminently well. Their poetry reveals, at times, an intense identification with God during which time they speak as if God Himself were speaking and, at other times, they are His strongest proponents, speaking on His behalf.

Hosea was one of the most personal of prophets. The poetry of the first three chapters is autobiography. It is masochism, with a touch of sadism, par excellence. God commands Hosea to marry a promiscuous woman named Gomer. They have one child together and then she leaves him and goes to the Temple of the Baals where she becomes a prostitute. Gomer's rejection of Hosea makes him pine and yearn for her all the more with the most intense of unrequited love. She has two more children apparently out-of-wedlock and they are given very derisive names which are really symbolic of the mother's depraved behavior as a temple prostitute. Gomer goes from temple prostitute to slave. Hosea purchases her back from her masters and puts her in solitary confinement until her lust for other men presumably will disappear. He eventually releases her from this captivity hoping that she will now settle down to be a loving wife and mother, but alas, character will out; she returns to prostitution and Hosea is devastated.

In beautiful poetic form, Hosea demonstrates rapid shifts in mood, from intense love to hatred and anger. He identifies the erring Israelites (or Ephraimites) with the faithless Gomer. They have behaved toward God as she has behaved toward him. Like her, they whored after strange gods. His perception of the world is refracted through the prism of his own experience. All the other prophets portray the relationship between God and His people as that of parent-child, but with Hosea it is husband and wife, with the latter being the Israelites.

In the most comprehensive and scholarly work on Hosea to date, Andersen and Freedman (1980) discuss the difficulties encountered in trying to understand the text. Hosea is about equal to Job in the number of unintelligible passages, more than in any other book of the Bible. This difficulty is to be borne in mind in the following discussion of the verses cited by Sellin (1924) as the source of his 'discovery'. Sellin (1924) writes:

> On the subject of the death of Moses, in the period following this event, for reasons that are known, a veil was dropped. But in my book on Moses (1922) I proved how the memory of the actual fact (or deed) has been maintained

through the centuries. We find, mainly, the repeated reference to this event in the prophet Hosea for whom Moses was the prophet most outstanding. I have previously brought attention to three places which in today's text nobody could reasonably explain. (p. 77)

The following are the verses cited by Sellin.[14] The order of the text cited here is the way Sellin has given it, presumably so as to make his point.

Chapter 9:7-13.

9:7a   The days of visitation have come.
        The days of recompense have come.
9:7b   Let Israel know—
        (They say) "The prophet is a fool,
        the man of the Spirit is insane,
        because your iniquity is great,
        and your hostility is great.
9:8a   The prophet is a watchman of Ephraim with my God,
9:8b   a trap set on all his paths,
        hostility in the house of his god.
9:9a   —that they have deeply defiled themselves
        as in the days of Gibeah.
9:9b   He will remember their iniquity,
        He will punish their sins.
9:10a O Israel, like grapes
        I found in the wilderness
        I discovered your forebears
        like a fig tree's best yield in its first season.
9:01b They came to Baal Peor.
        They dedicated themselves to shame.
        They became disgusting like the one who loved them.
9:11a O Ephraim, like a bird their Glory will fly away.
9:11b No childbirth. No gestation. No conception.
9:12a Even if they raise children,
        I will bereave them before maturity.
9:12b Yes! Woe to them also, when I turn from them.
9:13a I saw Ephraim as in that place, by the Rival—
        [a fig tree] planted in a meadow
9:13b Ephraim indeed brought his children to the slayer.

12:14a By one prophet Yahweh brought Israel up from Egypt.
12:14b By another prophet he was watched.
12:15a Ephraim has caused bitter provocation.
12:15b He will hold him responsible for his murders.
         His Lord will return his disgrace upon him.

13:1a   Truly He had spoken terrifyingly against Ephraim.
            He had lifted up (his voice) against Israel.
13:1b   He became guilty at Baal and died.

5:2a   The rebels are deep in slaughter.
5:2b   I am a chastisement to them all.

4:4a   Let no one dispute
           let no one debate.
4:4b   My contention is indeed with you, priest.
4:5a   You will stumble by day
           and the prophet will stumble with you by night
4:5b   and I will ruin your mother.

As the reader can see, with the possible exception of verses 12:15 and 5:2, there is absolutely no reference, direct or indirect, in these passages which would indicate that Moses was murdered. No biblical scholar agrees with Sellin. Sellin is mentioned only once in the *Anchor Bible — Hosea*, and that is in reference to an article he published in 1930 on a totally unrelated subject. It is disconcerting and surprising that Freud, the scientist, would accept this hypothesis without question, hesitation or doubt. We must look to Freud the man for an explanation.[15]

A strong case has been made against Freud's and Sellin's hypothesis. Nevertheless, there may be some elements of truth in it. It should be remembered that Sellin felt that Moses was murdered by rebellious Israelites who wanted to return to Baal worship. Freud carried this idea further by postulating that the Israelites wanted to rid themselves of a leader who had behaved like a tyrant in coercing them to accept his version of Egyptian monotheism. Freud felt that Moses had no choice but to behave in an authoritarian way so as to gain control over the rebellious Israelites. Though Freud may have been factually wrong, his intuition may have had some basis to it, though he was unaware of possible textual support.

If Moses was indeed murdered then there is the contingent possibility that he also may have been cannabilized. The immediate aftermath of the murder of Moses is conspicuous by its omission by Freud. To sustain an inherent consistency in his hypothesis, the possibility of cannabilism, as was the case with the Primal Father and the totem animal, and subsequently, in a symbolic form, with the crucifixion of Jesus, should have been considered by him. Freud makes more of a point by its omission than by its inclusion. The pointing out of the omission of the cannabilistic component of the sequence is not an attempt to either prove or disprove Freud's hypothesis. The omission does allude to the ambivalent emotional conflicts of Freud that are inherent in *Moses and Monotheism*. He either was being overly cautious and diplomatic in order to avoid further controversy or, possibly, he had to omit it so as to defend against his own primitive impulses toward his father. These impulses could be characterized in part as being cannibalistic in nature and with whatever unconscious fantasies are associated with them. There are probably elements of both, but it was probably more of the latter. If Freud had to interrupt his scientific attitude, as he does so often in this work, then underlying conflict of a highly personal nature may well have to be considered as a possible cause. Consistency in theory would have required inclusion of the cannibalistic component, otherwise the equation or formula set forth by Freud lacks any possible validity.

There is ample archeological and textual support for the possibility of both assassination and cannibalism, though more for the former than the latter. In Hosea 8:13, 13:2, and 13:12 the prophet states:

> 8:13a Sacrifices of my loved ones they have sacrificed.
> They ate flesh
> Yahweh does not accept them.
> 8:13b Now he keeps track of their iniquity.
> He will punish their sins.
> They have returned to Egypt.
>
> 13:2a Now they continue to sin
> They made a cast image for themselves.
> From their silver they made images
> according to their skill.
> 13:2b The whole thing is the work of artisans.
> Those who sacrifice people speak to them.
> They kiss the calves.
>
> 13:12a Ephraim's iniquity is wrapped up.
> 13:12b His sin is hidden away.

Why neither Freud nor Sellin used these verses as possible validation is puzzling. Sellin certainly knew the full text of Hosea but it is possible that Freud did not. There are a number of other relevant texts in the Bible which Freud could have used in support of the hypothesis of the murder of Moses and a possible cannabilistic aftermath. In Exodus 17:4 the Bible states:

> Moses cried out to the Lord, saying, "What shall I do with this people? A little more of this and they will stone me!"

In Hosea 2:2 the prophet states:

> 'The Judahites and the Israelites will gather themselves together, and they will appoint for themselves one head, and they will come up from the land. How great is the day, O Jezreel.'

On the words 'one head' in Hosea 2:2, Andersen and Freedman in the *Anchor Bible — Hosea* (1980) comment:

> 'As a token of reunification, this head must be modeled on a leader in the days before Israel was divided. This could be Moses (*or a second Moses*) especially if 'coming up from the land' is thought of as a new exodus, as in 2:17. Since Hosea makes extensive use of the traditions of the wilderness period, he may have in mind the insurrection described in Numbers 14, where the people reject Moses and try to appoint another leader ('head', Numbers 14:4) to lead a return to Egypt. Since the action described here is clearly constructive, it could be the antidote for the wilderness insubordination.' (p. 208, italics mine)

As can be seen from Hosea 8:13 quoted above, human sacrifice and cannibalism were practiced in his time, circa 750 B.C.E.[16] This phenomenon is cited elsewhere in the Bible. In Leviticus 18:21 God issues an injunction forbidding child sacrifice:

> Do not allow any of your offspring to be offered up to Molech, and do not profane the name of your God: I am the Lord.

The practice was rampant during the reign of King Manasseh (698-642 B.C.E.) in the Valley of Hinnom, just outside Jerusalem. It was officially banned by the reformist King Josiah (637-609 B.C.E.) as noted in II Kings 23:10:

> He also defiled Topeth, which is in the Valley of Ben-hinnom, so that no one might consign his son or daughter to the fire of Molech.

In Leviticus 26:29, God warns the Hebrews of what will befall them if they do not obey Him:

> You shall eat the flesh of your sons and the flesh of your daughters.

The prophet Ezekiel (5:10) wrote:

> Assuredly, parents shall eat their children in your midst, and children shall eat their parents. I will execute judgments against you, and I will scatter all your survivors in every direction.

The time of Moses was about five hundred years earlier, when presumably these practices were even more rampant. We know from studies in biblical archeology (Albright, 1969) that the assassination of leaders was indeed a very frequent and usual occurrence. In a short period of twenty years Hosea himself witnessed the demise of six monarchs by violent means.

Another Hypothesis of the Slaying of Moses

Freud makes reference to the German writer Goethe to support his hypothesis that Moses was slain by the rebellious Hebrews in the desert. Freud states:

> The killing of Moses by his Jewish people, recognized by Sellin from traces of it in tradition (and also, strange to say, accepted by the young Goethe without any evidence) thus becomes an indispensable part of our construction, an important link between the forgotten event of primeval times and its later emergence in the form of the monotheist religions. (S.E. XXIII: 89)

In a footnote reference to the 'young Goethe', Freud notes that his 'acceptance' appears in *Israel in der Wuste* [Israel in the Wilderness], the Weimar Edition, Volume 7, page 170. Freud nowhere else says anything further about Goethe's ideas in this regard.

In the chapter *Israel in der Wuste*, Goethe reveals his negative feelings for the biblical Moses, referring to him as lacking in leadership qualities, incompetent and indecisive, among other undesirable character traits.

> Meanwhile Miriam had died and Aaron had disappeared shortly after they had rebelled against Moses.
>
> Starting from the Arnon Creek, developments took a turn for the better. For the second time, the people felt that they were close to the fulfillment of their desires, in an area that put few barriers in their path; here they could advance in droves and overcome, destroy and expel the people who refused to their passing through this territory. One advanced further, thus Midianites, Moabites, Amorites were attacked inside their most beautiful estates. The first, and this was an action Jethro cautiously hoped to prevent, were even annihilated, the left bank of the Jordan was taken, and some impatient tribes were allowed to settle, and once again laws were passed, orders were given and one hesitated to cross the Jordan. While this was negotiated, Moses himself disappeared, as Aaron had disappeared, and we should be very much in error, if Joshua and Caleb had not considered it a good deed to terminate the regency of a limited man (a man of limited leadership quality), they had suffered for a number of years, and to send him the same way that he before had sent so many unfortunate people. Thus they would bring to an end this affair, in order to pursue in all seriousness the occupation of the entire right bank of the Jordan and of the country located on that side.[17]

Goethe did not give any reference so that we do not know whether the surreptitious and, possibly, calamitous and conspiritorial demise of Moses was his own brainchild or that of others. There is obviously no biblical basis for it. Though possible, it would nevertheless be totally out of character for Joshua and Caleb to have committed such an act. They were leaders of the tribes of Ephraim and Judah respectively. The two were among the twelve spies that were sent by Moses to do a reconnaissance of the land of Canaan. Out of the twelve they were the only ones to return with a positive impression of the land. The remaining ten spies had a distinctly negative impression and apparently were the recipients of mortal punishment for it. Joshua and Caleb were rewarded with large tracts of land after the conquest of Canaan. For Goethe, the rebellion against Moses was a question of dissatisfied leadership, but for Freud it was a compelling, regressive desire to rid themselves of their leader, the Father Figure, and return to idol worship. Neither would seem to apply to Joshua and Caleb. The sources of Goethe's ideas are unknown unless they are the products of his own youthful imagination.

It is difficult to understand why Freud would entertain a hypothesis only tangential to his own, unsupported by real evidence and one whose characterizations of the biblical characters Joshua and Caleb differ so greatly from the entirely positive biblical portrait. Though Freud often cites poets, especially Goethe, and had written that in the matter of psychological insight "the poets were here before us," this is a case where poetic intuition is hardly helpful.

A possible reason is that Freud wished to ally himself with the archetypal German poet while at the same time destroying the Jewish Moses, which, in a figurative sense, enacts the kind of family romance that characterizes *Moses and Monotheism*. A second reason for Freud's interest is also tied to his desire to escape the Jewish character of psychoanalysis. To this end he had appointed Jung as his "Joshua" (Freud's term), hoping to pass on the leadership of the psychoanalytic movement and to save it from what he feared would be an irradicable Jewish imprint. Betrayed by Jung, who went his own way theoretically, Freud suffered two fainting spells in the presence of this suddenly unfaithful Joshua.

The first fainting episode occurred in Bremen in 1909 just prior to their departure for America for Freud's lecture at Clark University. According to Jones (II:55), during a luncheon that included Freud, Ferenczi and Jung, the two successfully persuaded Jung to give up his abstinence and join them in drinking wine. Shortly after they all drank together, Freud fainted.

The second episode in 1912 is the more interesting one and one in which versions differ. It occurred at the Park Hotel in Munich during the International Psychoanalytic Congress being held there. Schur (1972) writes that it occurred at a luncheon just prior to which Freud and Jung had had a mild confrontation regarding a misunderstanding pertaining to Freud's visit to Binswanger (a mutual colleague) in Kreuzlingen, near Zurich, which resulted in Jung being slighted unintentionally by Freud. Jung felt that since Freud was in the area he should also have paid a visit to him. Jones (I:317), who was present at the event, recalls that as they were finishing their lunch, Freud began to criticize Jung for writing articles about psychoanalysis without mentioning Freud's name, thus symbolically disposing of the Master. Jung then responded that he thought it unnecessary to do so since Freud was so well known that nobody could conceive of psychoanalysis without Freud. Freud remained unsatisfied with this explanation and persisted in his criticisms of Jung when, suddenly, he fell to the floor in a dead faint. Jung, who was physically tall and strong, then carried Freud to a couch in the lounge. When Freud came to, the first words he uttered were, "How sweet it must be to die."

Jung (1965) remembered the event quite differently. He wrote:

> Someone had turned the conversation to Amenophis IV (Ikhnaton) The point was made that as a result of his negative attitude toward his father he had destroyed his father's cartouches on the steles and at the back of his great creation of a monotheistic religion there lurked a father complex. This sort of thing irritated me, and I attempted to argue that Amenophis had been a creative and profoundly religious person whose acts could not be explained by personal resistances toward his father. On the contrary, I said he had held the memory of his father in honor, and his zeal for destruction had been directed only against the name of the god Amon, which he had everywhere annihilated; it was also chiseled out of the cartouches of his father Amonhotep. Moreover, other pharaohs had replaced the names of their actual or divine fore-fathers on monuments and statues by their own, feeling that they had a right to do so since they were incarnations of the same god. Yet they, I pointed out, had inaugurated neither a new style nor a new religion. (p. 157)

In both versions the competitiveness between 'father' and 'son' is quite clear. Freud not only had what he thought was a disciple in Jung but also an arch rival for his leadership while Freud was still in his prime. According to Goethe, Aaron was disposed of because of his challenge to his more successful brother Moses. This was then repeated by Joshua and Caleb rebelling against Moses and causing him to disappear also. As noted, the Weimar Edition was published in 1888 and if Freud had read *Israel in der Wuste* prior to 1909 then a different, and more meaningful, explanatory light would be shed on these fainting episodes. If, however, Freud read it after 1912, then this explanation would be an exercise in playful fantasy, though, in some ways, partly relevant and possibly correct.

Freud's Ambivalence toward Christianity

What is rather perplexing were Freud's seemingly ambivalent views of Christianity.[18] Freud was of the opinion that for several centuries prior to the birth of Christ the inhabitants of the civilized world were in a state of malaise due to the unresolved conflicts pertaining to the murder of the primal father.

> The re-establishment of the primal father in his historic rights was a great step forward but it could not be the end. The other portions of the prehistoric tragedy insisted on being recognized. It is not easy to discern what set this process in motion. It appears as though a growing sense of guilt had taken hold of the Jewish people, or perhaps of the whole civilized world of the time, as a precursor to the return of the repressed material. Till at last one of these Jewish people found, in justifying a politico-religious agitator, the occasion for detaching a new — the Christian — religion from Judaism. Paul, a Roman Jew from Tarsus, seized upon this sense of guilt and traced it back correctly to its original source. He called this the 'original sin'; it was a crime against God and could only be atoned for by death. With the original sin death came into the world. In fact this crime deserving death had been the murder of the primal father who was later deified. But the murder was not remembered: instead of it there was a fantasy of its atonement, and for that reason this fantasy could be hailed as a message of redemption (evangelium). A son of God had allowed himself to be killed without guilt and had thus taken on himself the guilt of all men. It had to be a son, since it had been the murder of a father. It is probable that traditions from oriental and Greek mysteries had had an influence on the fantasy of redemption. What was essential in it seems to have been Paul's own contribution. In the most proper sense he was a man of an innately religious disposition: the dark traces of the past lurked in his mind, ready to break through into its more conscious regions. (S.E. XXIII: 86-87)

> The poor Jewish people, who with their habitual stubbornness contin- ued to disavow the father's murder, atoned heavily for it in the course of time. They were constantly met with the reproach 'you killed our God!' And this reproach is true, if it is correctly translated. If it is brought into relation with the history of religions it runs: 'you will not *admit* that you murdered God (the primal picture of God, the primal father, and his later reincarnations)'. There should be an addition declaring: 'we did the same thing, to be sure, but we have *admitted* it and since then we have been absolved.' (S.E. XXIII: 90)

It would seem that Freud wants to put Judaism and Christianity on the same plane, both having their origins in identical, but chronologically distinct, historical events, which were the violent death of their respective founders. Thus, from one perspective, there would be no inherent difference between the two religions. All that remains to achieve this equality is for the Jews to admit to the murder of Moses. The Jews' stubbornness in refusing to take this final step may be the reason for their persecution ever since the founding of Christianity.

A few lines further in this passage, with regard to anti-Semitism, Freud refers to "the city of Cologne, to which the Jews came with the Romans, before it was occupied by the Germans." In the above passage Freud, the presumed descendant of a Jew from Roman Cologne, identifies with Paul, the Roman from Tarsus. At the end of the book, however, Freud appears somewhat critical of Christianity when he states that Christianity had burst the framework of Judaism, that it had given up some characteristics of pure monotheism, and had adapted itself to the rituals of the other Mediterranean peoples.

> In some respects the new religion meant a cultural regression as compared with the older, Jewish one, as regularly happens when a new mass of people, of a lower level, break their way in or are given admission. The Christian religion did not maintain the high level in things of the mind to which Judaism had soared. It was no longer strictly monotheist, it took over numerous symbolic rituals from surrounding peoples, it re-established the great mother-goddess and found room to introduce many of the divine figures of polytheism only lightly veiled, though in subordinate positions. Above all, it did not, like the Aten religion and the Mosaic one which followed it, exclude the entry of superstitious, magical and mystical elements, which were to prove a severe inhibition upon the intellectual development of the next two thousand years. (S.E. XXIII: 88)

> ... We must not forget that all those peoples who excel today in their hatred of Jews became Christians only in late historic times, often driven to it by bloody concern. It might be said that they are all 'misbaptized'. They have been left, under a thin veneer of Christianity, what their ancestors were, who worshipped a barborous polytheism. (S.E. XXIII: 91)

In a brilliant stroke, Freud writes:

> It was as though Egypt was taking vengeance once more on the heirs of Akhenaten. It is worth noticing how the new religion dealt with the ancient ambivalence in the relation to the father. Its main content was, it is true, reconciliation with God the Father, atonement for the crime committed against him; but the other side of the emotional relation showed itself in the fact that the son, who had taken the atonement on himself, became a god himself beside the father and actually, in place of the father. Christianity, having arisen out of a father-religion, became a son-religion. It has not escaped the fate of having to get rid of the father. (S.E. XXIII: 136)

But then, in the next paragraph, which is also the penultimate paragraph of the book, he expresses the other side of his ambivalence toward Christianity:

Only a portion of the Jewish people accepted the new doctrine. Those who refused to are still called Jews today. Owing to this cleavage, they have become even more sharply divided from other peoples than before. They were obliged to hear the new religious community (which, besides Jews, included Egyptians, Greeks, Syrians, Romans and eventually Germans) reproach them with having murdered God. In full, this reproach would run as follows: 'They will not accept it as true that they murdered God whereas we admit it, and have been cleansed of that guilt'. It is easy therefore to see how much truth lies behind this reproach. A special enquiry would be called for to discover why it has been impossible for the Jews to join in this forward step which was implied, in spite of all its distortions, by the admission of having murdered God. In a certain sense they have in that way taken a tragic load of guilt on themselves; they have been made to pay heavy penance for it. (S.E. XXIII: 136)

In this passage Freud again parallels and confuses the group with the individual. It is as if the Jews as a group were a patient undergoing psychoanalysis and in order to be cured had to become consciously aware of the repressed memory of the murder of their Primal Father, the Egyptian Moses. Does he mean to say that if the Jews confessed as the Christians have, then all their problems would disappear? No more anti-Semitism? There is also a degree of naïveté here. He wonders why the Jews cannot overcome their unconscious resistance to awareness, as if this could be done by mere confession. Freud, resorting to a clinical paradigm, seems to be saying that if only the Jewish people, like the good male patient undergoing psychoanalysis, would accept the fact that they not only harbored, consciously in childhood, and still do unconsciously in adulthood, murderous wishes towards their Primal Father Moses but also had indeed murdered him, then they would be accepted (equal 'cured') by the entire world. Therefore, their refusal to do so results in the perpetuation of rejection and punishment by others and the suffering of pain and misery. This is contrary to everything he had ever said about the tenacity and persistence of unconscious resistances to awareness of repressed fantasies and memories of traumas. The distortion in Freud's usual clarity of thought may be another example of the imperative need to absolve himself of the sin and guilt of unconscious parricide.

In his conception of the psychodynamic origins of Christianity, Freud seems to have continued his fixed focus on only one aspect of the Oedipal conflict, the aggressive feelings of the son to the father. Loving and underlying erotic feelings receive little to no attention.[19] It seems that Freud was so tenaciously locked into battle with the Primal Father that he was not able to take a good look at the relationship of father to son. He has taken the basic tenet of 'Original Sin' out of its original context of the Adam-Eve-Serpent story and attached it to the drama of eternal emotional conflict between son and father, on both a group and an individual level. The 'Sin' of the gratification of forbidden sexuality is thus transformed into one of ultimate aggression, murder. In Freud's view, the son becomes the Father and then the Father is killed by his sons. The murder (or sacrifice) of Moses and Jesus are but major, almost epiphanic, examples of this phenomenon.

The Akedah and Christianity—A Link with Freud's Moses?

One of the hidden plot lines behind Freud's *Moses and Monotheism* can be found in Genesis 22, the story of the *Akedah* (the near, or possibly actual, sacrifice of Isaac by Abraham), one of the most moving and disturbing episodes in the Bible. Since the origin of the biblical Canon the story has moved poets, artists, theologians, among others, to the most sublime creative expression as well as to fear, anxiety and trembling. Every male child who has been exposed to the story has been effected by it because of the universality and timelessness of its theme. Sigmund Freud was no exception.

If Freud were to write about the father of the Jewish people why did he choose Moses? From a biblical perspective, it would have been more appropriate to select the first of the Patriarchs, Abraham. As a child, Freud must have heard the biblical Abraham referred to, as he always has been, among traditional Orthodox Jews, as *Avraham avinu, Abraham our father*. Moses has always been referred to as *Moshe rabeynu, Moses our teacher*. No patriarchal qualities were ever attributed to Moses!

Freud left a clue that might support the hypothesis of the Patriarch Abraham being a part of the latent content of his manifest interest in Moses. He is quite insistent about the institution of circumcision originating in Egypt and it being imposed on the Midianite Israelites by their Egyptian brethren as a categorical condition for their reunion into one religious and national group. He then states that in order to undo the historical fact of the Jewish religion beginning with the Egyptian Moses, the writers of the Bible, centuries later, decided to place the origin of both the religion and the rite of circumcision with the Patriarch Abraham. This helped lessen, if not totally suppress, the true significance of Moses, thus allowing for the supremacy of the religion of Yahweh and the forgetting of the earlier ethical monotheism of the Egyptian Moses. (The monotheism of Moses, according to Freud, was to emerge from repression much later through the medium of the Hebrew Prophets.) Freud seems to have been determined to make Moses, with whom he thoroughly identified, the father of the Jewish people, rather than Abraham.

> The fact that we find signs of efforts being made to deny explicitly that Yahweh was a new god, alien to the Jews, can scarcely be described as the appearance of a fresh tendentious purpose: it is rather a continuation of the

former one. With this end in view the legends of the patriarchs of the people—Abraham, Isaac and Jacob—were introduced. Yahweh asserted that he was already the god of these forefathers; though it is true that he himself had to admit that they had not worshipped him under that name. He does not add, however, what the other name was.

And here was the opportunity for a decisive blow against the Egyptian origin of the custom of circumcision: Yahweh, it was said, had already insisted on it with Abraham and had introduced it as the token of the covenant between him and Abraham. (S.E. XXIII: 44-45)

Shengold (1972) makes reference to a situation which is most intriguing. Karl Abraham (1955), who, according to Jones (1955, II) was one of the most faithful, devoted and normal of disciples, proposed an almost identical thesis to that of Freud about the origins of monotheism in ancient Egypt, and yet, Freud makes absolutely no mention of Abraham's work in *Moses and Monotheism*. What is further intriguing and somewhat perplexing is that Freud does make reference to Otto Rank, one of his most rebellious and eventually disowned disciples. Freud nevertheless refers to him in the most favorable manner, quoting extensively from Rank's study on the 'Family Romance'. Shengold attributes this lapse to Freud's unconscious feelings of competitiveness and annoyance with Abraham, because of his continued friendship with Freud's former friend Wilhelm Fliess. Both Abraham and Fliess lived in Berlin. Another contributing factor to Freud's displeasure was Abraham's suspiciousness of Jung. Freud desperately wanted Jung to eventually lead the psychoanalytic movement so that it would not be considered a mostly Jewish one. The omission of the biblical Patriarch Abraham from Freud's thinking and the exclusive focus on Moses as the source of Jewish monotheism are attributed, in part, by Shengold to the sharing of the name between Father Abraham and Karl Abraham.

Shengold's hypothesis leads to some very interesting speculative possibilities. Freud creates a direct link, to the point of identity, between the murder of Moses and the crucifixion of Jesus. Could the *Akedah*, the near or possibly actual sacrifice of Isaac, have served as the latent content for Freud's Mosaic hypothesis? Could the story, which illustrates the willing, passive submission of the son to what the son, as a child, perceives to be his omniscient, omnipotent father, which results in the direst consequences, have resonated with an identical conflict in Freud's unconscious? This conflict is so anxiety provoking that the entire complex of thoughts and feelings pertaining to it were repressed in childhood only to re-emerge in later life in the hypothesis of Moses' origin, rise to prominence and ultimate fate?

Briefly, this is the story of the *Akedah*. The character of Abraham, as presented in the Book of Genesis, is not only complex, but also incongruous.

This can clearly be seen by his argument with God concerning theodicy. The story begins in Genesis 18. Here, God, who in all of Chapter 18 is known as Yahweh, tells Abraham that he is going to destroy the wicked cities of Sodom and Gommorah. Upon hearing this Divine message, Abraham is transformed into a champion of justice. He argues with God to spare the innocent righteous inhabitants of these cities. He wins his case when God reassures him that even if there are ten such people (the argument and the bargaining started with fifty) the cities will be spared. There obviously were not even ten and the cities were destroyed. Four chapters later, in Genesis 22, God commands Abraham to take his son Isaac and sacrifice him as an offering to Him. There is not a whimper of protest out of Abraham. For total strangers he vehemently pleaded with God but for his own son—total silence! The character of Abraham certainly appears to be an inconsistent one; this is equally true of the Deity. A prominent theme in both Chapters 18 and 22 is Abraham's complete devotion and fidelity to God, but his trust in His judgment in the former is seriously questioned while in the latter it is totally unquestioned.

How can one explain this apparent inconsistency? There are obviously numerous theological explanations. However, the most reasonable one can be rendered on the basis of the Documentary Hypothesis [see Appendix II], the nineteenth century method of biblical exegesis, with which Freud was well acquainted. This method sees the Bible not as a unity, but as a tapestry of textual strands often reflecting very different authorial concerns. The inconsistency of character would lead one to conclude that we have here a merger of two different documents. The story of the near-sacrifice of Isaac occurs in Genesis 22:1-10 where God is referred to as Elohim (E Document) In verses 11-14, God is referred to as Yahweh (J Document). This means that the editor of the JE Document wove these two separate versions together but in a way that would maintain the integrity of ethical monotheism (though not undo the inconsistency of Abraham and God's characters). In verse ten, Abraham takes the knife, stretches his arm and hand and is about to apply it to his son's neck. But in verse 11 Yahweh comes to the rescue and the ram, sent by Yahweh, is substituted for Isaac. Verses 14-20 describes how Yahweh will reward Abraham for passing the test of faith. In verse 16 it is written:

> " . . . By Myself I swear, the LORD declares: Because you have done this and have not withheld your son, your favored son."

It may well be that in the original E Document Isaac was actually sacrificed and the verses 14-20 were added after the idea of human sacrifice was completely rejected by the Jewish religion. In support of this hypothesis of actual sacrifice verse 19 is cited:

> Abraham then returned to his servants, and they departed together for Beersheba; and Abraham stayed in Beersheba.

Abraham apparently came down the mountain without Isaac and both the name and character of Isaac receive no further mention in the E Document. This concept may sound quite heretical but the belief that Isaac was indeed sacrificed is found in the Midrash—the Aggadah, the story part of the Talmud. Now, why did Freud refer to Yahweh as the 'bloodthirsty demon Yahweh' when He appears, on the basis of this story, to be more merciful than the Deity known as Elohim?

The Apostle Paul, in his *Epistle to the Hebrews*, appears to have relied on this Midrashic tradition of the completed sacrifice of Isaac by Abraham:[20]

> 11:17. By faith Abraham offered Isaac, being tested and the one who received the promises offered [his] only one,
> 11:18. [with reference] to whom it was said, "In Isaac shall your seed be called,"
> 11:19. considering that God is able to raise [people] from [the] dead, from which he got him back, parabolically. By faith also concerning the things to come, Isaac blessed Jacob and Esau.

It is not known if Freud had ever read this passage in the New Testament. Aside from the question of the validity of Freud's hypotheses pertaining to the actual historic events, they do express his intuitive brilliance into the perception of biblical events as conceptualized by the early Christians. Indeed, in this passage Paul establishes an identity or equation between the sacrifices of Isaac and Jesus. The link of continuity thus appears to be between Isaac, not Moses, and Jesus. Paul then proceeds to cite the faith of Isaac in having blessed Jacob and Esau, the faith of Jacob in his blessing the sons of Joseph, the faith of Joseph in commanding the children of Israel to take his bones with them when they departed from Egypt. Paul, however, then goes on to equate the faith of Moses with that of Jesus:

> 11:24. By faith Moses, when he had grown up, refused to be called [let it be said that he was] a son of the daughter of Pharaoh,
> 11:25. choosing rather to be badly treated with the people of God than to have transitory enjoyment of sin,
> 11:26. since he considered the insult of the Messiah greater wealth than the treasures of Egypt, for he was looking out for the reward.
> 11:27. By faith he left Egypt, not having feared the wrath of the king, for he endured as [one who] saw the invisible.

It is noteworthy that Freud, in his hypotheses, gave primacy to the identity of Moses and Jesus and ignored that of Isaac and Jesus.

Shalom Spiegel, who was Professor of Medieval Hebrew Literature at The Jewish Theological Seminary of America, wrote a brilliant piece of work (1979) in which he convincingly places the origins of Christianity right back to its pagan fathers. He sees the *Akedah* and the crucifixion of Jesus as deriving from a common source in pagan idol-worship ritual.[21]

In the myths, legends and religious rituals of all the ancient peoples there are embedded thoughts, ways and means of coping with feelings of human sinfulness and mortality. The first-born were held to be property of the gods and were to be sacrificed to them by the father so that he can be cleansed of his sins and at the same time obtain absolution (or redemption) from the gods. The sons, like Isaac and Jesus, were deemed to be without sin or blemish just like the animal described in the Bible who was chosen as a candidate for sacrifice. (The stories of Isaac and Jesus are but two supreme examples in history, be they fictional or real events, of the willingness of the son to be the victim of the father and are expressions of that never-ending battle that the son fights in his attempt to cope with passive-feminine wishes towards his father.) With the passage of time, an unblemished animal was substituted for the unblemished son.

There are numerous biblical, mythological and archeological references to sacrifice of the first-born by the father. In the following four beautiful verses, the prophet Micah (6:6-9) summarizes the evolution from the lowest to the highest forms of religious expression:

6:6. With what shall I approach the Lord,
Do homage to God on high?
Shall I approach Him with burnt offerings,
With calves a year old?
6:7. Would the Lord be pleased with thousands of rams,
With myriads of streams of oil?
Shall I give my firstborn for my transgression,
The fruit of my body for my sins?
6:8. "He has told you, O man, what is good,
And what the Lord requires of you:
Only to do justice
And to love goodness,
And to walk modestly with your God;
6:9. Then will your name achieve wisdom."

In Greek mythology, Agamemnon was to sacrifice his daughter Iphigenia but the goddess Artemis had compassion and substituted an animal for the blameless girl. Artemis then carries her off in a cloud to become a priestess in her sanctuary. Sacrificial accounts pertaining to the first-born have been found preserved in Canaanite inscriptions.

... three votive stelae from the end of the second or beginning of the third century ... were discovered among the ruins of an ancient sanctuary dedicated to Saturn (equals Sabbathai!). On these stelae is engraved the god's image; he is pictured holding a knife in his right hand, and before him squats a ram—as in the Akedah story. Under the representation is a Latin inscription telling So-and-So and So-and-So, man and wife, wish to be remembered and inscribed for welfare, because they had carried out what in a night vision they were commanded to do, or what they vowed to do, and offered up as a burnt-offering a lamb in place of [the first born?] their children. Now, although in this Roman province Canaanite terms and beliefs persisted, and in the Latin inscription just referred to, the sacrifice mentioned above is called by a name which has survived from the Punic and occurs in Punic inscriptions—Molchomer or Morchomer, that is, Mlk'amr, to wit, a lamb sacrifice. (Spiegel, 1979, p. 62)

Therefore, there is a distinct textual possibility that Isaac was actually sacrificed and even though the rabbis in the Talmud and subsequent Midrashic commentators adhered to the unity of the sacred text, some of them took it for granted. But then, they faced the formidable task of justifying it. For this they resorted to a very primitive psychic defense mechanism, referred to as undoing. Though Isaac was sacrificed and burnt to ashes, the Deity, in His wondrous ways, brought him back to life again, whether here on earth or in Paradise. In a most bizarre twist of religious theme, Satan is given the role of trying to dissuade Abraham from his sacrificial intent. Never has Satan uttered such reasonable and rational words, but this only reflects the intense conflict of the rabbis over this whole issue. They dared not differ with God so they gave Satan the power of justice and reason which obviously reflects their own warded-off thoughts and feelings.

All this leads to the shared theme of both the *Akedah* and the Crucifixion, which is the concept of the resurrection of the dead. Satan is the angel of death and the individual who conquers Satan wins victory over death, and through him, others will gain eternal life. The recycling of the gods is a fairly common theme in pagan religions. It is also no accident that the Talmudic rabbis connect the willingness and submissiveness of Isaac, his righteousness, to the 'Resurrection of the Dead' Benediction which is part of the 'Eighteen Silent Blessings' (*Shemonah Esreh* prayer) and is required to be recited every day of the Jew's life.

Jesus was not the first deity to rise on the third day:

But it is certain that the very notion goes back essentially to times long before Christianity, and Judaism no less. This three-day season between the death and resurrection of the gods was well known to many nations in the ancient Near East. The Babylonian Tammuz and Osiris, the god of the

Egyptians—among others—go down to the netherworld and come up again on the third day. (Spiegel, 1979, p. 112)

The prophet Hosea refers to this theme in 6:1-2.

6:1a—Come let us return to Yahweh.

1b—Although he tore us apart, he will heal us
    Although he smashed us, he will bandage us.
6:2a—He will revive us after two days,
    and on the third day he will raise us up.
2b—We will live in his presence so that we know him.

Freud was quite correct in pointing out that the apostle Paul seized upon a seeming advance in religious thought and brought it back home to be infused with his own pagan sources. Spiegel comments upon this powerful regressive force in human thought and behavior:

It is very hard to drive out pagan spirits, and each generation must renew the battle against them. What is more, the very measures adopted to expel them are frequently themselves a partial admission of the vitality of pagan ways. (Speigel, 1979, p.77)

There is here a compound heavily freighted with pagan elements foremost of which is the ancient passion to 'be like God'—that dream and deep craving of the pagan world to have human beings delivered from the sentence of death and enjoying the radiance of eternity. But intertwining and amalgamating with the pagan inheritance are also hopes and expectations from the religion of Israel. In particular, there are here in fusion and confusion the story of the Akedah and the vision of the Servant of the Lord smitten by God and afflicted, crushed by sins not his own and by whose stripes others are healed. From these two channels the Christian idea of atonement drew its nourishment. Its founders and teachers drew quite consciously on the reservoir of Jewish thought and expression. And what the early teachers touch on lightly comes into full view in express statements of later ones.

... Despite all the echoes of theme and vocabulary from the Holy Scriptures with which the earliest Christian Fathers tried to surround their faith, in it there was a continuation and a return of ancient pagan beliefs. (Spiegel, 1979, pp. 83-85)

And yet, if Freud intuited the vestiges of a pagan drama in the Hebrew Bible, he also felt, in keeping with his ambivalent attitude, that Judaism proved fertile soil for ethical monotheism. The theme of the superiority of

Prophetic Judaism, which is derived from and equated with the Egyptian Mosaic concept of ethical monotheism, is often repeated and stressed.

> We reserve for discussion in later pages how the special peculiarities of the monotheist religion borrowed from Egypt affected the Jewish people and how it was bound to leave a permanent imprint on their character through its rejection of magic and mysticism, its invitation to advance in intellectuality and its encouragement of sublimations; how the people, enraptured by the possession of the truth, overwhelmed by the consciousness of being chosen, came to have a high opinion of what is intellectual and to lay stress on what is moral; and how their melancholy destinies and their disappointments in reality served only to intensify all these trends (S.E. XXIII: 85-86)

Indeed, Freud goes so far as to negate the importance of the Egyptian Moses by citing the role of the entire Jewish people in preserving the values of ethical monotheism.

> We cannot follow the chain of events further, but if we have rightly recognized these first steps, the monotheist idea returned like a boomerang to the land of its origin. Thus it seems unfruitful to try to fix the credit due to an individual in connection with a new idea. It is clear that many have shared in its development and made contributions to it. And, again, it would obviously be unjust to break off the chain of causes at Moses and to neglect what was effected by those who succeeded him and carried on his ideas, the Jewish Prophets. The seed of monotheism failed to ripen in Egypt. The same thing might have happened in Israel after the people had thrown off the burdensome and exacting religion. But there constantly arose from the Jewish people men who revived the fading tradition, who renewed the admonitions and demands made by Moses, and who did not rest till what was lost had been established once again. In the course of constant efforts over centuries, and finally owing to two great reforms, one before and one after the Babylonian exile, the transformation was accomplished of the popular god Yahweh into the God whose worship had been forced upon the Jews by Moses. And evidence of the presence of a peculiar psychical aptitude in the masses who had become the Jewish people is revealed by the fact that they were able to produce so many individuals prepared to take on the burdens of the religion of Moses in return for the reward of being the chosen people and perhaps for some other prizes of a similar degree. (S.E. XXIII: 110-111)

Symbolic Parricide and Suicide — Crime and Punishment

Moses and Monotheism, in essence, is a love story, in aggressive garb, between father and son. It is known from clinical experience that inter-marriage and conversion to a faith different from that of the parents are motivated partly by the Oedipal conflict, by the child's unresolved feelings of love and hate toward both parents. In intermarriage, the fact of the non-Jewish spouse being of a different religion or even color from the parents allows for a bypass (though not avoidance) of the imagined incest barrier which, in the particular instance, inhibits marriage to someone of the same religion as that of the parents. This is not to imply that such intermarriages cannot be happy ones. In this context Ostow (1982) describes the Oedipal dynamics in conversion of a male from one religion to another. On an unconscious level it would represent a murder of the father and the obtaining of the mother. It is possible that the only way Freud could have allowed himself to come to terms with the Judaism of his father on his return journey in old age was by de-Judaizing the primal father Moses and having him murdered. Even Freud's brief conversion wish in his youth was an early expression of this conflict. We can well imagine the effect of a conversion to Christianity on his parents. He must have known of the response of Martha's uncle, and probably her father, to the conversion of their brother to Christianity. Martha's uncle sat *Shiva*, the seven days of mourning, as if he had died. From this one can see the unconscious significance of the conversion experience on oneself and others, i.e., an unconscious suicide and homicide, alternately as well as simultaneously, appear to be involved.[22]

In this context it is significant that though *Studies on Hysteria*, co-authored with Josef Breuer, was published in 1895, psychoanalysis as we know it today, i.e., as a *psychological*, replacing an incipient *biological*, discipline, did not really begin until the late 1890s. This can be traced to the death of Jacob Freud in 1896 and the profound effect it had on his son.[23] The crucial discoveries, (e.g., the existence and etiological role of infantile sexuality, the Oedipus Complex, the investigative and therapeutic role of free association, elaboration of unconscious mental processes, resistance, and an earlier version of the concept of transference) all leading to the publication of his Magnum Opus, *The Interpretation of Dreams* in 1900, were motivated in large measure by the emotional upheaval precipitated by the demise of his ambivalently loved father. It is one of the pathetic aspects of the human condition that for some sons it necessitates the death of their father for their creative potential to be fully unleashed and realized.

Freud published his very perceptive essay on Dostoevsky in 1928. It served as an introduction to a German translation of *The Brothers Karamazov*. Freud felt that the three greatest works of literature were Sophocles' *Oedipus Rex*, Shakespeare's *Hamlet*, and Dostoevsky's *The Brothers Karamazov*. The central theme in all three is the murder of the father for which the underlying motive is sexual rivalry for a woman.

There is no question that the Russian author lends himself to a discussion of these subjects for, in the annals of world literature, very few have come as close as Dostoevsky in being able to plumb the depths of human sinfulness and guilt. Both had a glimpse of the terrifying nature of inner man, but Freud found a way to help overcome the unfortunate consequences of its manifestations. Dostoevsky became, for the most part, a victim of it but he left us a legacy of description of our nature that is difficult to duplicate. Nevertheless, what Freud tells us about Dostoevsky also tells us something about Freud.

> Parricide . . . is the principal and prime crime of humanity as well as of the individual. It is in any case the main source of the sense of guilt, though we do not know if it is the only one: researches have not been able to establish with certainty the mental origin of guilt and the need for expiation. But it is not necessary for it to be the only one. The psychological situation is complicated and requires elucidation. The relation of a boy to his father is, as we say, an ambivalent one. In addition to the hate which seeks to get rid of the father as a rival, a measure of tenderness for him is also habitually present. The two attitudes of mind combined to produce identification with the father; the boy wants to be in his father's place because he admires him and wants to be like him, and also because he wants to put him out of the way. This whole development now comes up against a powerful obstacle. At a certain moment the child comes to understand that an attempt to remove his father as a rival would be punished by him with castration. So fear from castration—that is, in the interests of preserving his masculinity—he gives up his wish to possess his mother and get rid of his father. In so far as this wish remains in the unconscious it forms the basis of the sense of guilt. We believe that what we have here been describing are normal processes, the normal fate of the so-called 'Oedipus complex'; . . . Thus both impulses, hatred of the father and being in love with the father, undergo repression. (S.E. XXI: 183-4)

The complicating factor, and one which certainly pertains to Freud's own state, is that the object of rebellion, the father, nevertheless becomes incorporated into the very fabric of the son's mental composition.

> But what has been said so far does not exhaust the consequences of the repression of the hatred of the father in the Oedipus complex. There is something fresh to be added: namely that in spite of everything the identification with the father finally makes a permanent place for itself in the ego. It is received into the ego, but establishes itself there as a separate agency in contrast to the rest of the content of the ego. We then give it the name of super-ego and ascribe to it, the inheritor of the parental influence , the most important functions (S.E. XXI: 184-5)

In Freud's Mosaic drama the theme of parricide is one that is central to his hypotheses. The scenario described in *Moses and Monotheism* can be viewed as any other mental production, be it dream, conscious fantasy, novel, or historical account based on scant data. They are all products of the author's mind. The scenery and cast of characters are all projected parts of their creator. The plot line is a reflection of his own unique psychic conflicts as expressed first in unconscious fantasy and then, in derivative form, in its conscious elaboration.

There is no doubt that Freud loved his father but, as with all father-son relationships, hated him as well. Aside from the usual positive Oedipal aspects, i.e., the wish to be rid of the father so as to have exclusive possession of the mother, in all such ambivalence there are the additional factors of Jacob Freud's religious, cultural, financial and societal status about which Sigmund had many conflict-laden feelings.

Freud plays numerous roles, simultaneously and alternately, in *Moses and Monotheism*. He is the royal Egyptian Moses who is the creator of a new ethical monotheism and a superb leader while at the same time he is the primitive and savage Israelite who can very quickly reject the father of his people and everything he stands for and turn to idol worship. Freud is the Hebrew prophet who brings about the return of the long-suppressed Mosaic religion. He is ultimately the crucified Jesus. Moses, like Jacob Freud, was also the father but in addition, an idealized one.

> There is no doubt that it was a mighty prototype of a father which, in the person of Moses, stooped to the poor Jewish bondsmen to assure them that they were his dear children. (S.E. XXIII: 110)

Parricidal wishes are present in all of us and they can be seen only in disguised, derivative form (with the exception of an obsessional thought where it can be clearly seen on a conscious level accompanied by much shame and guilt, and in situations of psychosis when it actually does take place). Equally intense feelings of love coexist with these wishes. One opposing set of feelings is often used to prevent the emergence of the other (Brenner, 1982). What is ultimately seen in reality, be it in thought or action, is an expression of a blend of these polar opposite wishes and feelings, with a degree of disguised eroticism attached to them. The quantity of the respective affect in this blend will determine the nature, that is, whether it be predominantly hateful or loving, of the ultimate expression. The frightening aspects of such wishes force us to maintain the repressive forces but they never disappear. In a treatment situation much analytic work on the psychological resistances has to be done by both therapist and patient before the outlines of these wishes can be 'visually', with the mind's eye, elaborated and felt in a consciously meaningful manner.

The emergence into consciousness of parricidal and infanticidal wishes can be seen clinically, in varying degrees of disguise, in waking fantasies, dreams and nightmares. I have seen this phenomenon most clearly in several male patients who have had what they deemed to be disappointing fathers and who, themselves, have far superceded them in their professional attainments. It was demonstrated most clearly in the form of the nightmare which would be the least disguised of all conscious mental productions. In this nightmare, which is a recurrent one, it is discovered by the police that the patient had murdered some unknown individual in the long-forgotton, distant past. He was now, after so many countless years, finally caught and had to face the consequences. All that he had striven for and attained during his entire life was now for naught. The patient would awake with feelings of dread and panic. In these nightmares it felt to the dreamer as if the catastrophic events had occurred in early historic, if not pre-historic, time. The discovery, in the dream or nightmare state, came as a complete and shocking surprise to him. The patient's associations to the specific content of the nightmare invariably led to paternal and/or sibling figures. The origins of the underlying wishes may well reside in early childhood perceptions and fantasies, which underwent repression only to return under the pressure of the therapeutic transference. The therapist, on an unconscious level, replaces the father or sibling and becomes the current day object of these hostile wishes. It is quite possible that in his conceptualization of the Primal Father and his fate Freud was operating with a similar, if not identical, set of unconscious wishes and fantasies.

Freud substituted Moses for his father but he was also Moses himself so that the inevitable accompaniment of this parricide is suicide. This represents crime and punishment. On an unconscious level there may be a fantasied sub-plot in which there is also a reunion-in-death with the father. This sequence can be seen in the crucifixion of Jesus and his reunion with God the Father. As Freud points out, the murder of the Primal Father, *the* Original Sin, had to culminate after a long interval in the crucifixion of the beloved son. A Father religion was replaced by a Son religion.

> But the fact of the parricide, in returning to the memory of mankind, had to overcome greater resistances than the other fact, which had constituted the subject-matter of monotheism [namely, the fact of the existence of the primal father]; it was also obliged to submit to a more powerful distortion. The unnameable crime was replaced by the hypothesis of what must be described as a shadowy 'original sin' (S.E. XXIII: 135)

Primal Murder as an Epiphany in Secular Garb

There are inherent contradictions in Freud's primal horde theory concerning the Egyptian Moses, which are neither noted nor addressed by him. It can be assumed that over many millenia there were *repeated* murders and cannibalizations of the primal father. Given the incorporation of the memory-traces of these external events into the psyche of each member which are then transmitted, in Lamarckian fashion, from generation to generation, why should the event with Moses have a higher value or power than any other single identical occurrence or the cumulative effect of all the preceding murders and cannibalizations? Freud appears to give the event an authority rivaling that of Divine Revelation. On Sinai, the voice of God erupted into history, fixing at a moment in time God's intervention in the fate of a people, and basing His claim upon them from that time forward on certain historical events: "I am the Lord your God who brought you out of the land of Egypt." Though the idea of the manifestation of the Divine Presence would be repellent to Freud, it would appear that that is precisely what he is doing in his theoretical framework. Though the conceptual frames of reference of both the natural and supernatural realms constitute two completely different worlds, these worlds often collide when we would like most, as Freud wished, to keep them separate. The Moses event, as Freud describes it, is an epiphany, a providential occurrence, in secular garb. As noted, the crucifixion of Jesus, another manifestation of Divine providence, was deemed to be a disguised replica of the murder of Moses. The catastrophic events pertaining to both Moses and Jesus thus, unalterably, changed the nature and course of Western Civilization. If the Moses event were really that special, etiologically, then this unique aspect of the primal horde hypothesis is in need of further elaboration and substantiation.

Another problem arises when we consider that one of the linchpins of classical psychoanalytic theory and technique is the concept of infantile psychic trauma, whether real, fantasied, or both, and its subsequent repression leading to neurotic symptom and character formation. The therapeutic technique that hinges on this hypothesis revolves around the analysis of the psychic resistances that prevent or impede recall, the consequent weakening and lifting of the repressive forces, and the emergence into consciousness of these memories with the feelings that were attached to them.[24] Now, if we were to accept the Lamarckian hypothesis, would there not be more than sufficient traumas in the pre-history and history of the race to account for all the fantastic variety of psychic and neurotic symptomatology and respective character flaws? Given the concept of determinism that is inherent in psychoanalytic theory, why the necessity to postulate a special class of trauma in the early years of the individual's life? Even if we were to attribute a special etiological role to infantile events, why should they be more significant than the almost infinite number of accumulated traumas in the predecessors on the particular geneological tree? To be consistent, with a technique that is anchored in the Lamarckian hypothesis, psychoanalytic insights and recon-struction of repressed and consciously forgotten infantile and early childhood events would be an exercise in futility. The most that can then be expected would be that the insight or interpretation might serve as a stimulus to a re-awakening, to use Freud's term in regard to the murder of the Egyptian Moses, of events in the prehistory of the race. The reason for noting these apparent contradictions in Freud's thinking is to show that in *Moses and Monotheism,* for very personal reasons, he was more interested in making a point rather than in proving it. As noted earlier, Freud wrote to Arnold Zweig on September 30, 1934 that he had originally given the following title to his essay, *The Man Moses, A Historical Novel.* Gay (1988, p. 648) is correct when he says that "He [Freud] would have done well to stay with his original intention" of calling it a novel.[25]

But even if it were a novel, it would have been dictated by the same mixture of the historical, the religious and the personal, in keeping with the book that played so central a role in Freud's thinking, the Hebrew Bible. Inscribed in his father's Bible, Freud could not write his way out of it, though he often tried. And though the effort no doubt increased the productivity and enriched the output of this remarkable thinker, it also tinged his later writing with violent, conflicted motives and led him to attribute to others—indeed to an entire people—what, at a deep level, lurked in himself.

There is a most perceptive example of this theme in the Talmud where one of the Talmudic sages, Rabbi Abaye (circa 279-339 C.E.) came face-to-face with his own evil temptations.[26] One day, he overheard a young man asking a girl to accompany him on a walk to a distant city on the following morning. On the basis of these few overheard words the rabbi concluded that this man was up to no good and that in an isolated spot he would attempt to seduce her. The rabbi felt that it was his solemn duty and obligation to arise early and follow the couple, unbeknown to them, and save them from committing sin. To his surprise and shame, but surely unconscious disappointment, the meeting between the two young people was purely social and innocent; the young man just happened to enjoy the maiden's company.

> *Because he hath done great things.* Abaye explained, against scholars more than against anyone (does the evil inclination act); as was the case when Abaye heard a certain man saying to a woman, "let us arise betimes and go on our way." "I will", said Abaye, "follow them in order to keep them away from transgression" and he followed them for three parasangs across the meadows. When they parted company (i.e., each one having to go in a different direction) he heard them say, "Our company is pleasant, the way is long." "If it were I", said Abaye, "I could not have restrained myself," and so he went and leaned in deep anguish against a doorpost, when a certain old man (Tradition identifies the anonymous old man with the spirit of Elijah) came up to him and taught him: *The greater the man, the greater his Evil inclination.* (italics mine)

In *Moses and Monotheism*, Freud set out to uncover a murder. Though the case is pinned on a rebellious horde of Hebrews, there is no question that at some level Freud understood he was himself the murderer, also the victim, also the accuser, also the judge.

CHAPTER 12

The Last Chapter

It has been a contention of this book that, for reasons that are unclear, Freud himself, his family and biographers have minimized the extent of his religious background and its influence on him. Neither was sufficient importance attributed to the attitudes of the Viennese middle class toward the *Ostjuden* and the effect this intense prejudice had on the self-esteem of these immigrants and their descendants.

Freud came from a mildly diminished, East European Orthodox milieu, rebelled against it in adolescence and continued this struggle to the very end of his life. He rebelled not in a clear-cut manner, but in what he would probably have referred to as a series of 'compromise formations', in which contending unconscious instinctual forces and the psychological defenses used to cope with them blend together in a unique solution to specific mental conflicts. In the last years of his life he returned to Judaism, on his own terms, and based on his own needs and abilities for compromise.

> A child's emotional impulses are intensely and inexhaustibly deep to a degree quite other than those of an adult; only religious ecstasy can bring them back. A rapture of devotion to God was thus the first reaction to the return of the great father. (S.E. XXIII:134)

Freud's attitude toward Judaism was not different from that toward members of his family, friends and colleagues who were close and meaningful to him. Its characteristic hallmark was ambivalence. There was love and hate, an attraction and a repulsion. The Orthodox Jews' passion for religion, in all its diverse ramifications, was replaced by an almost total, passionate immersion in Greek and Roman antiquities, as well as in the physical sciences, or more precisely, Freud's conception of them. This book focused on the genesis of his Jewish identity and his earliest identifications.[1] Freud's multiple identifications and the way he utilized them may well be an explanatory key to the generation and flowering of his creativity. As can be seen from his comments on the Hebrew language and Jewish identity in the latter years of his life, Freud was coming home again, even if he had to restructure, perhaps radically alter, its foundation.

On the surface level, Freud acted out his conflicts toward formal institutions which were associated with the primal figures in his life, his parents, and, later in life, with their surrogates. The struggle to overcome the presumed handicap of his parents' East European origins was never fully successful. On a deeper level, there were doubts about his self-image, his sexual identity, struggles for control over primeval impulses—factors that are critical in all of us. What makes for uniqueness is the way in which these conflicts are resolved.

Freud stresses the significance of the parent of the same sex in the formation of character. He describes how in childhood the individual admires and identifies with the parent. In adolescence, there is a rebellion against the parent and the person becomes everything the parent is not. When adulthood is reached, the formerly repressed identification with the parent emerges and the individual gradually manifests characteristics of the parent that had previously been condemned and rejected. Freud gives the example of Goethe who, in his period of genius, looked down upon his unbending and pedantic father but in his old age became just like him.

> In order not to miss the connection with our theme, we must keep in mind
> the fact that at the beginning of such a course of events [in the development
> of an individual's character] there is always an identification with the father
> in early childhood. This is afterwards repudiated, and even overcompen-
> sated, but in the end establishes itself once more. (S.E. XXIII:125)

Morris Raphael Cohen was another famous Jew who followed a developmental pathway similar to that of Freud. In fact, if we were to substitute 'philosophy' for 'psychoanalysis', we would see a remarkable parallel and many points of identity between their backgrounds, their feelings about Judaism and their own Jewishness, and the manner in which they returned to it toward the end of their lives. The outcomes were somewhat different, though they shared a common interest in the pursuit of truth, whatever the cost. Cohen's contributions to philosophy were considerable, but his fame rests more on his having served as a symbol, a model and an object of identification for those whose intellectual horizons were limited by the Eastern European Orthodox Jewish life style and mode of thought. Many of his students at City College did come from such a background but he also served the same function for those who knew of him only by reputation and his writings. Though Cohen was critical of the validating process of psychoanalysis, he and Freud shared a passionate commitment to the search for truth. It is to Freud's genius that we owe the knowledge that even such a noble pursuit is not without underlying motivations which may have little bearing on the lofty and sanctified expressions of the human spirit. Whereas Cohen set out to destroy myths and felt under no obligation to put a verity in their place, Freud sought to explain their origins, the reasons for their persistence and to place them within the context of life's experiences.

Freud, like Spinoza, was aware that there are levels of knowledge and truth and that the 'Amor Dei Intellectualis', the Intellectual Love of God, was the ultimate goal. But, unlike Spinoza, Freud realized that this was an ideal, that the inherent imperfections of man would not permit its attainment; that the highest duty of man, therefore, lay in the *pursuit* of this 'truth' and not necessarily in its attainment.

Leonora Cohen Rosenfeld, in a beautiful synopsis of her father's religious 'journey', describes a five-act play in which the important figures in his life, his teacher, his wife and Spinoza, exert significant influence (1962, p. 238):

> In the first act of Cohen's life, he was an Orthodox Jew; in the second, a rebel. During the third act, his youthful reflections about giving himself to some humanitarian cause were kindled by Davidson, the flame nurtured by Mary. In his fourth act, he developed a spiritualized naturalism, reminiscent of Spinoza's. In the final act, he sacrificed the unfinished writings and the remainder of his days on the altar of the Jews.
>
> To put it still more succinctly, the first and the last chapters of his life were Jewish.

And so it was, in his own idiosyncratic way, with Sigmund Freud.

APPENDIX I

Sigmund Freud's Formal Education

There appears to be some controversy over Sigmund Freud's primary school education. Anna Freud Bernays (1940), Sigmund's sister, has stated that he did not attend any primary school but was tutored at home by his parents. His formal schooling began at the age of nine and a half when he entered the *Gymnasium* in the Leopoldstadt section of Vienna. In order to be accepted he had to pass an entrance examination on elementary subjects (Knopfmacher, 1979).

The Freud family's insistence that Sigmund did not attend primary school is perplexing. It is hard to imagine keeping such a bright child at home until the age of nine and a half while the other children were in school. Also, since Jacob and Amalia Freud, as far as we know, never had any formal education in secular subjects, how could they have tutored him well enough to pass the entrance examination and then go on to be first in the class for the last six of his eight years at the *Gymnasium* (Jones, 1953, I:20)?

In a *Curriculum Vitae* that Freud submitted to the University of Vienna Medical School on January 21, 1885 (Figure 21) as part of the application process for appointment as *Privatdozent*, he wrote:

> I was born on May 6, 1856 in Freiberg, Moravia. When I was 3 years old my parents first moved to Leipzig and then to Vienna in which city we established permanent residence to this day. *The first schooling I received in my father's house and afterwards attended a private primary school* and in the Autumn of 1865 I entered the Real and Obergymnasium of Leopoldstadt ... (italics mine)

In Austria, primary school covered the ages of six to ten years. *Real* and *Obergymnasium* refer to the lower, which began at age ten, and upper schools respectively. In an unpublished letter of April 18, 1885 to his then fiancee, Martha Bernays, Freud states that first his mother gave him lessons, and then his father taught him before sending him to a private primary school, or *Volksschule* (Jones, 1953, I:18).

Even though compulsory education did not take effect until 1869 (Knoepfmacher, 1969) many parents sent their children to either public or private primary schools. Though there are no specific data, it would appear that most of the male children in the Leopoldstadt attended the private schools which were Jewish in sponsorship. The private schools were generally superior to the public ones, one reason being that the higher salaries attracted better teachers (Rainey, 1971). The Austrian government required that religious education be given in all schools, both public and private, starting with the first year of primary school through the last year of the *Gymnasium*. The authorities felt that ethics or morality could not be isolated from a religious frame of reference. The schools were given the responsibility to develop a student's piety (*Frommigheit*) as well as his academic skills. The subject of religion was on a par with all other academic subjects, with the students being graded on it (Rainey, 1971).

There were several ways a Jewish student could fulfill the religious studies requirement. If the child attended the Jewish primary school, then religion and academic subjects would be part of the total curriculum. The IKG supervised the religious instruction in both public and private schools. With the exception of the *Talmud-Torah* school, sponsored by the Orthodox Jewish component of the Leopoldstadt, most of the instructors in Jewish religion were the same for both public and private schools.

Prior to Emancipation in 1848 the predominant institution for the education of Jewish children was the Eastern European equivalent of the one-room schoolhouse, the *Ḥeder*, in which the basic goals were first, the development of skills in reading and writing Biblical Hebrew, the study of the Old Testament, and then, as the child advanced, an almost exclusive focus on the study of the Talmud. Secular academic subjects played a relatively minor role in the *Ḥeder*. Arithmetic, geography, and history were taught in Yiddish though the textbooks were printed in Hebrew. The brighter students usually went on to study in the *Yeshiva*, which had a tradition, hierarchy and status of its own, almost akin to the Ivy League system in the United States. Of course, all those students who followed this pathway came from strictly Orthodox families and were Orthodox themselves. For the most part, these institutions were located in Lithuania, Poland, or the Eastern part of the Austro-Hungarian Empire.[1]

Given the extent of Eastern European migration to the Leopoldstadt, there may well have existed a *Ḥeder* or *Yeshiva* for the children, but no records of such institutions exist. The curriculum of religious instruction in the Jewish *Primary* and *Gymnasium* schools from 1860s and early 1870s, which is the time frame of Freud's attendance was as follows: five hours per week,

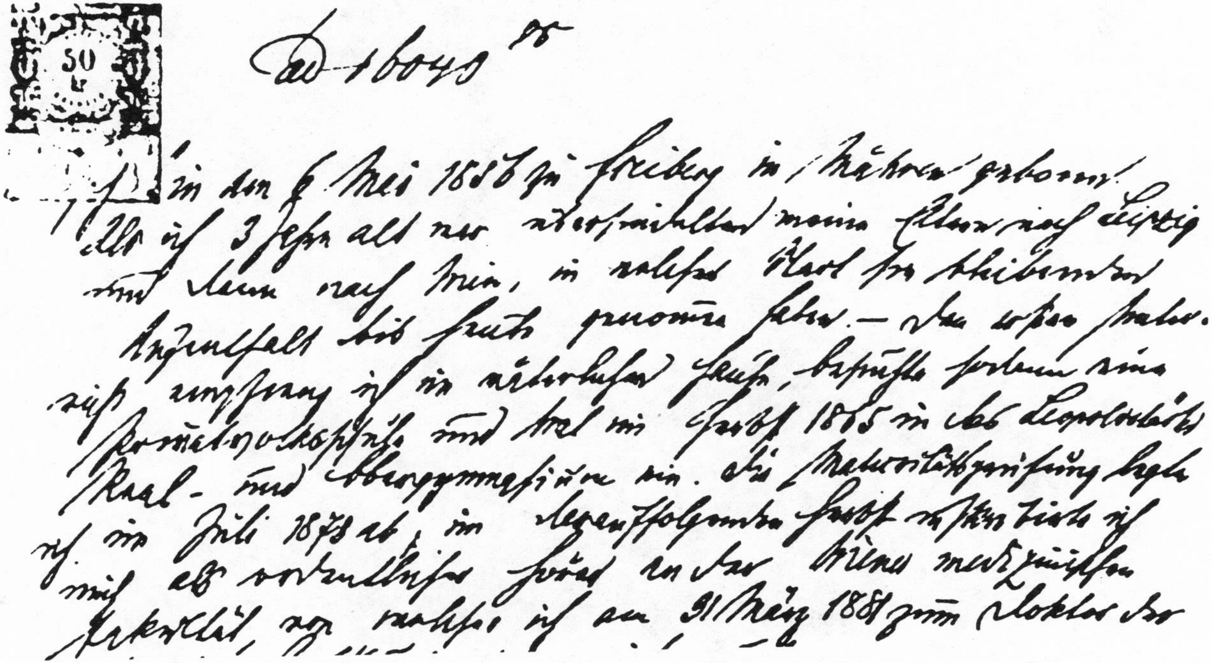

Figure 21. Segment of Sigmund Freud's Curriculum Vitae, dated January 21, 1885. Reproduced by permission of A.W. Freud et al., by arrangement with Mark Paterson & Associates, Colchester.

Figure 22. Sigmund Freud, at the age of eight (in 1864), standing along his father Jacob Freud. Reproduced by permission of A.W. Freud, et al., by arrangement with Mark Paterson & Associates, Colchester.

Figure 23. The Freud family in Vienna in 1876. *Standing:* Starting from left: Sigmund Freud's sisters Paula and Anna, Sigmund, his half-brother Emanuel Freud (who was then living in Manchester, England but visiting in Vienna), Sigmund's sisters Rosa and Marie ("Mitzi") and the man in uniform is his cousin, Simon Nathanson.

Seated: From left to right: Sigmund's sister Adolphine ("Dolphi"), his mother, Amalia, and his father, Jacob.

Seated in front: The boy who is seated in the chair may be Sigmund's brother, Alexander. The young girl who is standing to the right of Amalia and the boy who is seated on the floor are unidentified. Reproduced by permission of A.W. Freud et al., by arrangement with Mark Paterson & Associates, Colchester.

Figure 24. From left to right: Sigmund Freud, his mother Amalia, and his wife Martha. Photograph was taken while they were on holiday in Ausee in 1905. Reproduced by permission of A.W. Freud et al., by arrangement with Mark Paterson & Associates, Colchester.

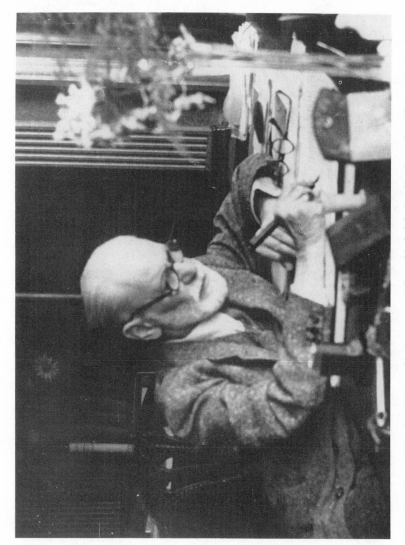

Figure 25. Sigmund Freud, in 1938, working on a manuscript at his desk in London. Reproduced by permission of A.W. Freud et al., by arrangement with Mark Paterson & Associates, Colchester.

ten months per year, were devoted to religious studies as compared to two hours in the public school system. The Hebrew language (reading, writing and grammar) was taught in every class, from the first through the fifth. The first five books of the Bible, the Pentateuch, received the most emphasis. The New Testament was not taught at all. Jewish history, proficiency in reading the prayers in Hebrew, laws and doctrines were additional subjects. Attendance at a brief worship service at school was probably required. Some elementary Hebrew was taught in the public schools through to the end of the *Gymnasium*, but the extent of the teaching was in no way sufficient to lead to mastery of the subject. Competence in reading simple Hebrew was probably attained by the more diligent and brighter students and they would have been able to read the prayers and the Bible. Adequate comprehension would have been another matter.

Samuel Hammerschlag was the instructor in the School of Religion as well as in the *Gymnasium* from 1870 to 1873, throughout the period in which Freud was a student there. Apparently there was no instructor in Jewish religion at the Gymnasium from 1865 to 1870. According to the law, Jewish students would have had to receive their instruction at the IKG school, of which Hammerschlag was the headmaster and principal instructor. So it would seem that Freud's contacts with him predated Hammerschlag's arrival at the *Gymnasium* in 1870, which allowed time for development of the close relationship that was to exist between them for many years thereafter.

From the following letters to Martha it appears that Freud perceived Hammerschlag as the unambivalently loved 'ideal' father. He represented a unique combination of Jewish and Western cultural, philosophic and religious values. When Freud would feel low in spirits he would visit with him. In a letter to Martha (November 15, 1883), he wrote:

> ... Today is a holiday and I have done no work whatsoever, in order to refresh myself. The weather is quite horrible; this evening I think I will go and see Hammerschlag. I am so weary that it will do me good, if someone is friendly to me. What's more, they will ask after you and I will have a chance to talk about you.

Freud's feelings for him are poignantly expressed in another letter he sent to his fiancee on January 10, 1884. After expressing resentment at his half-brothers Emanuel and Philipp for not sending adequate financial support to the Freud family in Vienna, he writes:

> ... I had been to see the Hammerschlags, where I was very warmly received. The old professor took me aside and charged me with a delicate mission concerning his young son Albert, who is a medical student; then he informed

me that a rich man had given him a sum of money for a worthy person in need, that he mentioned my name and he was herewith handing it to me. I am describing the situation to you in all its crudity. The good professor himself, as he has often told me, has experienced great poverty in his own youth and sees nothing shameful in accepting support from the rich. Nor actually do I, but I intend to compensate for it by being charitable myself when I can afford it. It is not the first time the old man has helped me in this way; during my university years he often, and unasked, helped me out of a difficult situation. At first I felt very ashamed, but later, when I saw Breuer and he agreed in this respect, I accepted the idea of being indebted to good men and those of our faith without the feeling of personal obligation. Thus I was suddenly in the possession of fifty florins and did not conceal from Hammerschlag my intention of spending it on my family. He was very much against this idea, saying that I worked very hard myself and could not at the moment afford to help other people, but I did make it clear to him that I must spend at least half the money in this way ... I don't know any people kinder, more humane further removed from any ignoble motives that they ... You mustn't forget that the Hammerschlags themselves are very poor, have nothing but his pension and what the eldest children earn, the son as a tutor and the girl as a school teacher ... I have always felt more at home with this family than with the wealthy Schwabs, quite apart from the deep-seated sympathy which has existed between myself and the dear old Jewish teacher ever since my school days ...[2]

The closeness between Freud and the Hammerschlags is further revealed by Freud's naming of his two daughters after a daughter and a niece of Hammerschlag (Jones, 1953, I: 163). Freud wrote an obituary for two newspapers in Vienna on the death of Hammerschlag in 1904:

S. Hammerschlag, who relinquished his activity as a Jewish religious teacher about 30 years ago, was one of the personalities who possess the gift of leaving ineradicable impressions on the development of their pupils. A spark from the same fire which animated the spirit of the great Jewish seers and prophets burned in him and was not extinguished until old age weakened his powers. But the passionate side of his nature was happily tempered by the ideal of humanism of our German classical period which goverened him and his method of education and was based on the foundation of philological and classical studies to which he had devoted his own youth. Religious instruction seemed to him a way of educating towards love of the humanities, and from the material of Jewish history he was able to find means of tapping the sources of enthusiasm hidden in the hearts of young people and making it flow out beyond the limitations of nationalism or dogma. Those of his pupils who were later allowed to seek him out in his own home were able to perceive that sympathetic kindness was the fundamental characteristic of his nature. Feelings of gratitude towards a revered

teacher—undiminished through the course of decades—received most
dignified expression over his grave from Dr. Friedjung the historian.
(S.E., IX: 255-6)

If Freud did attend a primary school, and it appears fairly certain that
he did, then the question remains, which one? There were two private schools
that were obviously Jewish in support and orientation in the Leopoldstadt.
Knoepfmacher (1979) accepts the Freud family contention that Sigmund did
not attend a primary school and abruptly dismisses Gicklhorn's (1965) assumption that he did on the ground that the school was strictly Orthodox.
Knoepfmacher was apparently unaware that a second Jewish primary school
existed. Rainey (1971) suggests that the most likely possibility was the *Erst
Offentliche Israelitische Haupt—und Unterreal—(Volks—und Burger) Schule* (a
rough translation being 'First Public Israelite Primary and Junior High
School'; 'Volks' refers to the first four years of school from ages six to ten and
'Burger' to the next four years of school from ages ten to fourteen) which was
founded in 1862 as the result of a merger of two Jewish primary schools. This
was the only Jewish school officially recognized by the government. The
approved curriculum facilitated eventual transfer of the students to the *Gymnasium*. A co-director of this school was Simon Szanto, whose ideological and
practical religious persuasion was in the direction of Reform Judaism.

In addition to the private primary schools there was a school of religion
sponsored by the IKG. Until 1857 the headmaster of this school was Leopold
Breuer, the father of Josef Breuer. Samuel Hammerschlag took over this
position in 1857 and stayed until 1873 when he retired for medical reasons
(some difficulties with his hearing). Leopold Breuer wrote the textbook on
religion used in this, as well as other, schools. According to Rainey (1971),
both Leopold Breuer and Hammerschlag propounded a moderate Reform
view of Judaism. Just how Reform it was is a matter of definition. Breuer, as
well as Ludwig Philippson believed in Divine Revelation of the Bible and in
a unified Mosaic authorship (though how they defined Revelation is not
quite clear), the primacy of the Hebrew language and the need to study
Bible as well as Talmud, though the stress was on the ethical or humanistic
aspects of religion.

However, their concept of Revelation differed from that of the Orthodox
Jew. Whereas the Orthodox believe that every word of the Bible was dictated
by God to Moses on Mount Sinai, the moderate Reformers believe that it
was the 'essential core' of the Bible that was revealed by God. Obviously,
this ambiguity leaves much room for positioning within the spectrum of
religious belief.

The Orthodox Jews of the Leopoldstadt did not send their children to
the schools mentioned above (just as it would have been unthinkable for the

Orthodox Jews of the Lower East Side of New York City to send their sons to
the co-educational *Talmud Torah*, which was obviously not quite as Orthodox
as the *Yeshiva*). In addition to the Orthodox primary school there was an
Orthdox *Talmud-Torah* school, which was not a *Yeshiva* but an after-school
religious program, in which both Bible and Talmud were studied, but with
greater emphasis on the Talmud[3]. Like Knoepfmacher, Rainey prematurely
forecloses discussion by stating:

> It is very unlikely that Freud attended this school since his family was not
> Orthodox and since in later life he described his instructors as free thinkers
> or 'liberals'. Therefore an account of the Talmud Torah school is excluded
> from the presentation of Jewish education in Vienna which follows.

Klein (1985), too, accepts the Freud family's contention that Freud did not
attend a primary school and discusses it no further.

Such premature closure of investigation and discussion is not justified.
We have to remember that we are describing the years 1862 and onwards. In
1856, the Freud family in Freiberg, and in 1872 in Manchester, showed signs,
scant though they may be, of being part of the Orthodox group and it does
not seem unreasonable that seven years later they might still maintain some
attachment to it. With the data available to us at present we cannot say with
any degree of certainty that the Freud family in Vienna during the early
years of their residence there was either moderate Reform or Orthodox, but
dismissal of the possibility of an Orthodox orientation does not appear to
be justified.

The specifics of the curriculum of the Orthodox *Talmud Torah* in the
Leopoldstadt is not known and it is doubtful if it is available. However, we do
know what happened to another Orthodox *Talmud Torah* in Hamburg,
Germany, in the early part of the nineteenth century. In order to counteract
the emergent popularity of Reform Judaism, the members of the Orthodox
community appointed a new Chief Rabbi in 1821. He was Isaac Bernays, the
paternal grandfather of Martha Freud. A university graduate, he attempted
to reconcile the conflict between religious and secular knowledge. He was
the first Orthodox rabbi to preach in German. One of the conditions he
stipulated prior to accepting the position was that he have complete control
over the parochial schools. In 1822 he made radical changes in the curriculum of the *Talmud Torah*. To the subjects of Hebrew, Bible and arithmetic he
added German, Natural Science, Geography and History. By 1827 the school
had been transformed from a strictly religious institution into a good primary
school that prepared its students for future studies in the secular school system.
It is possible that this school was a model for the Orthodox *Talmud Torah* in
the Leopoldstadt, but there is no evidence available that this was the case.

In *An Autobiographical Study* (S.E. XX: 7-8), Freud states the following:

> I was born on May 6th, 1856, at Freiberg in Moravia, a small town in what is
> now Czechoslovakia. My parents were Jews, and I have remained a Jew
> myself. I have reason to believe that my father's family were settled for a
> long time on the Rhine (at Cologne), that, as a result of a persecution of the
> Jews during the fourteenth and fifteenth century, they fled eastwards, and
> that, in the course of the nineteenth century, they migrated back from
> Lithuania through Galicia into German Austria. When I was a child of four
> I came to Vienna, and I went through the whole of my education there. At
> the 'Gymnasium' I was at the top of my class for seven years; I enjoyed
> special privileges there, and had scarcely ever to be examined in class . . .

Let us compare this quote with the first sentence of his *Curriculum Vitae*
(Figure 21) where there is no mention of his German ancestry. Freud may
conceivably be correct in tracing his roots to Cologne, but there is no way he
could have proved it or had any evidence of it. The notion that Eastern
Europe was merely a stopover on the Freud family's journey through time,
and that its real roots are in Germany, would therefore represent a bit of
Family Romance.[4] Given the adulation of all things German and the contempt
for Eastern European immigrants and what they represented that existed in
Vienna in the late nineteenth and early twentieth centuries, this fantasy
makes much sense. Just as Freud had done with his own life, in retrospective
fantasy he elevated his geneology from the lower middle class to the high
bourgeoisie. What is more significant for our purposes is the conspicuous
omission of any mention of the *Privatvolksschule* and the beginning of his
formal education in the *Gymnasium*. If this primary school was the liberal or
Reform one, would he have omitted mention of it? Or was it the Orthodox
primary school, which did not have official government authorization?

Freud's tracing his genealogy to the fourteenth century and the heartland
of Germany reflected not only an attempt to create a Family Romance
fantasy, the dynamic significance of which he himself discovered, but also the
painful conflicts that he, like many other Jews, must have lived through in
medical school and thereafter. These conflicts revolved around not only the
general anti-Semitism that was all-pervasive, but specifically the perception
of the East European Jews who were emigrating in massive numbers from
the provinces to Vienna. It was difficult enough being an Austrian Jew, but to
have an Eastern European tag attached to you compounded the felony.
Added to this was the general inferiority the Austrians felt in comparison to
the Germans. In their minds Germany represented the ultimate in intellect,
culture and civilization. (According to Henry Bondi, to this day, one of
Amalia Freud's great-grandchildren insists, despite overwhelming evidence to
the contrary, that she was born in Vienna, not in Brody, which is in Galicia.)[5]

In the early 1860s, the *Ostjuden*, the Jews from Hungary, Galicia and the rest of Eastern Europe, began a slow but steady increase in emigration to Vienna with most of them settling in the section known as the Leopoldstadt. As the pace of emigration to this Jewish enclave intensified, the *Sperlgymnasium* was opened in 1864 (Freud was in the second class when he entered in 1865). In 1865, 44% (68 students) of the student body was Jewish; in 1869, 63% (227 students), and in 1873, 73% (300 students) (Kneopfmacher, 1979). These Jewish youths from the provinces were viewed by the existing Jewish student establishment, and also by those who had emigrated earlier from these same areas, as threats to their complete assimilation into German culture. Klein (1865) maintains that Freud shared these views and that this may have been why he changed his first name on the records of the *Gymnasium* from Sigismund to Sigmund in 1869 or 1870. In this manner he presumably severed his tie with his provincial Jewish background and identified with the progressive German-liberal culture. Though the student population at the *Gymnasium* was preponderantly Jewish, Freud did have first hand experience with anti-Semitism:

> And when in the higher classes I began to understand for the first time what it meant to belong to an alien race, and anti-semitic feelings among the other boys warned me that I must take up a definite position, the figure of the semitic general [Hannibal] rose still higher in my esteem. (S.E. IV: 196)

At the medical school, discrimination against East European Jews was quite rampant and intense. In the liberal student groups only those Jewish students who were of German origin were allowed to join. Part of the reason for the prejudice against East European Jewish students was that there was a limit on the number of students admitted to medical school and competition for admission and graduation was intense. The Jewish students from the provinces were presumed to be (for the most part, correctly) not as well prepared culturally and academically as the native Viennese or Germans and were looked down upon because of this deficit by many faculty and students. Though Freud himself was reared in Vienna, his parents, relatives and friends must have served as a constant reminder of his East European origins.

Shortly after entering medical school in 1873 Freud joined the radical German student society, the *Leseverein der deutschen Studentens Wiens*. From its founding in 1871 it served as the symbol and representative of German interests. One of its major goals was the complete integration of the Austro-Hungarian Empire with Germany. If such a union did take place they would enjoy the same civil liberties as the Germans. An additional factor was the boost in self-esteem that would result from their official identification with their idealized Germany. Spurred by the economic crash of 1873, the organization became more militant in its anti-establishment approach. The government, perceiving its radical socialist militancy as a threat to its stability, dissolved the *Leseverein* in 1878. Freud was never enamored of the political and economic goals of the *Leseverein* and doubted the feasibility of a socialist solution to economic and cultural difficulties.

Many Jewish students who later achieved prominence belonged to the *Leseverein* or its successor, the *Akademische Leshalle*. Among them, aside from Freud, were Viktor Adler, Theodor Herzl and Arthur Schnitzler. The ideological godfathers of the *Leseverein* included Schopenhauer, Wagner and Nietzche; their works were the object of heated discussion and widespread acceptance. It was one of the most prominent student societies on campus. It had 135 faculty members, including Theodor Billroth, the world-renowned surgeon, and Theodor Meynert, Chief of Psychiatry, as well as 500 student members. Its meetings were attended by three or four times that number (McGrath, 1967).

Ernst Jones has been criticized by McGrath (1967, p. 184) for not having mentioned in his three-volume biography that Freud was a member of this society. McGrath infers that this omission may have been due to Jones' embarrassment over what eventually became of the pan-Germanic movement in Austria. In McGrath's overview of the *Leseverein* and its successors he suggests that there was a line of inexorable development leading to an intensification of political anti-Semitism, which ultimately became the object of Hitler's admiration and contributed to the ideological foundations of the Austrian Nazi party.[6]

Despite their attempts to be 'good' Germans, the Jewish students were never fully accepted as equals in the mainstream of Viennese academia. An episode occurred in 1875 that sent shock waves through the medical school. Surprisingly, there is no mention of it in Freud's writings. Theodor Billroth, who was born and trained in Germany, was assigned to evaluate and report on the status of medical school education at the German-speaking universities in 1875.[7] Billroth was one of the most prominent members of the faculty of the University of Vienna Medical School, having begun to teach there in 1867. It was the first time that a man of his stature not only questioned but also attacked the policy of open admissions—specifically, for admitting Jews from Hungary and Galicia to the school. He felt that these impoverished Jews lacked the talent to become scientists or physicians, could not overcome cultural and academic deprivation and endangered the standards of the school.[8] He suggested that a quota be imposed for Jewish students from the eastern provinces. In a footnote (p. 154) he made the following comment (taken from Klein, 1985, p. 51):

It is often forgotten that the Jews are a well-defined nation and that a Jew—just as little as a Persian, Frenchman, New Zealander or African—can never become a German. Whatever is meant by Jewish German, it is only coincidental that they are educated in Germany ... They lose their [Jewish] national tradition just as little as the Germans lose their German manner no matter where they lived ... It is thus neither expected nor desirable that the Jews ever become German-nationalists or participate in the national struggles like the Germans themselves. Above all, they cannot possibly be sensitive to the accumulated influence of medieval romanticism, upon which our German sensibilities—more than we want to admit—are based; for, the Jews, have no occasion to ponder with special delight the German middle ages ... It is certainly clear to me that, in spite of all reflection and individual sympathy, I deeply feel the cleavage between pure German and pure Jewish blood.

Klein (1985, p. 51) aptly comments:

Under different circumstances, an argument against the policy of open admission would not have had to go beyond the problems of insufficient academic preparation and financial support; but, because circumstances had already defined the problems in cultural terms, Billroth directed his argument against the culturally deprived immigrant Jews.

After release of the report, violence erupted, Jewish students were attacked by their classmates with shouts of *Juden hinaus* ("Jews get out") and physical abuse. Since Billroth was a supporter of the *Leseverein*, one can well imagine the effect of this frightening situation on the idealism of the members of this student organization. Some Viennese colleagues have informed me that such shouts were heard quite regularly at the medical school up until World War II, after which, of course, there remained no Jews to shout at.[9]

The Jewish members of the *Leseverein* reacted to Billroth's study in a self-negating way, exemplifying the self-hatred that was so common among members of the upwardly mobile Jewish middle classes in Vienna. The priorities of their idealism were reflected in their placing their German identity above their Jewish one. Viktor Adler (1852-1918), the future leader of the Social Democrats, was the head of the *Leseverein* at the time. He organized a response to Billroth's report and all the commotion that resulted from it. The response, was overwhelmingly approved by the members of this student fraternity. Adler agreed with Billroth that the Jews had not been active participants in German life and culture, but argued that this isolation was in the process of being undone. Surprisingly, or maybe not so surprisingly, the members supported the Billroth report as well as the author, Viktor Adler, by repeating the differences between them and the Eastern European Jewish immigrants, reaffirming their commitment and loyalty to German national-ism. They passed a resolution condemning the severe criticism of Billroth by the Jewish students. Klein (1985) is of the opinion that Freud's position was similar to Adler's. (There is no direct evidence of this as the group's records for that year are missing from the collection in the *Oesterreichisches National-bibliotek.*) Jones (1953, I:43), however, notes that Freud and Adler were once debating opponents at a student meeting and that Freud behaved rudely toward him. The issue was not the Billroth report but a philosophic dispute, Adler favoring the views of the pantheistic *Naturphilosophie* and Freud that of radical materialism.

We do not know the nature and the degree of direct contact, if any, that Freud may have had with Billroth himself. When Freud was rotating through Billroth's surgical service the chief was away from Vienna (Jones, 1953, I:63), though Freud did attend his lectures in Clinical Surgery in 1877-78 (Bernfeld, 1951). On February 7, 1894, Freud wrote to Fliess, "Billroth's death is the event of the day around here. How enviable not to have outlived oneself." (Masson, 1985a)

APPENDIX II

Higher Biblical Criticism and the Documentary Hypothesis

The British philosopher Thomas Hobbes (1588-1679) raised some questions about the Mosaic authorship of the Bible, but Baruch Spinoza (1632-1677) was the first to publish a systematic critical study of the Bible, a distinct forerunner of the School of Higher Biblical Criticism that was to flourish in the nineteenth century. This type of criticism concerned itself with issues of authorship, date of composition, literary style and content. (The 'Higher' is in contrast to the 'Lower', or textual criticism, which aims at the establishment of a 'truer' wording of the text.) In his *Theological-Political Tractate*, he raised questions about biblical authorship that had never been raised before, at least not publicly. In essence, he denied the Divine authorship and brought the sacred text down to the level of man. He suggested that the Prophet Ezra was the ultimate compiler, in the fifth century B.C.E., of the biblical texts. (Spinoza's tractate was published anonymously in 1670; his heretical views were already known prior to it and he was excommunicated by the Jewish Community of Amsterdam in 1656.)

However, intensive critical scholarly studies of the Bible did not really begin until the eighteenth century, when three investigators, independently of each other, discovered and elaborated upon its multiple authorship and duplication of stories and deities, i.e., God being known as Yahweh in one document and as Elohim in the other. The first was a German minister, Henning Bernhard Witter, who made his discovery in 1711. The second investigator was the French physician attached to the Court of Louis XV, Jean Astruc, who published his findings secretly in Paris in 1753. The third was a German scholar, Johann Gottfried Eichhorn, who published his work in 1780. It was also in the latter part of the eighteenth century that the writings of Spinoza were rediscovered by the German writers Lessing and Goethe. The nineteenth century school of Biblical Criticism, which really represents an intensified continuation of the work of the earlier researchers (with the exception of the above-mentioned Witter whose work was forgotten and not rediscovered until 1924) with a much greater degree of organization and synthesis of their own and prior theories and findings, was initiated by the German professor, Julius Wellhausen (1844-1918).

There were, and are, many scholars of the Bible who, for obvious reasons, do not consider themselves part of the school of Biblical Criticism. The 'Higher' biblical critics were most numerous and prolific in nineteenth and early twentieth century Germany so that Freud had easy access to them. Very few of these critics were Jewish.

Julius Wellhausen is probably the most significant figure in the organization, synthesis and promulgation of the modern school of Higher Biblical Criticism. As Friedman (1987) notes, he was to Biblical Criticism what Freud was to Psychology. He made many important contributions to biblical scholarship. His writings were known to Freud. He resigned his academic position in Germany as a theologian when he realized that his scholarly pursuits were inherently and, at times, blatantly inconsistent with the teachings of the Church.

> I became a theologian because I was interested in the scientific treatment of the Bible; it has only gradually dawned upon me that a professor of theology likewise has the practical task of preparing students for service in the Evangelical Church, and that I was not fulfilling this practical task, but rather, in spite of all reserve on my part, was incapacitating my hearers for their office. (as quoted in Friedman, 1987, p. 65)

There were also prominent nineteenth century British Bible critics like William Robertson Smith, often quoted by Freud, who was Professor of Old Testament in the Free Church of Scotland College at Aberdeen and editor of the Encyclopedia Brittanica. He was charged with heresy, put on trial before the church and expelled from his chair (Friedman, 1987). American critics in the twentieth century include William Foxwell Albright at Johns Hopkins University, among many other such luminaries.

In order to separate the constituent documents that together formed the Old Testament, these critics used the particular designation of the Divine name as one of the 'keys' to authorship and origin. They developed what is known as the 'Documentary Hypothesis'. The earliest document is known as the J (Jahwist or Yahwist) since Yahweh is the name used to refer to God. This dates from the ninth century, B.C.E. Dating from the eighth century, B.C.E. is the E (Elohist, i.e., the use of Elohim for the name of God) document. The fifth book of the Pentateuch, Deuteronomy, which dates from the seventh century, B.C.E. is known as D (for Deuteronomist, i.e., the author of Deuteronomy) document. The letter P (for Priestly, the author of the priestly code) refers to the P document which dates from the fifth century, B.C.E. The letter H (Holiness code) refers to a part of the Book of Leviticus, which itself is considered to be within the P code. Lastly, there is the JE document in which both names for God are used interchangeably; this is thought to be due to the efforts of an editor in the seventh century, B.C.E. The Pentateuch and the *Book of Joshua* were unified in the form as we know it today in the fifth century, B.C.E., presumably by the Prophets Ezra and Nehemiah. This union is also referred to as the Hexateuch.

APPENDIX III

Review and Further Elaboration of Freud's Mosaic Hypothesis

What follows is a review, with some appropriate amplification and comment, of the major theses proposed by Freud in *Moses and Monotheism*.

1. Moses was an Egyptian of aristocratic lineage who allied himself with the iconoclastic Pharaoh, Akhenaten. The pharaoh had rebelled against his father's religion, obliterated all traces of it and instituted a new monotheistic religion based on a deified heliocentric conception of his universe.

2. The alliance by Moses with the Israelites occurred either late in the reign of Akhenaten or afterward. In order to perpetuate the monotheistic religion Moses 'adopted' the enslaved Jews, made them heirs to the new monotheism, and then led them out of Egypt.

3. When the escaping Jews arrived in the wilderness they rebelled against their leader Moses, slew him, and regressed to their idol-worshipping ways.

4. For two or three generations after the killing of Moses, the Egyptian Jews wandered in the desert. They then encountered their long-lost brethren who had never been to Egypt and who had been resident in the wilderness for some time. The city of their meeting was called Kadesh (which is the same as Kadesh-barnea). There they bowed to the leadership of a second Moses, a Midianite, and presumably not a Hebrew, who had introduced them to another form of monotheism, the worship of the volcano god, Yahweh. An indispensable condition for the union of the two tribes was the retention of the Egyptian rite of circumcision. The monotheism of the slain Egyptian Moses was almost completely suppressed by the newly unified Yahweh worship. Yahweh was considered by Freud to be a 'demon' God with a religion focused primarily on ritual and ceremonial practices. The monotheism of the Egyptian Moses re-emerged centuries later when it achieved expression

by the Hebrew prophets, thus re-establishing the hitherto interrupted continuity between the Egyptian Mosaic religion and Prophetic Judaism.

5. The murder of the Egyptian Moses was a repetition or re-enactment of the murder of the Primal Father.

> It would be worthwhile to understand how it was that the monotheist idea made such a deep impression precisely on the Jewish people and that they were able to maintain it so tenaciously. It is possible, I think, to find an answer. Fate had brought the great deed and misdeed of primaeval days, the killing of the father, closer to the Jewish people by causing them to repeat it on the person of Moses, an outstanding father-figure. It was a case of 'acting out' instead of remembering, as happens so often with neurotics during the work of analysis. To the suggestion that they should remember, which was made to them by the doctrine of Moses, they reacted, however, by disavowing their action; they remained halted at the recognition of the great father and thus blocked their access to the point from which Paul was later to start his continuation of the primal history. It is scarcely a matter of indifference or of chance that the violent killing of another great man became the starting-point of Paul's new religious creation as well. This was a man whom a small number of adherents in Judaea regarded as the Son of God and as the Messiah who had been announced, and to whom, too, a part of the childhood story invented for Moses was later carried over, but of whom in fact we know scarcely more with certainty than of Moses — whether he was really the great teacher portrayed by the Gospels or whether, rather, it was not the fact and circumstances of his death which were decisive for the importance which his figure acquired. Paul, who became his apostle, had not known him himself. (S.E. XXIII:88-9)

Let us examine what Freud means by 'Fate' in the above passage. He is referring to his concept of the 'repetition compulsion', the need to re-enact an unremembered trauma of childhood. In the beginning was the 'wish'. The child is not maturationally and cognitively capable of formulating such a wish until the Oedipal phase of psychosexual development, roughly between the ages of three and six. The wish is then 'father' to the formulated thought or fantasy. Given the mental makeup of such a young child, the thought is then equated with the deed and, on a mental level, they are interchangeable. The anticipated punishment by castration, as well as fear of loss of the father's love and even loss of the father himself, causes a repression to the unconscious of the whole constellation of fantasies which have by now incorporated the anticipated punishment. Though repressed, they continue to retain their intense power and press for overt expression and gratification in disguised form. As long as these 'memories' stay repressed and unavailable to consciousness, there remains a compulsion to translate them into action repetitively. Freud is here applying a phenomenon that is seen clinically in the psychoanalytic therapy of every individual male to the group, in this instance to the Jewish people, by endowing it with the transcendent quality that is inherent in the word 'Fate'. Once recalled and resident in consciousness, the power behind these fantasies is lost, thus obviating the need to repeat them in action.

The sacrifice of the totem animal, which served as a replacement for the Primal Father, and the totem feast, occurred at a point in millenial time between these two major parricidal events. Freud reinterpreted the Christian concept of 'Original Sin', which originated with the Apostle Paul, by attaching it to the murder of the Primal Father. The memories of these traumatic events, i.e., the murder of the Primal Father and later the Egyptian Moses, another Father-Figure, were repressed for centuries, resulting in enormous guilt and a compelling need for penance and atonement. This was achieved by the coming of a Messiah, i.e., Jesus, and his crucifixion, the sacrifice of the son for the slaying of the Father. Jesus thus atoned for the guilt of all men. The new trauma of crucifixion, really a repetition of the original 'Primal Father' and Moses traumas, further intensified the need for atonement and redemption.

> The killing of Moses by his Jewish people . . . thus becomes an indispensable link between the forgotten event of primeval times and its later emergence in the form of the monotheist religions. It is plausible to conjecture that remorse for the murder of Moses provided the stimulus for the wishful fantasy of the Messiah, who was to return and lead his people to redemption and the promised world-dominion. If Moses was this first Messiah, Christ became his substitute and successor, and Paul could exclaim to the peoples with some historical justification: 'Look! the Messiah has really come: he has been murdered before your eyes.!' Then, too, there is a piece of historical truth in Christ's resurrection, for he was the resurrected Moses and behind him the returned primal father of the primitive horde, transfigured and, as the son, put in place of the father. (S.E. XXIII: 89)

There appears to be a gap in Freud's hypothesis of the continuous and repetitive chain of disguised, identical and putative historical events. In order to sustain internal consistency, the four major events—the slaying of the Primal Father, the totem animal, Moses, and then Jesus—all have to be identical in quality and structure. In other words, first the slaying and then the cannibalization. Freud is very specific about the cannibalization of three of these figures but the omission in the case of Moses is conspicuous. True, in the case of Jesus it is disguised in the ritual of Holy Communion.

> We have already said that the Christian ceremony of Holy Communion, in which the believer incorporates the Saviour's blood and flesh, repeats the

content of the old totem meal—no doubt only in its affectionate meaning, expressive of veneration, and not its aggressive meaning. (S.E. XXIII: 87)

Though Freud does not make reference to it, there is further confirmatory, but disguised, evidence for the identity and equation of sacrifice and cannabilism in Paul's *Epistles* where he portrays Jesus as the apotheosis of the Paschal Lamb. When the Temple in Jerusalem was in existence the paschal lamb was sacrificed on the eve of Passover and was then, after being burnt, eaten on the first night of the holiday. Following the destruction of the Temple in 70 C.E., this ritual, as has been the case with the whole institution of animal sacrifice in the Temple, was replaced by prayer and in this particular instance, the reading of the Haggadah at the Passover Seder.

Therefore, the question remains why did Freud omit mention of the Mosaic component of this sequence. Was he fearful of an even greater outcry on the part of Jews to this idea than to his postulate of Moses being an Egyptian and being murdered by the Israelites in the desert? Could the inclusion of the cannibalization of Moses have made Freud run the risk, on an unconscious level, of bringing him closer to the frightening primitive impulses, both sexual and aggressive, toward his thoroughly Jewish father? Would having done so resulted in a kind of acknowledgment of an identification with his father? Freud gives us a clue.

> The first decisive step towards a change in this sort of 'social' organization seems to have been that the expelled brothers, living in a community, united to overpower their father and, as was the custom in those days, devoured him raw. There is no need to balk at this cannibalism; it continued far into later times. The essential point, however, is that we attribute the same emotional attitudes to these primitive men that we are able to establish by analytic investigation in the primitives of the present day—in our children. We suppose, that is, that they not only hated and feared their father but also honored him as a model, and that each of them wished to take his place in reality. We can, if so, understand the cannibalistic act as an attempt to ensure identification with him by incorporating a piece of him. (S.E. XXIII:81-82)

Freud's conflicts over his cannibalistic impulses towards his father date back, in his writings, to 1912 when he wrote *Totem and Taboo*, a work that is crucial to the hypotheses formulated in *Moses and Monotheism*. It is of significant interest that in neither work does Freud make any mention of cannibalistic impulses toward the maternal figure. Gay (1988) astutely comments that

> ... both Jones and Ferenczi confronted him with the possibility that the painful reservations he expressed after publishing *Totem and Taboo* might

have deeper personal roots ... The two had read proofs of the book ... "We suggested he had in his imagination lived through the experiences he described in his book," Jones writes, "that his elation represented the excitement of killing and eating the father and that his doubts were only the reaction." ... Whatever the objective value of Freud's attempt to discover the foundations of religion in the Oedipus complex, then, it is highly plausible that some of the impulses guiding Freud's argument in *Totem and Taboo* emerged from his hidden life; in some respects the book represents a round in his never-finished wrestling bout with Jacob Freud. It was an episode, too, in his equally persistent evasion of his complicated feelings about Amalia Freud. For it is telling that in his reconstruction Freud said virtually nothing about the mother, even though ethnographic material pointing to the fantasy of devouring the mother is richer than that for devouring the father ... Still, like so much else in Freud's work, *Totem and Taboo* productively translated his most intimate conflicts and his most private quarrels into material for scientific investigation. (pp. 334-335)

Freud seems to be either diplomatic, facetious, or disingenuous in the above comment of the Holy Communion having solely affectionate and venerable significance. *Moses and Monotheism* was written at least a decade after his postulation of the dual instinct theory, i.e., the existence of the instinctual drives of sex *and* aggression. He well knew that every thought and action must have elements of *both* instincts and never to the total exclusion of one or the other.

6. Christianity, presumably having accepted the responsibility of the murder of the Primal Father, as re-enacted with the crucifixion of Jesus, now was felt by Freud to have superceded Judaism, thus reducing the latter to the status of a 'fossil'.

The triumph of Christianity was a fresh victory for the priests of Amun over Akhenaten's god after an interval of fifteen hundred years and on a wider stage. And yet in the history of religion—that is, as regards the return of the repressed—Christianity was an advance and from that time on the Jewish religion was to some extent a fossil. (S.E. XXIII:88)[1]

7. Freud felt that anti-Semitism and the persecutory behavior that accompanied it, were the result of the Jews not having acknowledged the murder of Moses as the Christians acknowledged that of their own deity, Jesus. This admission is deemed to be equivalent to an acceptance of culpability which in turn would entitle the believer and confessor to absolution. Freud seems to have buried his otherwise acute awareness of anti-Semitism under his ambivalent attitude towards Judaism, for, as he well knew, the ultimate responsibility for the crucifixion was placed on the Jews.

Notes

Chapter 1

1. Since the subject of assimilation will be a recurrent topic in this book, an operational definition is in order. The one that will be used is patterned after that of Rozenblit (1983) and Gordon (1964). Rozenblit, in her historical study of the assimilation of Jews in Vienna, follows the formulation of Gordon in his sociological study of assimilation among American Jews. Gordon views the phenomenon of assimilation as a continuum or spectrum. It begins with the process of acculturation, i.e., the adoption of the economic, political and cultural patterns of the majority group while one's friendships, marital choices and family relationships continue to exist within the minority group. The end of the continuum would be represented by 'marital assimilation' leading to its disappearance within the majority culture. Between these two ends of acculturation and total assimilation Gordon posits an intermediary stage which he defines as 'structural assimilation,' i.e., the establishment of ever-increasing relationships in all areas of human endeavor between the majority and minority groups. Both Rozenblit and Gordon do not specifically consider within their definition the precise role of the nature and degree of religious belief and ritual observance and how they may facilitate or hinder the interaction of the minority group member with the majority group. The intense religious orthodoxy of Jacob Freud, which certainly existed in the first half of his life, necessitates its inclusion in the consideration and determination of the point on the assimilation continuum on which he could be placed in the second half. As will be shown in this study of the religious identity of the Freud family, when one is so deeply 'anchored' early in life, as Jacob Freud was, in the Jewish cultural, scholastic and religious traditions then the positioning on any point in the outermost reaches of the assimilation continuum becomes, emotionally and realistically, an impossibility.

2. Reprinted by permission of the publishers and Sigmund Freud Copyrights, Ltd. from the *Freud-Silberstein Correspondence*, forthcoming from Harvard University Press, Cambridge, Massachusetts. All rights reserved.

3. I will be refering to Bondi throughout this book so that some biographical information about him is in order. Henry Bondi was born in 1921 in Hamburg and

his father died when he was eight years of age. Oscar Philipp, the son of Elias Philipp (Martha Bernays Freud's maternal uncle), was appointed his guardian. Oscar, and his brother Julius Philipp, were founders of the well-known international commodities firm, Philbro. Bondi's parents, grandparents, and extended families were all very close friends of the Freud's but more so of the Bernays. His mother and her ancestors came from Hamburg while the father's were from Mainz. (The Bernays' family were originally from Mainz and eventually settled in the Hamburg area.) They used to visit Vienna quite often, the family metals and mining business having had a branch there. Henry Bondi's great-great grandfather was one of the founders of the synagogue in the Hamburg area in which Martha Freud's grandfather was the rabbi. His great-grandfather, Samuel Bondi, was the Chief Rabbi of Mainz. His grandfather, Marcus Bondi, moved to Vienna in the early 1870s where he managed the family business. He soon became the *Parnas*, i.e., the senior, honorary and unpaid, official of the leading Orthodox synagogue in the Leopoldstadt. His father had two brothers who were well-known physicians in Vienna. Samuel Bondi, born c. 1871, was a specialist in Internal Medicine and may have been Sigmund Freud's physician in the early part of the century. Joseph Bondi, born c.1865, was an obstetrician-gynecologist, among whose patients were Amalia and Martha Freud. According to Henry Bondi, both physicians knew Jacob Freud well.

Some of the information that Bondi has given me can be subsumed under the rubric of anecdotal or hearsay evidence and it is important to bear that in mind. However, the closeness of Bondi and his family, which would include his parents, grandparents, uncles, aunts and cousins to the Bernays families in both Hamburg and Vienna dating back to the early nineteenth century and subsequently to the Freud family, beginning with the courtship of Sigmund and Martha, would appear to add a substantial degree of validation to this data.

Parenthetically, Bondi had no knowledge of either my work or hypotheses. Sophie Freud was very kind to send me a copy of this letter after the completion of an early draft of this book. I then contacted Bondi and subsequently met with him for very extensive discussions.

4. Except for the *Book of Hosea* and St. Paul's *To the Hebrews* which are taken from the Anchor Bible Series, the quotations from the Bible are taken from the new Jewish Publication Society translation, *The Tanakh — The Holy Scriptures*, 1988.

5. The term *Ostjuden* is a comprehensive one in that it refers to those Jews who had emigrated to Austria and Germany from all the countries in Eastern Europe. *Ostjuden* in Vienna were mostly from the eastern parts of the Empire, Galicia and Hungary. The term did not come into common use until after 1914 (Wertheimer, 1987).

Chapter 2

1. The *Gymnasium*, a school attended from approximately ten to eighteen years of age, is equivalent to the combined American intermediate and high schools and, in

terms of curriculum, probably the first year or two of college. Only boys were permitted to attend.

2. Bertha Pappenheim's Catholic school education did not appear to have any negative effect on her Jewish identity. In 1930 she translated the Yiddish classic work, *Ze'enah U-Re'enah*, into German. The title of this book is taken from the Bible, the *Song of Songs*, 3:11, "Go forth, O ye daughters of Zion, and behold King Solomon". It is a commentary on the Old Testament, in Yiddish, and was written expressly for women, who had less Hebrew education than the men. This was their only access to a study of the Bible. It was first published in 1600 C.E. and has gone through over 200 editions with translations into many languages (Schultz, 1987). A copy of this work was present in practically every Jewish home. The best-known German translation is that of Pappenheim.

I recently had the opportunity of reading a letter, written in 1956, by Edward Bernays to the noted Jewish scholar Willy Aron who, in the process of writing a history of the Jews of Hamburg, had contacted him for information on the Bernays family. In this letter Bernays tried to impress Aron with the fact of the assimilated status of the family of Jacob and Amalia Freud by stressing that his mother Anna (Sigmund Freud's sister) was sent to a Catholic girls school for her education. Edward Bernays may not have been aware of the common practice in nineteenth-century Vienna of middle-class Orthodox, as well as Reform or assimilated, Jewish families sending their daughters to Catholic schools for their education since there were no adequate public facilities for them. Privately sponsored secondary schools did not come into existence until the last decade of the 19th Century (Rozenblit, 1983). Sigmund Freud's daughter Anna, for example, attended the '*Cottage-Lyzeum der Salka Goldman*' (Young-Bruehl, 1988). These schools were open to both Jews and non-Jews. By itself, therefore, attendance at a Catholic school for girls is not sufficient evidence to establish an assimilated status for the family.

3. A woman who grew up in Berlin prior to World War II told me of some very painful experiences which are relevant to this subject of intra-ethnic prejudice. Her parents were professional, middle class, educated and assimilated Jews who were born and raised in Poland. They emigrated to Berlin right after World War I. This woman was born in Berlin. Her parents spoke a flawless German. Though they, all their relatives and friends, were completely assimilated, their social lives never mixed with those of the German Jews. Their only contacts were in the course of professional or commercial needs. After Hitler came to power, Jewish children were no longer permitted to attend the public schools. The Jewish community then organized schools that were exclusively for them, obviously not by choice. For the first few months this woman, who was then a young girl, mingled well with her classmates and close friendships were established. One day, one of her German-Jewish (I do not know how many generations of German habitation were required to qualify one as 'pure German') discovered that this woman's parents had originally come from Poland. This woman then became the object of the most intense ridicule, verbal cruelty and prejudice, far worse, according to her, than she experienced from her former, non-Jewish, German girl friends. Her Jewish classmates held her, and what she represented to them and

their parents, responsible for the intensified anti-Semitism that radically disrupted their comfortable life style.

There is, however, another side to German Jewry which merits much deserved praise. It served as a model and inspiration, in large measure, for the flowering of Judaism and Judaic scholarship in America. In a review-essay on Peter Gay's book (1978), *Freud, Jews and Other Germans: Masters and Victims in Modernist Culture*, Alfred Jospe (1979) writes:

> In his discussion of Jewish aspects and issues, Gay deals primarily with the psycho-and socio-pathological responses of Jews to their condition and experiences in Germany. These are important, not only for an understanding of the German-Jewish era in Jewish life, but of Jewish pathology wherever it exists—including the United States— and not only in the past but in the present as well. But he says only half of what has to be said. His focus disregards the fact that the German-Jewish community possessed an extraordinary amount of Jewish creativity. I do not mean to say or imply that German Jews were all fine human beings, great scholars, superb intellects, or deeply committed Jews. Many were; many others were not. The whole range of attitudes described by Gay did, of course, exist, and he is quite right when he declares with a measure of asperity that "there is a historical and sociological study that desperately needs to be undertaken: that of stupid Jews." But no matter how brilliantly the story is told, it is poorly told if it disregards the fact that the century before Hitler was a unique chapter in Jewish history—a period of incredible vitality, creativity and intellectual ferment in German-Jewish life. In this brief span, German-speaking Jewry became the seed-bed of the most significant movements affirming the viability and continuing validity of Jewish life in the face of the tensions and challenges involved in the Jewish encounter with the cultural, social forces of modernity: Neo-Orthodoxy, which is still being nourished by the spirit of Frankfort in its efforts to harmonize strict adherence to Jewish tradition with modern culture; Reform Judaism, which cannot be understood without its German roots; Conservative Judaism, which received its formative impulses from the men at the Breslau Seminary; Zionism, which more than Gay is prepared to concede, was not just a peripheral phenomenon in Germany but an authentic response to the inner and outer dislocations produced by the Jewish condition; and, above all, the *Wissenschaft des Judentums*, the scholarly study of Judaism as a legitimate academic discipline. No history of the Jewish intellectual effort can ignore the products of this Wissenschaft which, in the words of Salmon Rubaschoff (later known as Zalman Shazar [a Past President of Israel]), "is the most important gift which German Judaism has made to the whole of Jewry." Notwithstanding an identification with Germany that was often as passionate as it was uncritical, there was a strong and equally passionate identification with Judaism, which a balanced assessment must not bypass.

4. According to Klein [1985], the name was chosen because of the phonetic equivalence with the Nietzchean word, *rang* which means 'struggle'. It may have other mean-

ings too. As a noun it means a rank in the army. It also can have a negative connotation. *Eine rank* is a devious kind of scheme in which one twists one's way into a conspiratorial situation. There was also an historian named Rank who was known for his right-wing, anti-Semitic views. In any event, one can well see the depth of Jewish self-hatred in this identity conflict. Rank's ideological masters prior to his involvement with Freud were the composer Richard Wagner and the philosopher Nietzsche, neither of whom he knew personally.

5. There is, in all probability, a scribal error in Figure 2 in regard to the Hebrew word '*hamkhuna*'. The scribe, i.e., the official of the IKG who was in charge of entering the names of the newborn in the Registry, inserted the letter 'ahyin' instead of the letter 'mem'. The word as written, i.e., '*ha-a-huna*', does not exist in the Hebrew language.

6. 'Sigismund' was the name of a sixteenth-century Polish monarch who was known and admired for his tolerant attitude toward Jews. In class and ethnic conscious Vienna the name was also the butt of anti-Semitic humor and abuse. (Klein, 1985)

7. If the family patriarch's first name were really Abraham then it would have a much deeper significance as discussed in the section on Moses later in this book. It should be noted that it is the custom among Orthodox Jews to add more Hebrew surnames during the course of one's lifetime, at the time of a life-threatening illness, so as to deceive and confuse the Angel of Death who was presumably on his way to fetch the stricken person at the appropriate moment.

8. I am indebted to Prof. Menahem Schmelzer of The Jewish Theological Seminary of America for information pertaining to the name 'Alexander Ziskind'. In the German edition of the Encyclopedia Judaica (Eschkol Publishing Co., Berlin, 1928), Vol. II, columns 216 and 217, there are three individuals listed (unrelated to Freud), two with the name 'Alexander Ziskind' and a third 'Alexander Susslin', a derivative of 'Ziskind'. Personally known to the author are men with the paired name of 'Alexander Ephraim' which is derived from their ancestors and passed down through many generations.

9. Josippon (or Yosippon), a popular chronicler of Jewish history, dealt with events that occurred during the period from the return of the Babylonian Exile to the year 70 C.E. He wrote in Hebrew and he excerpted and paraphrased legends and stories from the writings of the ancient historian Josephus, the Talmud and unknown sources. The book was written in Italy in the Tenth Century, C.E. The statement referred to above is found in Josippon, Venice ed. (1544), p. 17d; Berdichev ed. (1896-1913), p. 63.

The quotation of Simon the Just is taken from *Seder Hadorot* (448), a work of later origin than Josippon which is also a chronicle of events in Jewish history.

10. For a more detailed examination of the *Leseverein*, and a general discussion of Freud's secular education, see Appendix I.

11. Translation reprinted with permission from *Jewish Social Studies*.

There is a sad story attached to the vicissitudes of this letter. The daughter of Dr. Feuchtwang, whose name is not given, is a survivor of the Concentration Camp and somehow was able to preserve the letter until two years prior to giving the copy to

Hes. At that time she asked someone to make a photocopy of the letter. The unscrupulous individual to whom this request was made apparently took advantage of her weakened mental faculties due to old age and returned only the copy, keeping the original for himself. She was unable to find this person after she noticed the theft.

Chapter 3

1. As quoted in Gay (1988), p. 390. Freud's feelings for the loss of his father, twenty-four years after his death, were apparently not dimmed by the passage of time. He erred in that both Freud and Jones were forty years of age, not forty-three at the time of the demise of their respective fathers. As for the specific motivation of this slip of the pen, more would have to be known about Freud's underlying thoughts.

2. I have known many men from the same East European background who, when given two or three words from the Bible, could immediately cite chapter, verse and commentary. All of this was done in Hebrew.

3. With the help of a photograph of specimen pages, Menahem Schmelzer, Professor of Medieval Hebrew Literature at The Jewish Theological Seminary of America, was able to identify it by comparing it to a duplicate copy in the seminary library, as being the 1839 edition.

Chapter 4

1. Reproduced by permission of A.W. Freud et. al., by arrangement with Mark Pateson & Associates, Colchester.

2. Classes were held at the religious school of the IKG in the primary school years and later at the *Gymnasium*. Religious instruction was given five hours per week, ten months per year. Since there was no instructor in religion assigned to the *Sperlgymnasium* until 1870, instruction was given at the *Religious School* from 1865-1870.

Chapter 5

1. This practice is nowadays fairly common and is used in non-Orthodox writings as well; for example, the Anchor Bible Series, the newest and perhaps of the best English translations and commentary and which has been authored by Jews non-Orthodox and Gentiles, do use B.C.E. and C.E. Whether this is now generally accepted practice or represents an accommodation to Jewish Orthodox sensitivities, I do not know.

2. In the Sigmund Freud Archives in the Library of Congress there is a Residence Certificate attesting to the good character of the Freud family handwritten and signed by the Buergermeister of the hamlet of Klogsdorf, which is adjacent to the city of

Freiberg, on February 26, [1]859. In the body of the certificate are written the years 1815 (the year of Jacob Freud's birth, and 1857 (the year, an obvious error, of Sigmund's birth), and 1858 (the year of Anna's birth). At the end of the certificate there is written the following: 'Gemeinderath Klogsdorf am 26 Feb 859 Jos. Herrmann, Buergermeister'. Either the omission of the '1' is an error or it may express a practice among some Europeans, Jew as well as non-Jew, of omitting the '1' without it having any religious connotation. However, the fact remains that it has always been a practice among Orthodox Jews. This, coupled with Jacob Freud's omission of the Hebrew letter, 'heh' preceded by an apostrophe would incline me to believe that his use of the omission of '1' was based in Orthodox Jewish tradition.

Chapter 6

1. In his book *Moses and Monotheism*, published in 1937, Freud wrote:

> For natural reasons, youngest sons occupied an exceptional position. They were protected by their mother's love, and were able to take advantage of their father's increasing age and succeed him on his death. We seem to detect echoes in legends and fairy tales both of the expulsion of elder sons and of the favoring of youngest sons. (S.E. XXIII:81)

2. Israel is another name that the Bible uses for Jacob.

3. 'Shekhem' does not necessarily refer to the entire city as it does in other parts of the Bible but to a plot of land that Jacob had bought from Hamor, the father of Shekhem. (Genesis 33:19). Some time after the purchase the plot was, presumably in an illegal fashion, taken back by the Amorites, i.e., the clan of Hamor. Jacob then reacted quite aggressively to this seizure and by force of action, "with my sword and my bow", retook the land. Incidentally, this aggressive and victorious military feat by Jacob is not mentioned anywhere else in the Bible.

Chapter 7

1. In some editions of the Bible this verse is 31:19.

2. McGrath (1986) has offered a most interesting example of the significance of the Jacob and Joseph relationship to Freud. In Freud's dream, 'My son, the Myops' (S.E. V:441), he finds himself visiting Rome with two of his sons. Due to certain dangerous events that have been taking place in the city it became necessary to get the children to a safe place. He is sitting on the edge of a fountain, 'almost in tears'. Then, "A female figure— an attendant or nun—brought two boys out and handed them over to their father, who was not myself. The elder of the two was clearly my eldest son; I did not see the other one's face." The dream continues with the woman asking the eldest son to kiss her good-bye, his refusal to

Notes

do so but, in the process of extending his hand in farewell, said, "Auf Geseres" to her and then followed by "Auf Ungeseres" to his father and/or the younger son.

Freud's association to this dream were to the play by Theodor Herzl, *The New Ghetto*, which he saw the same night in which the dream subsequently occurred. The protagonist of the play is a Jacob Samuel, an heroic figure who attempts to make the transition from the cultural and religious beliefs and traditions of the old ghetto to the new world of the Vienna of 1893. Unfortunately, due to the intense anti-Semitism that pervades the city, the outcome is only the establishment of a new ghetto. The aggressive behavior of Jacob in his attempts at overcoming this ingrained prejudice is closer to that of his biblical counterpart, and in marked contrast to what Freud perceived as the passivity of his own father Jacob as demonstrated in his confrontation with the Gentile who knocked the fur cap off his head.

In his battle with the anti-Semitic world of the Gentiles Jacob Samuel used as his model a fourteenth-century young Jew who was known as Moses of Mainz. While Moses was studying he heard ominous cries for help from outside the ghetto. Disregarding the danger implicit in leaving the ghetto, he went to offer aid but in the process was himself brutally murdered. Jacob Samuel felt that such a fate of martyrdom was preferable to living in the ghetto. In the course of the play's unfolding drama Jacob was challenged to a duel by an anti-Semite who had insulted him. Jacob was mortally wounded and, in his final words to his Christian friend, declares, "Dear Franz . . . Tell the Rabbi: like Moses of Mainz!" (as quoted in McGrath [1986, p. 238])

Herzl's play opened on the night of January 5, 1898, not too long after the death of Jacob Freud on October 23, 1896. As McGrath (1986) perceptively notes, the mirrored contrast between the part of the 'Myops' dream in which a female figure "brought two boys out and handed them over to their father, who is not myself. The elder of the two was clearly my eldest . . ." is a striking one. That the Bible figured in the latent content of the dream is made evident by Freud's association to his "being almost in tears" while sitting at the fountain in Rome to the phrase from the *Psalm* 137, "By the waters of Babylon we sat down and wept." McGrath relates the phrase "I did not see the other one's face" to the biblical Jacob's visual difficulties in blessing and differentiating between Joseph's two sons and behind that story that of the near-blindness of Isaac when he blessed Jacob and his brother Esau. We see in this dream a prefiguring of the three biblical characters who played a most important role in his life, Jacob, Joseph and Moses. Hidden behind these three major heroic figures of Judaism, in Freud's mind, may well lie those of the Patriarchs Abraham and Isaac—a subject which will receive much attention later in this book.

Oring (1984) suggests the interesting hypothesis that the dream may be an expression of Freud's underlying conflict about his Jewish identity along with the persistant, sometimes overt, and at other times dormant, wish to convert to Christianity.

3. In some editions of the Bible this verse is 31:2.

Chapter 8

1. Other than comments by Sigmund's son Martin (1958) and his niece Judith Bernays Heller (1956) there is no evidence that ritual observance in the elder Freud's

household was either extensive, absent, or erratic. As has been, and yet will be, shown in this book there is sufficient evidence from which can be inferred a greater degree of observance than heretofore has been believed to have existed.

Bergmann's (1982) comments on the birthday benediction appear to be in the process of becoming part of the Freud biographical 'canon'. Vitz (1988) and Gay (1988) quote them verbatim and in their entirety and accept them without question. Bergmann writes: "However, if the dedication is analyzed as a Hebrew document it becomes apparent that Jacob Freud was neither a religious nor a nationalist Jew, but a member of the Haskala, a movement that saw Judaism as epitomizing the religion of the enlightenment. No Orthodox Jew would speak lightly about the Spirit of God speaking to a seven-year old. Nor would any religious Jew see the Bible as belonging to mankind as a whole. Biblical flowery language ('melitzot' in Hebrew), also marks Jacob Freud as a member of the Haskala."

In regard to the question of the 'Spirit of God speaking to a seven-year old', I have never heard of any kind of prohibition against it. The 'Spirit of God', i.e., the 'Ruaḥ Ha-Shem', is a most oft-quoted and referred-to phrase among Orthodox Jews. I discussed the matter with a scholarly member of a famous Austrian-Galician Ḥasidic dynasty and he, too, had no knowledge of such prohibitive qualities. As for the 'Bible and mankind', there does not appear to be any mention of it in the birthday benediction; Bergmann's reference to it is puzzling. It is true that the use of 'melitzot' among the enlightened Jews, the Maskilim, was prominent but that fact in itself did not automatically identify one as an assimilated or unobservant Jew. There was a spectrum of enlightened belief and ritual observance among the Maskilim. There were Orthodox Jews who wrote in this flowery style.

2. Among the many psychodynamic motivations that were essential to this activity, a notable one was that the Haskalah became a vehicle for rebellion against the religious traditions and beliefs of their parents.

3. I am certain that this had an equal effect on the women in the family but, unfortunately, no outlet was provided for their formal education.

4. The Mishnah represents the first codification of Judaic Oral Law since the closing of the biblical Canon in the second half of the third century B.C.E. It was compiled by many scholars under the leadership of Rabbi Judah the Prince (ca. 135-217 C.E.). As with the Talmud, which was its successor in legal codification, it has both legal and storytelling (Halakhic and Aggadic) parts, often commingled with each other. The Mishnah is divided according to topic into six orders which, in turn, are then subdivided into tractates, chapters, and finally into smaller divisions called 'mishnayyot'. All aspects of religious, civil and criminal law are covered by the Mishnah.

5. There is also a 'Jerusalem Talmud', i.e., the Talmud Yerushalmi in contrast to the Talmud Bavli, i.e., Babylon, which was composed by the rabbis and students who lived in Jerusalem during the same period but, though a significant and important work, it never attained the status or degree of importance of the Babylonian Talmud. It is about one eighth the size of the Babylonian Talmud and is considered to be inferior to it in terms of its comprehensiveness, composition, brilliance of thought and codification.

Following the Babylonian Exile in 586 B.C.E. the use of Hebrew as a spoken language began a steady decline to a point where it was utilized mostly as a literary medium while slowly being replaced by Aramaic, to the point of almost total exclusion of Hebrew, in verbal communication. The desire to sustain and perpetuate the use of Hebrew in all modes of communication may well have been one of the motives of Rabbi Judah Ha-nasi in his exclusive use of Hebrew in the writing and redaction of the Mishnah. He was ultimately not successful in perpetuating Hebrew as the rabbis of the Talmud, in the centuries following the close of the Mishnah, obviously preferred Aramaic. Throughout the ages, and especially during the medieval period, Hebrew was used extensively as a literary medium. However, the renaissance of Hebrew as both a spoken and literary language did not really begin in earnest until the end of the latter half of the nineteenth century in Eastern Europe. It was an inevitable consequence of the combined forces of the Haskalah and the emergent Hebrew nationalism.

6. Abraham may well have been describing his own mental processes more than that of Freud. He came from an Orthodox Jewish family that had been settled in Germany for generations. Karl Abraham was born in Bremen. His father was a teacher of religion who, nevertheless, was apparently quite tolerant of his son's emerging liberal theological views. The younger Abraham was strictly observant of religious ritual into adulthood. When he began the practice of psychiatry he informed his father that he could no longer observe the Sabbath as well as other religious practices. These practices certainly included the laws of Kashruth and, most probably, daily prayers with *Tefillin*, i.e., phylacteries, among others. His father advised him to follow the dictates of his own conscience (Gay, 1988, p. 180). Given a father who was Orthodox (and a German Jew who was Orthodox was really 'Orthodox' in the ultimate sense of the word) as well as being a teacher of religion, which would include the teaching of the subjects of Hebrew, Bible and Talmud, among others, and a son who was himself observant until his adulthood, it is therefore safe to assume that Karl Abraham must have been quite well versed in all of these subjects.

7. David Weiss Halivni (1986), one of the world's foremost scholars of the Talmud, has convincingly validated his hypothesis pertaining to the penchant of Jews in post-biblical times for *justified* law, i.e., the marked preference for justifying the formulation, promulgation and execution of a law rather than accepting it as a dogmatic assertion without further discussion. This preference for discursive argumentation and elaboration is seen as early as the *Book of Deuteronomy*, the last of the five Books of the Bible. The Midrash, which was composed over a period of one thousand years beginning in the second century, B.C.E., or possibly earlier, as well as the Talmud, whose composition began in the early part of the Common Era down through to its final redaction in the sixth century, C.E., were expressions of *justified* law even though much of the latter was based on the *apodictic* laws of the Mishnah. The Mishnah, which was composed circa 50-200 C.E., was a regressive anomaly in that it represented a return to the apodictic style of the earlier portions of the Bible. Halivni attributes this transient deviancy to the religious and political conditions that existed after the destruction of the Temple in 70 C.E. In all probability, much prior rabbinic discussion preceded the final formulation of the laws of the Mishnah but it was either never recorded

or the records were recorded but subsequently lost. That this authoritarian and categorical mode of thought of the Mishnah was relatively brief in duration is an indication of its being antithetical to the evolving Talmudic mode of thought. Regressive phenomena have an inherent tendency to return, and so it was with the Mishnaic mode of thought which reappeared with Maimonides in the twelfth century, C.E. but it was met with much opposition.

Though circumscribed by theologically imposed restraints, the free mode of Talmudic thought would appear to be a cognitive forerunner to the completely unfettered mode of thought that inheres in the sciences and, more specifically for our purposes, in the search for cause, motivation and mechanism in human thought and behavior, i.e., psychoanalysis. Abraham's comment to Freud about their mutual mode of Talmudic thought would thus appear to be more than just an idle metaphor. We have only to add the basic humanism that permeates the Talmud and the 'free association' mode of transcription and the result is a veritable entree to a psychoanalytic mode of thought.

8. The concept that the Written (i.e., the Bible) and Oral (i.e., Midrash, Mishnah, and Talmud) Laws are of Divine Origin has resulted in the almost complete absence of the study of their historical background, as well as the obvious Greek and Roman influences on the Talmud, even in the most advanced of Orthodox *Yeshivot*.

Though nearly completely focused on the American version of *Yeshivot* since World War II (which in their theological and behavioral orientation have decisively swung further to the right of their Lithuanian forerunners), an excellent description and discussion of how the Talmud is taught and studied in such institutions of higher learning has been given by Helmreich (1986).

9. The translator of the Babylonian Talmud into German, Lazarus Goldschmidt (1871-1950), was born in Lithuania and spent much of his life living in Berlin from whence he emigrated to London in 1933. The translation, entitled '*Der Babylonische Talmud*', was begun in 1896 and was completed, with a total of twelve volumes, in 1936.

The ready availability of the Babylonian Talmud in the original Aramaic and Hebrew was facilitated by advances in printing and paper manufacturing technology in Germany which made it possible to print classic Hebrew and Talmudic texts on very thin paper and small print. The original pages were photographed and then reduced in size. That is why it was possible to condense into four volumes the entire 20 volume set of the Vilna Edition of the Babylonian Talmud.

10. The word '*Hatam*' is an acrostic that is derived from a collection of his writings which are entitled, '*Hiddusche Torat Moshe Sofer*', which, in translation, means 'Innovations of the Torah of Moshe Sofer'. The word 'Sofer' is the Hebrew translation of the German word 'Schreiber', i.e., scribe or writer. (Patai, 1988, p. 62)

11. In this quotation we see the awe and admiration that a son expresses for his beloved father. As will be discussed later, Josef Breuer was known for many virtues, not the least of which was his empathy, decency, objectivity and reasonableness. And yet, this second generation Jew of culture and accomplishment could not escape the prevalent prejudice against East European Jews. As with Sigmund Freud, this prejudice

may have served as a displacement and a vehicle for the expression of the negative side of the ambivalence toward his father, who was of Eastern European origin.

12. We see here what may be an example of the hierarchies of prejudice which even religious piety could not eliminate. One would have thought that the educated and cultured German Jew would have been perceived as the peak of attainment of status, but no, for the Sephardic Jews, i.e., those who claimed direct descent from pre-Inquisition Spain and Portugal, were considered to be the cream of the religious aristocracy. The arduous climb up the ladder of 'status' began with the Galician, Polish, or Russian Jew on the bottom rung; next came the Lithuanian Jew; then the German Jew; and on the top step was the Sephardic Jew; from this lofty peak the Deity was within easy reach!

13. The reason for the choice of 'Bernays' is unknown. I believe that family names for Jews in Western Europe were not initiated or required until the late eighteenth and early nineteenth centuries.

14. The second offspring of Adolphus, Leopold John Bernays (1820-1882), studied at Oxford University and was ordained as an Anglican priest in the Church of England in 1845. He was the headmaster of the Hackney Grammar School (1846-7) and of the Elstree School (1847-60). He was also the Rector of St. John's Great Stanmore Church near Harrow, in Middlesex from 1860 to the time of his death in 1882. The Reverend's grandson, Robert Hamilton Bernays (1901-1945), became a member of Parliament and was killed in an airplane crash off the coast of Italy. He had been flying to visit the front-line troops in Italy, at the personal request of Winston Churchill, when the aircraft, for reasons unknown, fell into the sea. Another son of Adolphus, named Albert James Bernays (1823-1892) was educated at King's College and received a Ph.D. in Chemistry. He taught at various medical schools in London. He made many contributions in the field of food chemistry, environmental medicine and pharmacology (cited in the Dictionary of National Biography). Another son, Louis Adolphus Bernays (1831-1908) was also educated at King's College, emigrated to Australia where he was a botanist and served as a clerk in the Queensland Legislature (cited in 'Who Was Who').

15. Information on the Bernays family was obtained from Henry S. Bondi and the Harry Freud Collection of the Sigmund Freud Archives in the Library of Congress. I am indebted to Leli M. Freud, the widow of Harry Freud (who was the son of Alexander, Sigmund's younger brother), for allowing me access to the collection. Additional information on the Reverend Leopold John Bernays was obtained from the Allumni Cantab. and Oxon.

16. The Ashkenazi Jews lived in Altona and Wandsbeck, suburbs of Hamburg. The triangle of Altona-Hamburg-Wandsbeck formed a unified Jewish community, in a limited sense, known colloquially as AHU. Altona and Wandsbeck were in the more liberal Danish territory. The Ḥakham was the Chief Rabbi of AHU but his synagogue and ministry were in Altona. He subsequently lived in Wandsbeck.

The Sephardic Jews have always considered themselves to be an aristocratic entity, separate and apart from the larger Jewish community which falls under the rubric of Ashkenazim. Their privileged residential status in Hamburg proper in the first half of the nineteenth century was, in part, due to their early arrival in that city as well as their financial and commercial success and influence.

The city of Vienna had its own Sephardic history with the bulk of their very early Jewish immigrants coming from the Balkan countries. The oldest Jewish settlers in Vienna date back to the mid-eighteenth century, if not earlier. They were Sephardic Jews who came mostly from Turkey and who enjoyed the protection of the Sultan of Turkey. (In Vienna the Sephardim referred to themselves as *Turkish Jews* while the Sephardim in England and Northern Europe called themselves *Spanish-Portuguese Jews*.) They formed their own communal organization, identical in structure and function to the IKG, which was known first as the *Turkish-Israelitische Gemeinde*. The name was later changed to *Verband der turkischen Israeliten*. Only Sephardic Jews were permitted to join their *Verband* and synagogue, thus effectively locking out or severely limiting the involvement of Ashkenazic Jews in the affairs of the Sephardic community (Papo, 1967). This state of affairs existed until the onset of World War II.

Though the prayers in both the Sephardic and Ashkenazic traditions are almost identical, the chants, melodies and synagogue architecture differ, all displaying a strong Moorish influence. Their origins go back to pre-Inquisition Spain and Portugal and the desire to preserve them may, in part, explain their elitism. The attachment to the memories and traditions of the pre-Inquisition Golden Age of Spanish Jewry as well as the perpetuation of the Spanish language spoken in the fifteenth century, known as *Ladino*, passed on from generation to generation, may be additional factors.

The Sephardic presence in Vienna in the twentieth century was distinguished by the award of the Nobel Prize for Literature to Elias Canetti. His parents were Sephardic Jews from Bulgaria who lived in Vienna from 1913 to 1916 during which time the young Elias was sent to Hebrew school for religious instruction (Rozenblit, 1983).

17. The rank of *Privatdozent* is the lowest rank on the academic ladder, the equivalent of an Instructor in the American University system. To be granted this rank one had to read a paper before a group of students and a faculty committee. The *Privatdozent* is obliged to teach an elective course each year as long as at least three students sign up for it. (Curriculum Vitae of Josef Breuer, footnote by translator, Gerhart Piers, 1964. This document is available at the A.A. Brill Library of The New York Psychoanalytic Institute.)

18. Julius Wagner-Jauregg (1950), a colleague and friend of both Breuer and Freud, wrote, after attending a lecture given by Freud on October 15, 1886,

> A man whom I respected more than any other colleague with whom I had had any contact, showed pity on him (Freud): Josef Breuer . . . He kept Freud busy by sending him patients for treatment. From this activity originated Psychoanalysis.

Chapter 9

1. It must also be noted that Freud's uncomfortableness with the Hebrew word *ruah* ('spirit'), that at times disrupted his thinking and his otherwise lucid prose style,

may be more than a religious anxiety. The confusion may reside in the uncertainty of the concept of 'spirit' that is inherent in Jewish tradition. Meissner (1984) aptly comments:

> It is interesting that Hebrew belief did not include a clearly developed notion of immortality. It was impossible for the Hebrew mind to conceive of the ruach, or spirit of man, existing without his body. The distinctions that later Greek thought produced had no place in the Hebrew conception of living man as a concrete totality. The concept of afterlife is simply absent from the earlier books of the Old Testament. References to the restoration of Israel (*Ezekiel* 37:1-4) or other references to the servant Yahweh (*Isaiah* 53:10-12) cannot be taken as expressions of a doctrine of personal return to life. The belief in personal resurrection emerges with startling abruptness in the Maccabean period (*2 Maccabees* 7:9, 11, 23), and there only in reference to the just. (p. 132)

2. Personal communications from Rabbi Max Grunwald and Silvia Heiman.

3. Herman Nunberg, a psychoanalyst who was a close friend of Freud and his family, told this to my colleagues Sidney Furst and his son Henry Nunberg, both of whom kindly passed this information on to me.

Chapter 10

1. Much has been made by nearly all of Freud's biographers of the negative influence of his Catholic nanny on his religious beliefs and identity. She cared for him until he was three years old. (Jones [1957, III: 349-350] believes the upper limit to have been two and a half years) I tend to agree with Jones that *too* much has been made of it. In letters to Fliess on October 3, 4, and 15, 1897, Freud relates how he 'recovered' memories during the course of his 'self-analysis' (a concept that, according to Freud's subsequent writings, is a contradiction in terms and which Gay (1988, p. 96) has appropriately referred to as "the cherished centerpiece of psychoanalytic mythology") that dated back to early childhood experiences with her. They were, in reality, not memories but 'reconstructions' which were theoretical constructs based on the analysis of his dreams. The only validation he had for anything to do with his nanny was when he asked his mother about her more than forty years later and she replied that the nanny had taken him to church, had preached to him about God and had been arrested for stealing some of his money. Vitz (1988), on the basis of his knowledge of Catholicism in nineteenth-century Austria and Freud's analysis of his dreams, believes that she secretly baptized him and that Freud had a strong unconscious affinity to Catholicism. Harden (1988) attributes Freud's ambivalent feelings toward his biological mother to her having abandoned him to the real nurturing mother, i.e., the nanny, because she had to devote most of her efforts to the newly arrived siblings, first Julius and then Anna. The evidence that is available is too scant and uncertain to warrant the attribution of such significance to this relationship.

2. It consists of a series of the three Gustave A. and Mamie W. Efroymson Lectures, with some further elaboration, that were delivered during December 1986 at the Hebrew Union College—Jewish Institute of Religion—in Cincinnati, Ohio,—the first home of Reform Judaism in America.

3. Diderot, Voltaire and Feuerbach were certainly not lacking in anti-Semitic sentiment, a character flaw of which neither Freud nor Gay make any mention. The enlightened, critical attitude of these thinkers appears to have had no effect on their own prejudice. Overt nobility of expression sometimes blinds us to the possible ignobility of the underlying motives and character flaws of the expressor.

4. Reprinted by permission of the publisher and Sigmund Freud Copyrights Ltd. from the FREUD-SILBERSTEIN CORRESPONDENCE, forthcoming from Harvard University Press, Cambridge, Massachussetts. All rights reserved.

5. While a Seminary student, I sat in a seminar led by the revered theologian Abraham Joshua Heschel. He started his presentation with the comment that there are two kinds of neuroses; one is the medical neurosis and the other is the result of turning away from God. This was contrary, at the time, to all that I knew about disorders of the mind. At that point, the empiricist in me won over, for I then abruptly tuned out and did not hear anymore of the presentation. In retrospect, I should have been more tolerant and patient for had I paid attention I might have appreciated a possible dynamic element of truth underlying this statement.

Heschel's equation of mental health and consequent happiness with closeness to God is inherently not that different than what was written by Spinoza but, obviously, within a drastically different frame of reference. Spinoza's family origins were in Portugal from which they fled to The Netherlands at the end of the sixteenth century. They were Orthodox, Sephardic, Jews and Benedict Spinoza was the first to rebel against the family's religious traditions. His father, Michael, was an officer of both the synagogue and the Hebrew school which his son attended. Spinoza was born in 1632 and his mother died in 1638 when he was six years old. The father died in 1654, two years prior to the son's excommunication by the Jewish religious hierarchy in Amsterdam in 1656. It can safely be assumed that Spinoza had rather strong ambivalent feelings towards his father. For Spinoza, the ultimate goal of man's quest for truth, as stated in the 'Ethics' (1949), is the 'intellectual love of God':

> As each person therefore becomes stronger in this kind of knowledge, the more is he conscious of himself and of God, that is to say, the more perfect and the happier he is . . . the intellectual love of God which arises from the third kind of knowledge is eternal . . . Hence it follows that God, in so far as He loves Himself, loves men, and consequently that the love of God toward men and the intellectual love of God are one and the same thing. (Ethics, pp. 272-275)

Though, on a conscious level, Spinoza's concept of God has been de-personified and then abstracted, in essence, it is still a supreme entity which possesses, simultaneously, both transcendent (insofar that it is an ideal that can never really be reached) and natural qualities. He attempts to blend two distinct frames of reference and universes of discourse, i.e., those pertaining to concepts that traditionally have been applied to both the supernatural and natural realms. They are inherently unblendable if one is to maintain a logical consistency that is appropriate to a scientific endeavor. It is an excellent example of the difficulties involved in fully surrendering the thoughts and beliefs that were instilled in us in childhood. Doing so would have the unconscious implication of disowning and discarding our parents, a task that the child persisting within every adult could not possibly allow to be completed.

God is an object who has to be loved and the love is rendered with the anticipation of obtaining something equivalent in return. There is not much difference, on a psychodynamic level, between loving the highest form of knowledge, which is about Nature wherein Spinoza's Pantheism resides, or the personified God of the Judeo-Christian-Islamic traditions. These religious traditions require that God be loved. The rendered love to God can manifestly be felt as love, but since we are dealing with the human species, the 'conatus' (the inherent, unstoppable, natural tendency, or instinct), to use a term of Spinoza's, has to carry with it all the negative, i.e., hostile, feelings pertaining to the Supreme Father as well. This results in a potentially unstable emotional equilibrium, due to unconscious psychic conflict. This will then necessitate the establishment of a new equilibrium which is manifestly different than the previous one but the latent psychic conflicts, nevertheless, remain the same while surrendering none of its instinctual power. A mind in conflict is a basic 'given' in human nature and it is the intensity and unique configuration of the conflicting psychic forces that will determine its ultimate content, form and expression (Brenner, 1982).

6. A personal anecdote might illustrate this dilemma. Most seminary students spend the first year or two trying to personally resolve these very fundamental religious conflicts. I had thought that by the end of my freshman year I had achieved the desired resolution, for me, that is, and that I was now free to pursue religious studies unencumbered (or so I thought) by conflicts of Theism vs. Atheism, Divine or human authorship of the Bible, the relevance of Talmudic law, the significance of ritual and prayer, etc. . . . In my third year I happened to pass a table in the dining room with four freshmen engaged in intense discussion and argumentation about these very same profound subjects with almost the very same words—a 'deja vu' experience indeed. My reaction was one of surprise. For a fleeting moment I naively thought to myself, 'gee, weren't these conflicts satisfactorily resolved a year ago?'

7. In 1933 Eitingon emigrated to the then Palestine and founded the first psychoanalytic institute there.

8. Freud had obvious difficulty with the concepts and definitions of 'spirit' and 'spirituality'. His English translator, James Strachey, even goes so far as to point out, in a footnote on page 114 of *Moses and Monotheism*, that the lengthy paragraph in which the usually pellucid Freud tries to explain the concept of 'Geist' is untranslatable. Strachey notes that Freud uses the words 'Geist' and 'Seele' interchangeably. 'Geist' can mean 'intellect', 'spirit', and 'soul', but 'Seele' also means 'soul', 'spirit' and 'mind'. Freud states that the word 'Geist' is derived from the idea of a breath of wind as, for example, in the Greek word 'anemos', the Latin 'animus', 'spiritus', and the Hebrew

'ruaḥ which can also mean 'breath'. The equation between 'Geist' and 'Seele' can be seen in the reference to the moment of death when the dying man 'breathes out his spirit [Seele]'. (S.E. XXIII:47, 86, 111, 114)

This problem of translation can be seen in Figure 9, the translation of Jacob Freud's Hebrew poetic dedication to his son, where he uses the word, 'ruaḥ. Either 'spirit' or 'wind' would be correct in expressing the 'spirit' of the poem. The ambiguity, if not the definition, is quite clear.

The meaning and significance of the concept of 'spirit' in early Christian thought might shed some light, speculative though it may be, on the question of Freud's uneasiness and uncertainty in his use of this seemingly conflict-laden concept and its verbal representation. One of the putative motives of the Apostle Paul for attempting to replace Judaism with Christianity was to stress the New Testament primacy of Faith over that of the Judaic Law, i.e., an adherence to the belief that God sent His only and most beloved Son to suffer and be sacrificed for our sins rather that the emphasis on the rule of religious law and the performance of ritual associated with it. Faith, not the Law, would lead to redemption and salvation, to a state free of the feelings of sin, guilt, despair, unworthiness and hopelessness—in essence a rebirth. With the passage of time this theological process was deemed insufficient as a means of attaining this sublime transformation into a state of grace and blessedness. The early Christian theologians, taking their cue from St. Paul, introduced the additional notion of 'union' with the Deity as the basic requisite for this ultimate state.

Here we see the introduction of religious mysticism into the mainstream of theological thought. Such mysticism represents a kind of road-map which will lead the believer to the most intimate contact with the Deity, leading to a state of union. Glimmerings of such thoughts were already evident in the closing days of the Biblical Canon before the birth of Jesus. In Judaism, the effect of this tendency did not really reach full-blown proportions until the Middle Ages with the writings of the Kabbalists.

But how, in early Christian thought, was this union with God going to take place, what steps did the believer have to take? The proposed solution necessitated a shift toward the instinctual drive of sexuality which was deemed to be the bane of mankind and the source of all evil and sin. God was described as the Holy Trinity, God, the Son, and the Spirit (or Holy Ghost). Father and Son were the 'physical' entities while the Spirit was non-substantial and described in a neuter gender, the Greek word *pneuma*. The Gnostics, as shown in their Gospels however, were closer to the Hebrew sources and relied on the Hebrew word *ruaḥ* which is in the feminine gender (Pagels, 1979). (The word that the Kabbalists used to describe the Spirit of God was *Shehinah*, literally 'the Divine Presence', which represents the feminine component of the Divinity.) As Christianity developed further the Divinity came to assume a bisexual nature with the establishment of the Spirit as His feminine aspect (Pagels, 1979). God was now both Father and Mother all wrapped up in One (Brown, 1988).

The Spirit was thus the non-substantial, feminine part of the Deity. It was the part that descended to earth, made 'physical' contact, and entered the body of the elect, i.e., the one who was purified of all sexual desires and practice, and united with his or her soul. The union that then occurred was between the Spirit, i.e., Divine Mother, and the human soul.

In the third century, C.E., the Syrian Christian, Tatian, described the union between the Spirit and the soul in ecstatically erotic poetry (as quoted in Brown, 1988, p. 91):

> As the Wind moves through the harp
> And the strings speak
> So the Spirit of the Lord speaks through my members
> and I speak through His love.

For Tatian, the Lord was both Father and Mother, i.e., God and His Spirit. In fact, in the Syriac language the word for Spirit is in the feminine gender.

The search for inner purity, a body totally devoid of sexual desire, lead to the cult of the virgin. Only a body and soul as pure as that of the virgin could be a receptacle for God's love and thence to become an object of worship and adoration. This idealized goal, however, was not a sexually biased one. In the Armenian Church the bearded monk was also referred to as a virgin (Brown, 1988). The third century Christian father Origen felt that the Divine encounter with man could occur not only with the female virgin but also with men who were purified of sexual desire. In order to attain this sublime state, Origen had himself castrated at the age of twenty. He described his encounter with the Divine Spirit in terms of the marriage bed (as quoted by Brown, 1988, p. 174):

> "We find there a certain sensation of an embrace by the Spirit ... and, oh, that I could be the one who yet might say: His left hand is beneath my head and his right arm reaches around me."

It was not until the fifth century that the Desert Father, John Cassian, expressed sharp disagreement with St. Augustine and his focus on the evils of sexual desire. Cassian pointed out that the over-emphasis on sexuality was really a defense against the awareness of the evils of human aggression. The early Christians 'aggressively' pursued their suppression of sexuality without allowing themselves the awareness of its inherent instinctuality. But then again, it wasn't until the late 1920s that Freud allowed himself to finally consolidate his discovery of aggression and to formulate it as part of a dual instinct theory of sex and aggression.

The reader may now ask as to how this digressive discussion relates to Freud's difficulty with the concept of 'spirit'. Though Freud's conflicts appear to mostly concern his ambivalent relationship with his father, it is tempting, in light of the above, to raise the possibility that on a deeper level there were conflicts with his mother that were not adequately resolved and which expressed themselves in his preoccupation with the importance of not only his own father but also with all fathers in terms of their contribution to the genesis of emotional conflict. As will be seen in the subsequent discussion of Freud's work, *Moses and Monotheism*, women play little, if any, role in his theoretical elaboration of the history of the Jewish people and religion.

9. The books of the Kabbalah, the classic texts of Jewish mysticism whose origins date from the Middle Ages but whose sources derive from Canonical and non-Canonical

biblical as well as Talmudic literature, were rarely studied by the rational Talmudists. Study of these books was not permitted or encouraged until adulthood for fear it would distract from the main object of study, the Talmud. The most outstanding Talmudists infrequently made references to the Kabbalah. (However, there were some exceptions. Though I have not seen any research on this aspect, I have the impression that, in nineteenth-century Europe, forays into the study of Kabbalistic literature were more prevalent in the Austro-Hungarian, Polish and southern Russia areas than in northern part, e.g., Lithuania.

The late eighteenth and early nineteenth-century talmudic giant, the Ḥatam Sofer, who headed the renowned *Yeshiva* in Pressburg, Hungary, did not shy away from the study of the Kabbalah. He also gave literary expression to it in one of his Hebrew poems:

> Embers of fire, the flame of God, is the love of
> my Lover,
> He cleaved to me, desired me, and encompassed me
> on the day of *Sh'mini Atzeret*,
> The King spoke to me and thus addressed me: Be
> thou my Mistress.

(This quote was translated by Patai, 1988, pp. 63-64, and is taken from: Solomon Alexander Sofer (ed.), *Moshe Sofer: Shirat Moshe*, Vienna-Budapest, Jos. Schlesinger, 1902, p. 13.)

The words *Lover* and *King* are synonyms, in the literature of the Kabbalah, for God. The holiday of *Sh'mini Atzeret* concludes the harvest festival of *Sukkot* (Tabernacles). Since it is conjoined with the holiday of *Simḥat Torah*, i.e., the celebration of the Torah given by God to the people of Israel, a mystical significance has been attributed to it whereby it serves as an expression of the enduring love between God's chosen people and the Torah.

Though the tendency towards mystical thought has been ever-present in Jewish history, the rabbis of the Talmud and their successors down through the generations have always attempted to control this impulse by placing severe restrictions around its study. There always has been the fear that gratification of this compelling need to discover the innermost secrets of God, life and the universe through the irrational and non-empirical modes of thought implicit in mysticism (all of which stem from a deep, conscious or unconscious, desire for some kind of contact with God), would lead to total immersion in mystical study and activity with the serious risk of departure from the rational and legal, i.e., halakhic, aspects of Judaism. They feared a result ranging from heresy to insanity (Ostow, 1988). The Talmud cites specific examples where such sequelae presumably did occur (Babylonian Talmud, Tractate *Hagigah*, p. 14b). Study of these books was not permitted or encouraged until adulthood for fear it would distract from the main object of study, the Talmud. Jacob Freud appears to have been too much of a Talmudist and Rationalist to have concerned himself with the subject; at any rate, there is no evidence of such interest. Neither is there evidence that Sigmund Freud was involved in the subject unless one wants to consider his life-long interest in parapsychology and in the significance of numbers, e.g., his tendency to look upon the latter as predictive of the year of his demise, as a derivative of the same tendencies that motivated the creation of, and sustained interest in, the writings of Jewish mysticism down through the centuries to the present time. I once met an Orthodox Rabbi, of East European origin, whose life was devoted to the study of the Kabbalah but with little or no interest in the Talmud, and who had what appeared to be an almost ingenious ability to select words from the Bible, translate them into their numerical equivalent and come up with a specific date for the occurrence of some catastrophic or cataclysmic event in the near or distant future. Needless to say, the predicted day came and went without any such occurrence.

10. Reproduced by permission of A. W. Freud et. al., by arrangement with Mark Paterson & Associates, Colchester.

This poem was translated by my colleague Silvia Heiman who noted the poetic license, in the form of a double-entendre, in Martha using the name 'Freud' instead of the expected word 'Freude', both of which mean 'joy'. The 'Kiddush' is the blessing that is recited over wine immediately prior to the Sabbath and Holiday dinners.

11. This is reminiscent of the time of the courtship between Sigmund and Martha when he was in Vienna and she in Hamburg. As Jones (I, 1953, p. 116) notes, Martha's mother would not allow her to write to her fiance on the Sabbath, so Martha, unbeknownst to Mrs. Bernays, went to the garden and wrote in pencil rather than in pen which would have had to be done in her mother's presence.

I am indebted to Israel Friedman and Rabbi Samuel Dresner for helping me establish contact with Mrs. Aron and, needless to say, to her for her graciousness in allowing me to read the extensive correspondence of her late husband with the Freud and Bernays families.

12. Personal communication from Roazen, 21 September 1989. The interview with Mrs. Oschner took place on 14 August 1965.

Chapter 11

1. These are not the only instances where Freud reveals, often unknown to himself, ideas in an early period of life which germinated and came to fruition many years later. In the 1890s, during the time of his intense friendship with Wilhelm Fliess, he wrote the *Project for a Scientific Psychology* which was not meant for publication but only for the eyes of Fliess. The manuscript came to light many years later with the discovery of the Freud-Fliess correspondence. A careful reading of this germinal work will reveal crucial ideas which Freud did not elaborate on until many years later.

2. The oasis of Kadesh was located in the southern part of the Negev, while Midian, a much larger area, was located further south on the eastern part of the Gulf of Aqaba. The Midianites were desert nomads and traders who travelled far and wide.

3. It should be noted that a time frame of 'forty years' is a biblical symbol for a 'generation' (Numbers 32:13, Psalms 95:10).

4. Breasted (1933) uses the name Amenhotep rather than Amenophis. Freud, following Breasted, translates it to mean 'Amen rests' or 'is satisfied'. Akhenaten, when translated, means 'Aten is satisfied' which represents a transposition of the pharaoh's old name into a corresponding idea in the faith of Aten. In order to effect as complete a break as possible from the faith of his father, Akhenaten left the old capital of Egypt, Thebes, and built a new capital at a point midway between Thebes and the sea which he called Akhetaten, which means 'Horizon of Aten'. This place is now called Tell el-Amarna.

5. For reasons that are not at all clear, Freud makes very short shrift of the Midianite Moses for he is not discussed again; he also does not explain how this Midianite came to have an Egyptian name. On May 2, 1939 Freud wrote to Rafael da Costa that the "second Moses" was "wholly my invention." (Gay, 1988, p. 647)

6. Friedman (1987), though not mentioning Freud's hypothesis concerning the possible union of the Egyptian and Midianite Israelites in the desert, suggests another possibility that Yahweh had always been the deity of the Egyptian Israelites and that the deity of the Israelites in the desert who had never been to Egypt was El. At the subsequent reunion in the desert the merger of the two deities occurred by which they were declared to be one in the same.

> Some investigators doing research on early Israelite history have concluded that historically, only a small portion of the ancient Israelites were actually slaves in Egypt. Perhaps it was only the Levites. It is among the Levites, after all, that we find people with Egyptian names. The Levite names Moses, Hophni, and Phineas are all Egyptian, not Hebrew. And the Levites did not occupy any territory in the land like the other tribes. These investigators suggest that the group that was in Egypt and then in Sinai worshipped the God Yahweh. Then they arrive in Israel, where they met Israelite tribes who worshipped the God El. Instead of fighting over whose God was the true God, the two groups accepted the belief that Yahweh and El were the same God. The Levites became the official priests of the united religion, perhaps by force or perhaps by influence. Or perhaps that was their compensation for not having any territory. Instead of the land, they received, as priests, ten percent of the sacrificed animals and produce. (p. 82)

7. On the subject of the Bible, Freud was not alone in his affection for 'two's'. Three students of the Bible in the eighteenth century, Witter, Astruc and Eichhorn, independently of each other, discovered a basic structure in it, the 'doublet'.

> A doublet is a case of the same story being told twice. Even in translation it is easy to observe that biblical stories often appear with variations of detail in two different places in the Bible. There are two different stories of the creation of the world. There are two stories of the covenant between God and the patriarch Abraham, two stories of the naming of Abraham's son Isaac, two stories of Abraham's claiming to a foreign king that his wife Sarah

is his sister, two stories of Isaac's son Jacob making a journey to Mesopotamia, two stories of a revelation to Jacob at Beth-El, two stories of God's changing Jacob's name to Israel, two stories of Moses' getting water from a rock at a place called Meribah, and more. (Friedman, 1987, p. 22)

In addition, they noticed that in one version of the Bible, God is known by the name of Yahweh and in the other by Elohim.

8. See Appendix II for a discussion of the 'Documentary Hypothesis' pertaining to the origins and writing of the Bible.

9. These cultured Egyptian Jews were presumably descended from the Levites, a priestly class who were Moses' closest followers, scribes and domestic servants, as well as those Israelites who were able, after the passing of two or three generations, to transcend the primitiveness and savagery of their ancestors. The Levites were the cultural aristocrats, who Freud considered superior to their non-Levitic brethren, and who retained their loyalty to the memory, traditions and religious innovations of Moses. They were chiefly responsible for perpetuating the Mosaic legacy down through the centuries.

10. The roots of the new Egyptian religion, whose origin is attributed to Akhenaten, go far back into the country's history. We see their presence in hymns to the sun god which date from the twenty-fifth to the twenty-first centuries, B.C.E. Heliopolis (Sun City), which was situated in lower Egypt, became a very important city. In the Bible the city is referred to as On, the birthplace of Joseph's wife. Its founding preceded the date postulated by Freud by one thousand or more years. Temples to the sun-god Re, Re-Atumk, or Re-Harakhty were built in Heliopolis and soon achieved a position of power that almost approached that of the temples of Amun, whose center was in the city of Thebes in Upper Egypt. The word 'Aten', referring to the sun-god, has been found to have been in use between the twenty-first and eighteenth centuries, B.C.E., but did not reach its point of historical significance until the reign of Amenophis (Amenhotep) I, in the early part of the sixteenth century B.C.E. The concept of the sun-god underwent further development by his successors. The expansion of power by Egypt into other countries fostered a universalism which influenced its religious ideas. By the early part of the fifteenth century B.C.E., Aten was already a universal deity. Freud viewed the contrast and conflict between Aten and Amun as polar extremes, but as Albright (1949) points out, the latter was affected by the former. In the fourteenth century B.C.E., hymns were written in which the god Amun-Re was exalted as the father of all the other gods, the maker of heaven, earth and creator of mankind, indicative of the syncretistic tendencies of all religious phenomena. It thus appears that the attributes of the sun deity Aten were neither novel nor revolutionary.

The infusion of foreign influences facilitated by Egypt's expansion of political and economic power resulted in revolutionary tendencies among the ruling hierarchies. The father of Akhenaten, Amenophis III, broke with tradition by marrying a commoner named Teye. She appears to have been quite ambitious and has been considered to be the power not only behind her husband but also her son. The switch from Amun to Aten served not only religious needs but also political ones as well.

11. The association between religion and ethics is a relatively recent phenomenon in the story of man. Religion does not appear to have originally been considered as a vehicle for a system of thoughts and practices that related to relationships between man and man. The relationship between man and God (or, more appropriately, the gods), and man and man were perceived as distinct, dichotomous and unrelated entities. As far as we know, in terms of Western Civilization, it was Moses (and possibly his Egyptian and Mesopotamian forerunners, though convincing evidence for their contribution is meagre) who served as 'matchmaker'. Sarna (1986), commenting on one of the significant uses of the theme of the Book of Exodus, writes:

> Finally, with the historicizing of religion comes the ethicizing of history. That is to say, history is used as a source of ethical teachings and as a motive force for social ethics. God's redemptive acts demand a corresponding imi- tative human response. A host of biblical passages give eloquent expression to the idea that the experience of the slavery and the liberation must become the wellspring of moral action. (pp. 3-4)

12. Within the total context of this tradition, Moses could well be considered to be the prime initiator of Hebrew prophecy. Though the Midrash credits the young Abraham with the breaking of his father's idols, the Bible, however, credits Moses as being the first to fight against the pagan tendencies of the rebellious Israelites.

The notion that Prophetic Judaism, the concept of religion propounded by the Hebrew prophets, is an outgrowth, an advance, over ritual, ceremonial, or cultic Judaism is an imaginative idea created by the liberal Protestant and Jewish clerics (with some help from Spinoza) of the late eighteenth, nineteenth and twentieth centuries. It has little basis in reality. It was never the intent of the Hebrew prophets to create a new movement or religion. They were like prosecutors whose responsibility it was to ensure that the Jews fulfilled the terms of the Covenant, the contract that was made between God and Noah, Abraham, Moses and David. Though they may have decried the focus on ritual and ceremony it was never their intent to do away with them, but to bring them into harmony with the biblical ideals of social justice.

> The prophets should be considered conservative reformers, who wished to restore an earlier form of society, rather than as revolutionaries. They called for a radical return to, not a radical departure from, the tradition of Israel's earliest days. They sought to infuse ritual and legal regulations with spirit- ual integrity and a deep sense of moral justice and in this way to revitalize the existing order. They carried God's message to repent, to return to God's commandments to which Israel had bound itself at Sinai. (Cornfeld and Freedman, 1976, p. 140)

Man's need to know the future has been ever-present and history has shown that those who claimed an ability to satisfy this hunger have never been in short supply.

From the oracles of Greece, the prophets and soothsayers of the Middle and Near-East, to the astrologers and palm and card readers of today we see an unchanging and insatiable expression of this need. However, the Hebrew prophets are in a class by themselves. Though predictive ability was important, it was a relatively minor factor in the choice, power and influence of a particular individual's prophecy. The prophet's role was primarily a religious and ethical one. Basically, the aim of the prophets was to fight against the regressive pull toward paganism and primitive rituals and to direct the Hebrews' efforts toward an ethical monotheism as expressed in the worship of Yahweh. In fact, the raging and never-ending conflict between the Hebrew prophets and pagan religion was due, in large measure, to the inherent perverse and destructive nature of paganism. Though significant, the worship of idols was a relatively minor concern; it was the worship service *itself* that was of primary concern to the prophet.

> The struggles of nature formed the basis of the plot played out among the deities in the Canaanite cult drama. Priestly men and women enacted the major roles of gods and their consorts. Actual union of the male and female actors was believed to bring about, through mimetic magic, the union of the lord of nature, Baal, and mother earth to ensure great harvests and herds for the community. The use of wine and beer often turned the proceedings into bacchanalian festivals. Sacred prostitutes, both male and female, were designated by the same words in Ugaritc and Hebrew, *qedeshem* and *qedeshot*. In Hebrew the word for a temple attendant is different from that for a common prostitute, but the distinction is lost in tradition. (Cornfeld and Freedman, 1976, p. 147)

The pagan gods represented the powerful forces of nature—the sky, the storm wind, the sun, the sea, fertility and death. (The novelty of Yahweh was that He was a force *outside* of nature to Whom the forces of nature were subordinate.) These were forces that were felt to be uncontrollable by any other means but by the performance of specified rituals. Surprisingly, there was a universality about them in the Mediterranean, Middle and Near Eastern countries. Though they carried different names which varied from country to country, they were in reality identical and interchangeable. For example, the wind was represented by Zeus in Greece, by Marduk in Babylon and by Baal-Haddad in Canaan (Haddad, or Hadad, comes from a common noun meaning 'thunder, or storm'). The goddess of fertility was Aphrodite in Greece, Ashtoreth in Canaan and Ishtar in Mesopotamia.

As disturbing as the sexual practices of pagan worship were, they did not match in primitivism and ferocity the perverse aggressive component of human behavior. This was expressed in human sacrifice and cannibalism which somehow had been incorporated into the religious system, probably since the dawn of mankind. A turning towards Yahweh meant not only a substitution of the One for the Many but that the worship of the One God would facilitate the elimination of these perversities and barbarities.

And yet, in our protaganist, there are those elements of ambivalence, of paradox and of contradiction. Freud, the prophetic fighter against the paganism of the unconscious, surrounded himself in his study with the statuettes of those very same

Egyptian idols whose worship k   ıelites prompted the wrath of Moses. On his
desktop he kept a statuette of the   n god Amun-Re, whose temporary riddance
by Akhenaten presumably pave   for the establishment of monotheism and its
subsequent amplification by Mc   he one hand he identifies with Moses, the
arch enemy of paganism and th   ˙ of ethical monotheism, and on the other
hand there is Moses, the father   aelites, who is the object of rebellion and
destruction. Freud's hobby of cc   egacies of antiquity began soon after the
death of his father in 1896 (Spi   bviously, his passion for the collection of
antiques did have other underlying motivations that may or may not have had to do
with emotional conflicts pertaining to his father.

13. Man's phylogenetic inheritance appears to endure eternally. There was a
report published in *The New York Times* on April 3, 1988 in which is described the
phenomenon of the 'Bull Spree'. In the late eighteenth century, Portuguese fishermen
from the Azores migrated to the southern Brazilian state of Santa Catarina and
brought with them a strange Easter Week ritual in which a bull symbolizing Judas
Iscariot, the betrayer of Jesus to the Romans, was tied up and sadistically taunted. (In
this instance, on an unconscious level, Judas Iscariot may well be serving as a
displacement object from the person who was betrayed and crucified and who thus
became an intrinsic component of the deified Trinity.) Over the last thirty years or so
this practice has degenerated, or, more accurately, become more regressive, whereby
the bull is now beaten, stoned, stabbed, and then slaughtered by the participants in
this frenzy. The bull is then eaten in a community barbecue. This practice is in conflict
with the Portuguese tradition of bullfighting, in contrast to the Spanish one, where
the bull is never mortally wounded. The question can appropriately be asked as to
why the bull, rather than any other animal, has been chosen as the object of such
sadism? The answer may lie in the symbolic significance that has, since time imme-
morial, been attributed to the bull. The bull was a supreme object of deification and
worship in pagan religion. Its large size, strength and aggressiveness facilitated its
becoming the symbol of the father. It was thus an 'appropriate' object for selection as a
totem animal though Freud does not mention the specific animal that was used in the
totem feast.

What is most instructive about the progressive (and, at times, regressive) transitions
from one religion to another is that the break was never complete, abrupt or
dichotomous. Some object and beliefs from the old are always incorporated in the
new. One would have thought that with the severe denunciation of idols that not a
trace would be found in monotheism. But that does not appear to have been the case.
For example, there were two winged creatures, called 'Cherubs' that resembled a
sphinx and whose wings served as a cover for the Ark of the Covenant in the Temple
in Jerusalem. These creatures were quite common in the mythological art and
iconography of the ancient Near East (Cornfeld and Freedman, 1976). Jeroboam, a
king of Israel (the Northern Kingdom) substituted two molten golden calves for the
cherubs. Friedman (1987) stresses the point that the word 'calf' is not the correct
translation of the Hebrew word. The word really means 'young bull', a symbol of
strength rather than weakness, as connoted by 'calf'. The Canaanites had a chief god
whom they referred to as 'Bull El'. Israel adopted the name 'El' for its name for an

abstract, though 'real', God which was above the bull. What were formally all-powerful gods of the highest level became, nethermost, the thrones, footstools, or guardians for their successor gods and in the case of the Temple, the invisible God. It was common practice in these times to name designate nobles, lords or heroes with the names of male animals as can be seen in Old Hebrew and Ugaritic texts (Cross, 1973, p. 4).

Among the Canaanites, as well as the Egyptians, the sacred idols were representative of the fish, bull and serpent. In the Book of Numbers 21:5-9, the story is told of how Moses makes a bronze snake which would heal any Israelite bitten by a real snake. In 2 Kings 18:4, King Hezekiah broke this bronze snake into pieces, presumably to diminish the power of the priests descended from Moses, who were powerful in the Northern Kingdom and enhance the power of the Aaronid priests whose power-base was in the Southern Kingdom of Judah where Hezekiah was the ruling monarch; all was not too friendly between the northern and southern brethren. This destruction of the serpent was presumably carried out because the children of Israel were burning incense to it.

There is an oft-told Jewish legend which states that when the Messiah arrives God will go into battle with the world's largest and most powerful fish, the Leviathan, and its counterpart in the animal world, the Great Ox (or Bull). He will defeat and slaughter them and then prepare the most fabulous dishes for all those Jews who will merit entree to this banquet. Thus it will come about that Yahweh will conquer His major competitors, slaughter them and then have them eaten. (According to the Babylonian myth of creation, the God Marduk slew the dragon Tiamot, which is Leviathan in the Bible, cut it in two and formed heaven and earth out of each part.)

Expressions, on a more overt and less disguised level, of this seemingly primitive phenomenon of cannabilistic incorporation of the father and/or deity also can be seen in severe, regressive, mental states. I recall an acutely psychotic male patient in the hospital who, when informed of his father's sudden death expressed neither sorrow nor remorse but did voice regret that he was not present with the corpse prior to burial so that he could have eaten its genitals. In all probability, the unconscious fantasies that accompanied this primordial wish pertained to an identification with the powerful father by the process of orally incorporating the symbol of his strength and power, his genitals. In addition, fantasies of a passive-feminine nature are invariably conjoined with the violent incorporative fantasies and acts. Needless to say, the guilt that results from this complex of fantasy and activity must be enormous.

14. The translation is from the *Anchor Bible — Hosea*, edited and translated by Andersen and Freedman.

15. Sellin was also a renowned archeologist and led many German-Austrian excavation teams to the then Palestine. He also taught and lived in Vienna for some time and given Freud's interest in archeology and the antiquities, it would not surprise me if they were personally acquainted.

16. Somewhere in the course of the development of Judaic civilization, human sacrifice to propitiate the gods was completely replaced by animal sacrifice as the medium of worship of the monotheistic God. Animal sacrifice ceased abruptly with the destruction of the second Temple in the year 70 C.E. and was replaced by prayers

which included reference to the sacrificial system. In pagan cultures, human sacrifice continued to exist for several centuries into the Common Era in the Near and Mid-East and, at least up until the fourteenth century among the Aztecs in Mexico. In Phoenician civilization, child sacrifice to propitiate the gods, Baal Molokh and his consort Tanit who supposedly demanded such acts of violence, prevailed for a number of centuries into the Common Era. Excavations of ancient Carthage have revealed the remains of thousands of these victimized children.

It does give cause to wonder what happened to impulses and behavior that gave rise to the institution of child sacrifice which had prevailed, uninterruptedly, for so many centuries. Unfortunately, the set of unconscious wishes and impulses from whence these barbaric pagan practices derive has not disappeared. Human and animal sacrifice are, after all, a projection of the worshipper's wishes onto the deities, thereby, among other motivations, avoiding responsibility for them. Through the centuries, to this very day, it has re-emerged, periodically, with varying degrees of intensity, in the form, for example, of the so-called 'blood libel', which is a creation of a segment of Christianity that is characterized by primitivity and regressivity. The 'blood libel' pertains to the delusional idea that the blood of a male Christian child is an indispensable ingredient in the manufacture of unleavened bread, the *matzot*, that is eaten by Jews during the Passover holiday. In order to obtain this blood the child had to be sacrificed. Many pogroms, resulting in severe injury and death of many Jews, were carried out all through Europe, especially Eastern Europe, because of the malignant spread of such malicious and devestating rumors. The baking and eating of unleavened bread, obviously without the mention or use of blood, is derived from Divine command in the Bible.

It would thus appear that all the phenomena pertaining to human, and especially child, sacrifice have persisted in the unconscious only to re-emerge periodically, in projected form as with most anti-Semitic accusations, by accusing the Jew of the practice and thereby rendering the accuser purified, albeit transiently, by this defensive repudiation and self-deceptive riddance of the consciously rejected wish. In essence the Christian accuser is saying: "It is not I who has this wish to sacrifice a Christian child so as to satisfy the demands of God so that I can gain favor with Him, it is the Jew!" It is more than just coincidence that Passover and Easter, which is a celebration of the crucifixion and resurrection of Jesus, occur at about the same time of the year. 'Blood libel' pogroms nearly always occurred before, and during, Passover.

Though charges of sacrifice of Christians being leveled against Jews date from the second century of the Common Era, it was not until the Middle Ages that some Christians created the charge that the Jews sacrificed a male child as an act of mockery of the Passion of Jesus, i.e., his suffering on the night of the Last Supper and the next day on the cross. It did not take long for this idea to be elaborated with the additional component of the child's blood being used in preparation of the *matzot* or in the rites of the Seder on the first night of Passover. The first such recorded charge was made in England in 1144, C.E. In view of the above, it is not difficult to see beneath the transparency another version, in projected form, of human sacrifice and cannibalism.

The more recent phenomenon of the Holocaust is another expression of the ultimate in the perversion of man's ever-present and natural 'religious' inclinations. The Germans, and their all-too-willing participating colleagues, seemed to have felt an almost 'religious', if not exactly just that, obligation to purify the world races in the name of some higher ideal which was formulated by, and embodied in, their living deity whose name was Hitler. This was an example of the exaggeration of the process of idealization to the point of a thinly disguised deification. The German nation was conceptualized in transcendent, ethereal and abstract terms and imagery. (The composer Richard Wagner and the philosopher Friedrich Nietzsche laid the essential groundwork for this pathological, quasi-religious, frenzy though it is doubtful that it was ever Nietzsche's intent that his ideas be misused in this manner.) The completion of this murderous task, when practiced on a daily basis, left the participants with a feeling of virtue which is the consequence of the fulfillment of the command of the 'deity'. One can well imagine the enormity of guilt that would have been felt by them if the defensive disguise and self-deception were taken away. This helps explain the unrepentant attitude of so many of those who participated in the most horrendous episode of human history. Inherent in the human propensity for religious quest and identity is the potential for a life most noble or most base; anti-Semitism, with all its passion, has always found a secure home in the latter.

17. I am indebted to Ms. Ingeborg von Zitzewitz of Goethe House, New York, for locating and translating this passage.

18. An early example of this ambivalence occurred when Freud, at the time of his wedding, remarked to his friend and mentor Josef Breuer, that he would have preferred to convert to Christianity rather than have to suffer through the Orthodox marriage ritual. With the return to his religious roots in late life, the same emotional conflicts seem to have reappeared but this time they were projectively expressed in *Moses and Monotheism*.

19. This is all the more remarkable when one considers the significance that Freud attached to erotic feelings that a son has towards his father, whether he be imagined (as in the case of Leonardo Da Vinci [S.E. XI] or real (as in the case of Schreber [S.E. XII].

20. The translation of St. Paul's *Epistle to the Hebrews* is taken from the *Anchor Bible*, 1972. As can be seen in the commentary of the following verses in the *Anchor Bible*, there is some controversy over the issue of whether Paul relied on the Old Testament version of the binding and near-sacrifice of Isaac or on the specific Midrashic tradition of the sacrifice having been completed. So that the thematic consistency be maintained, i.e., the identity between God resurrecting Isaac by means of a 'parable' and Jesus in a literal manner, it would appear that Paul had the Midrashic tradition in mind. The meaning of the word 'parable' in this context is not clear.

21. Bergmann (1988) has hypothesized that the origins of both Judaism and Christianity lie in the institution of infanticide of which the binding and/or sacrifice of Isaac and the crucifixion of Jesus are the most prominent expressions.

22. An analogous situation can be seen with one of Freud's heroes, Charles Darwin. His father was a devout, believing Christian whom the son felt would be hurt by the atheistic implications of the results of his biological research. His findings

made the younger Darwin question his theological beliefs but he never did fully surrender them. Darwin having an obsessional character structure only made the situation worse for him. One can well imagine the emotional and physical pain that he must have endured while struggling with his doubts and the guilt accruing from them. He is known to have had numerous psychosomatic symptoms (Greenacre, 1963). Acceptance of the implications of his research was tantamount to an attack not only on his father's beliefs but also perceived to be a mortal blow to the father himself. In 1844 he wrote a letter to his botanist friend Joseph Hooker (as quoted in Ritvo, 1965):

> I am almost convinced ... that species are not (*it is like confessing a murder*) immutable ... I think I have found out (here's presumption) the simple way by which species become exquisitely adapted to various ends. (italics mine)

23. This fateful and dramatic change in psychoanalytic theory from a presumed, *actual*, sexual seduction of the child by a parent (or surrogate) to a *fantasied* one may partly be responsible for Freud's fundamental shift in focus and orientation from biology to psychology. The hypothesis that Freud effected this change for fear that the intense opposition of some of his medical colleagues to his theories pertaining to the sexual etiology of neurosis might serve as a devestating threat to the emerging field of Psychoanalysis (Masson, 1984) has to remain in the realm of conjecture for lack of convincing evidence.

24. Novelists and dramatists have unfortunately overly dramatized the process by picturing a radical transformation or a re-birth of the protaganist after such a recall. The 'feeling' experience resulting from genuine psychoanalytic insight is not revelational nor apocalyptic; if it appears to be so then we must suspect the presence of intensified resistance to real awareness rather than true insight. Emotional growth subsequent to insight comes in gradual, almost imperceptable increments and not in one dramatic leap.

25. Yerushalmi (1989) has read the original manuscript of *Moses and Monotheism*, dated by Freud '9 August 1934,' which is in the Sigmund Freud Collection in the Library of Congress. This manuscript corresponds roughly to Parts I and II of the final published version of *Moses and Monotheism*. Yerushalmi found that the title that Freud gave to the manuscript was indeed *Der Mann Moses — Ein historische Roman* (The Man Moses — A Historical Novel). Freud apparently did consider the title '*Moses und der Monotheismus*' in the 1934 manuscript but deliberately rejected it. He also found an unpublished preface for the book which Yerushalmi has now had translated and published. The reason for its omission may be due to Freud subsequently changing his mind and bringing his study closer to the factual or historical realm. Part III was the result and the entire work thus became a historical study rather than a fictional account of a biblical and, presumably, historical character.

Yerushalmi focuses on the conscious, rather than unconscious, intentionality that motivated Freud to give his manuscript the abortive subtitle of *A Historical Novel*. A psychoanalytic study by Yerushalmi is avoided. From the unpublished (but now published) preface it seems clear that Freud felt that, in 1934, he did not possess sufficient reliable data pertaining to Moses that would qualify his work as scientific and that it would be safer to center it in the realm of fiction. Freud was of the opinion that he would have to rely more on the probability of the veracity of a fact or the occurrence of an event since the proven reality is often if not entirely absent. If one can conceptualize a continuum, with the novel on the left and a frank historical work on the right, then Parts I and II (in 1934) of *Moses and Monotheism* could be considered to fall somewhere after a quasi-historical novel like Thomas Mann's tetralogy *Joseph and His Brothers* but still far short of a work of historical verisimilitude.

Yerushalmi makes the significant point that the final title of *Moses and Monotheism* was the responsibility of the first English translator, Katherine Jones, and that it was retained by James Strachey in the Standard Edition. The German title given by Freud was *Der Mann Moses und die monotheistische Religion* (*The Man Moses and the Monotheistic Religion*), a title more in keeping with an historical study than a work of fiction. It is also of interest that the German word for 'novel', *Roman*, is also part of the phrase 'Family Romance', i.e., *Familienroman*.

26. The Babylonian Talmud, English translation taken from the Soncino Edition, Seder *Mo'ed*, Tractate *Sukkah*, page 52a; published by The Soncino Press, London, 1938, edited by Rabbi Dr. I. Epstein and translated by Rev. Dr. I.W. Slotki; see also Levine, 1987

Chapter 12

1. There may possibly have been some experiences in Freud's early childhod, when the family lived in Freiberg (a city now in Czechoslovakia), that contributed to his intensified interest in the statue and character of Moses in adulthood. Harold P. Blum, Executive Director of the Sigmund Freud Archives, has informed me that while in the company of E. Blum, E. Laible, and J. Sajner, there was found a statue that is now in the external rear of St. Mary's Church, outside the church and close to the back wall, in Freiberg. During the nineteenth century this statue stood in the town square in the midst of Catholic religious icons and statues. (In this area of the country the major focus of worship was on the Virgin Mary.) The child Sigmund Freud, who lived in that city until the age of three and a half, must have seen this statue on many occasions while in the company of his parents or nursemaid and also on his return visit as an adolescent. This statue is by an anonymous sculptor. It appears as an imposing figure, as one might imagine the biblical Moses (but, realistically, in accordance with the biblical text, his older brother Aaron), wearing the breastplate of the High Priest of Israel and a helmet with horn-like projections. This figure is presented as being in the process of writing on a stone tablet. One can well imagine the visual and emotional effect of this statue of an imposing figure from the Old Testament amidst the Catholic statuary and icons on an impressionable, sensitive and bright child as young Sigmund must have been.

This statue has been identified by Czechoslovakian monument authorities as being that of Zechariah, a Minor Prophet in the Old Testament. They are in error.

Though Zechariah may have been a priest, he was not the High Priest. Only the High Priest was permitted to wear the breastplate. This breastplate was framed in solid gold and contained twelve gemstones of different colors. It was the medium, along with two stones or tablets (known as the *Urim and Thummim*), for divination. According to I Samuel 28:6, there are three ways in which God could communicate with man: dreams, *Urim* (priestly oracle), and the prophetic utterance. In the Book of Zechariah we see expressions of all three modes.

Zechariah describes eight specific visions which appear to be a dream within a dream. Of special interest is the fact that it is the only place in the Bible where dream phenomena receive so much emphasis and attention. The dream sequence is introduced by the prophet, in what seems to be a hypnotic state:

> 4:1. The angel who talked with me came back and woke me as a man is awakened from sleep.

This statue is really that of the High Priest Joshua seen by Zechariah in his fourth vision and described by him in the following verses:

> 3:1. He further showed me Joshua, the high priest, standing before the angel of the LORD, and the Accuser standing at his right to accuse him.

> 3:5. Then he gave the order, "Let a pure diadem be placed on his head." And they placed the pure diadem on his head and clothed him in [priestly] garments, as the angel of the LORD stood by.

> 3:9. For mark well this stone which I place before Joshua, a single stone with seven eyes. I will execute its engraving—declares the LORD of Hosts— and I will remove that country's guilt in a single day.

In all probability, the reason for the presence of this statue in the town square of Freiberg may be due to the Messianism that pervades Zechariah's prophecies, as seen in 3:8, 9:9, and 12:10. There are some traditional Jewish commentators who regard the 'stone' in 3:9 as a jewel in the diadem of the Messiah who will arrive at some point in the future. However, these same prophecies have been interpreted by believing Christians as foretelling the coming of their Messiah, Jesus Christ.

Appendix I

1. I am indebted to Hyman Grossbard, Emeritus Professor of Social Work at Columbia University and a graduate of one of the most illustrious of Lithuanian *Yeshivot*, for providing some of this information.

2. One of the mysteries of the Freud family history that has never been clarified is exactly what Jacob Freud did for a living and how he did, or did not, support his family. In Freiberg he presumably carried on some kind of trade in textiles. Nowhere is there any mention of what he did in Vienna. In an unpublished letter to Martha

Bernays, Freud described his father in Micawber-like terms as being "always hopefully expecting something to turn up" (Jones, 1953, I:2) My colleague Charles Fischer informed me that Max Schur, Freud's personal physician and biographer, was shocked by what must have been the impoverished living situation of the Freud family when he visited their former home. The entire apartment consisted of one room. In his biography of Freud, Schur (1972) toned down his reaction by referring to the entire family being 'crowded' into one room. Anna Freud Bernays (1940) engaged in some romanticization of her family's past when she described her father as owning a textile mill (which was not true) and her father's being thirty-six years of age, rather than forty when he married the nineteen year-old Amalia.

Though the *Gymnasium* was a public institution all of the students were required to pay tuition. Rozenblit (1983 p: 112) cites data from 1890 through 1910 which shows that in 1890 30.2% of the Jewish students in the *Erzherzog-Rainer-Gymnasium* in District II (the Leopoldstadt) received tuition waivers. In 1910 this figure jumped to 50.4%. On the basis of these data it can be inferred retroactively that in the 1860s and early 1870s, the years of Sigmund's attendance, a substantial number of Jewish students did not pay any tuition. Yet Jacob Freud paid full tuition for Sigmund though it obviously would have been quite easy to obtain a waiver. Rozenblit (1983, p: 112) notes that a prestige factor may have been attached to the payment of tuition in that those students who did receive tuition waivers came from families who were perceived to be of lower social status than those who paid tuition. Ellenberger (1970) suggests that he did not apply for a waiver as this would have necessitated his submitting a record of his income. While in medical school, and for a time thereafter, Sigmund did receive some financial support from his immediate superior in the physiology laboratory, Ernst von Fleischl-Marxow, his classmate Josef Paneth, who had inherited wealth, and from Josef Breuer.

Another possible source of financial support for the Freud family was revealed to me by Henry Bondi. As noted earlier, his grandfather, Marcus Bondi, was the senior lay official of the leading Orthodox synagogue in the Leopoldstadt and he told his family that several well-to-do members of this synagogue, realizing the dire financial situation of the Freud's, would periodically give money to Jacob Freud. Marcus Bondi, himself, may well have been one of these contributors.

3. The Leopoldstadt section of Vienna had a large Orthodox immigrant contingent from Eastern Europe and it would appear almost certain that they would have established the kind of educational institution, i.e., the *Yeshiva*, that was so central to their lives in the cities and towns of their origins. However, I have not been able to find any record of the existence of a Galician-style *Yeshiva* in Vienna in the nineteenth century. The Leopoldstadt was, in essence, a Jewish ghetto, not unlike the Lower East Side of New York or Williamsburgh section of Brooklyn; it was not too long after their arrival that the Orthodox Jews did establish *Yeshivot* in these areas.

4. Prior to settling in the Rhine Valley, these Jews had lived in France and Italy, having been forced into an eastward and northern migration by prevailing anti-Semitism. The Rhine Valley was the start of the Yiddish language which included not only the native dialect which evolved into the German language but also words from

the Romance Languages (Samuel, 1956). Apparently, Freud got this idea of his family's geneology from his father. It seems that, on a visit to Cologne, Jacob Freud met the secretary of the Jewish community there who, very imaginatively, 'traced' the family back to its fourteenth century roots in Cologne. (Gay, 1988, p.5) There was obviously no documentation. Gay is being very charitable when he refers to the evidence as 'slender'.

5. Freud's need to sustain this Family Romance appears to have lessened in his old age. At the age of eighty, when he was in the midst of writing *Moses and Monotheism* he wrote in a letter to a Dr. Fehl: "I hope it is not unknown to you that I have always held faithfully to our people and never pretended to be anything but what I am: a Jew from Moravia whose parents came from Austrian Galicia." (Letter to Dr. Siegfried Fehl, November 12, 1935; Sigmund Freud Archives, B2, Library of Congress; as quoted in Gay (1988), p. 597.) The idea of his families' original settlement in old Cologne was no longer necessary for maintenance of his self-esteem, or so it seemed, for he returns to the subject of Jews in Cologne, without mentioning his own familial antecedents, in *Moses and Monotheism*.

6. McGrath's impression of the ominous, interlocking, vicissitudes of the worship of all things German is of significant interest. The postulation of a connecting link over a fifty year span between the *Leseverein* and the Nazi Party would thereby exemplify the unfortunate, all too frequent phenomenon seen throughout history, and especially in our times, where the extension and intensification of any ideological movement into its psychopathological extreme will always result in the creation of its perverse and destructive image.

7. The report was released in mid-December, 1875 but carried an 1876 postdate. It was entitled, '*Uber das Lehren und Lernen der medizinischen Wissenschaften an den Universitaten der deutschen Nation nebst allgemeine Bemarkungen uber Universitaten: Ein culturhistorische Studie*', and published in Vienna by Carl Gerolds Sohn.

8. The relevant passages appear in pp. 148-54 of the Billroth report.

9. Billroth later expressed regret over the racial hatred that was precipitated by his report (Klein, p. 52). He was not really an anti-Semite in the classical sense. He shared the prejudices toward the East European Jews that were pervasive among the second- and third-generation middle-class Viennese Jews as well as the German Jews.

An excellent example of these shared prejudices is what occurred in the 'Duisberg Affair' which began in the Prussian city of Duisberg in 1909 and ended in 1914. The Representative Assembly of the *Gemeinde* of the city had always consisted exclusively of liberal, Reform-affiliated, native-born German Jews. The gradually increasing immigration of East European Orthodox and Zionist Jews resulted in a clamor on their part for some representation. An election was called and the liberal Jews suffered a stunning defeat. The losers then petitioned the government to nullify the election results because of fraud. An investigation was then undertaken and the government found no evidence of the alleged fraud. Just before their term of office expired the liberal incumbents changed the voting rules by restricting the franchise to men of 'German citizenship' who were resident in the city for at least a year and were earning enough income to warrant an assessment for the communal tax. In an attempt to justify this move, they sent a memorandum to the government in which they stated that the East European Jews were:

> of a lower culture ... whose hearts cannot beat in unison for Germany ... they are fully alien to German Jews by virtue of their customs and habits ... This is the question: In the future should the community be led and represented by German-feeling men or by men who ... want to reverse world history to reestablish a national Judaism and who do not partake of the German national sensibility [*Volksempfinden*], its thinking, feeling and aspirations? (As quoted in Wertheimer, 1987, pp. 139-140)

Billroth demonstrated his philo-Semitism in regard to his relationship to Joseph Breuer and, through Breuer, to Freud. He was quite friendly with Josef Breuer and recognized his potential for a brilliant career. In 1871 he wanted to propose Breuer for an appointment in the medical school as Professor Extraordinarius (Breuer, Curriculum Vitae, 1928). This was an honorary title with no privileges or teaching responsibilities. Breuer, however, refused the offer, went into private practice and became the most successful internist in Vienna, with a large non-Jewish as well as Jewish clientele. On July 3, 1883, Billroth wrote a letter to a friend (cited in Pulzer, Peter G.J., *The Rise of Political Anti-Semitism in Germany and Austria*, John Wiley and Sons, New York, 1964, p. 252) condemning the prejudice against Jews in the granting of faculty appointments and in the 1890s, he was one of the few professors who played an active role in the '*Verein zur des Antisemitismus*' ('Society to Combat Anti-Semitism') (Klein, pp. 65-66). In 1885, when the impecunious Freud needed money to go to Paris to study with Charcot, Breuer enlisted Billroth's help and influence to obtain a grant for him (Jones, 1953, I: 74).

Appendix III

1. When I read the word 'fossil' I immediately recalled another use of this word in precisely the same context from a book that I had read over thirty-five years ago. The noted British historian, Arnold J. Toynbee, wrote a ten volume opus entitled, "A Study of History", the first three volumes having been published in 1933. In Volume I Toynbee writes:

> On a closer inspection, we can also discern two sets of what appear to be fossilized relics of similar societies now extinct, namely: one set including the Monophysite Christians of Armenia, Mesopotamia, Egypt, and Abyssinia and the Nestorian Christians of Kurdistan and Malabar, as well as the Jews and Parsees; a second set including the Lamaistic Mahayanian Buddhists of Ceylon, Burma, and Siam, as well as the Jains of India. (p. 35)

Freud wrote Part III of *Moses and Monotheism* in which the word 'fossil' appears some time prior to 1938 when it was published but certainly a considerable period of time after 1933. Toynbee created quite a stir of animosity among Jews for his reference to Judaism and its adherents as a fossil religion and society, almost as intense as that to Freud after his *Moses and Monotheism*. I have often wondered whether the adverse reaction to Toynbee would have been as intense if he had only described his thoughts without the use of the word 'fossil'. In this context the word certainly has a pejorative connotation but it also serves as a kind of 'lightning rod' for the most intense feelings. I wonder if Freud had read Toynbee and obtained the idea from him. After all, the idea of culture, civilization, or religion being a 'fossil' is rather an uncommon one. In all of my own readings I have seen it used only twice, in Toynbee and Freud. (Toynbee was not the most philo-Semitic of historians; the noted Jewish writer and translator Maurice Samuel (1956), has written a masterful response to Toynbee.)

Bibliography

Abraham, Karl. 1955 "Amenhotep IV: A Psychological Contribution Towards the Understanding of His Personality and of the Monotheistic Cult of Aton (1912)." In *Clinical Papers and Essays on Psychoanalysis*, Vol. II. Basic Books, Inc., New York.

Albright, W.F. 1949 "The Biblical Period." In '*The Jews — Their History, Culture and Religion*', ed. by Louis Finkelstein. Harper and Brothers. New York, pp. 3-69.

———. 1957 *From The Stone Age To Christianity. Monotheism and the Historical Process.* 2nd Edition. Doubleday Anchor Books, Doubleday & Co., Inc., Garden City, N. Y.

———. 1969 'Moses As Monotheist.' In *Monotheism and Moses — The Genesis of Judaism.* Ed. by Robert J. Christen and Harold E. Hazelton. D.C. Heath and Co., A Division of Raytheon Education Co., Lexington, Mass.

———. 1969 *Archaeology and The Religion of Israel.* Anchor Books, Doubleday & Co., Garden City, N. Y.

Anchor Bible — Hosea. 1980 *The Book of Hosea. A New Translation with Introduction and Commentary* — Francis I. Andersen and David Noel Freedman. Doubleday & Co., Inc., Garden City, N. Y.

Anchor Bible — To The Hebrews. 1972 *To The Hebrews. Translation, Comment and Conclusions* — George Wesley Buchanan. Doubleday & Co., Inc., Garden City, N. Y.

Arlow, Jacob A. 1951 "The Consecration of the Prophet." *The Psychoanalytic Quarterly,* 20: pp. 374-397.

Aron, Willy. 1956-57 "Notes on Sigmund Freud's Ancestry and Jewish Contacts." *YIVO Annual of Jewish Social Sciences*, 11: pp. 286-295.

Auerbach, E. 1975 *Moses.* Translated by I.O. Lehman and R.A. Barclay. Wayne State University Press, Detroit.

Bakan, David. 1958 *Sigmund Freud and the Jewish Mystical Tradition.* D. van Nostrand Co., Princeton, N.J.

Baron, Salo W. 1939 Book Review of 'Moses and Monotheism'. *American Journal of Sociology,* pp. 471-477.

Bavli, Hillel. 1949 "The Modern Renaissance of Hebrew Literature." In *'The Jews— Their History, Culture and Religion',* ed. by Louis Finkelstein. Harper and Brothers, New York, pp. 567-601.

Bergmann, Martin S. 1982 "Moses and The Evolution of Freud's Jewish Identity." In *Judaism and Psychoanalysis.,* ed. by Mortimer Ostow. Ktav Publishing House, Inc., New York.

_____ . 1988 "The Transformation of Ritual Infanticide in the Jewish and Christian Religions with Reference to Anti-Semitism." In *Fantasy, Myth, and Reality—Essays in Honor of Jacob A. Arlow, M.D.* H.P. Blum, Y. Kramer, A.K. Richards, A.D. Richards, eds., International Universities Press, Inc., Madison, CT., pp. 233-257.

Bernfeld, Siegfried. 1951 "Sigmund Freud, M.D., 1882-1885." *International Journal of Psychoanalysis,* 32: pp. 204-217.

Bernays, Anna Freud. 1940 "My Brother Sigmund Freud." *American Mercury,* 51: pp. 335-342.

Breasted, James Henry. 1906 *A History of Egypt.* London.

_____ . 1933 *The Dawn of Conscience.* Charles Scribner's Sons, New York.

Brenner, Charles. 1982 *The Mind In Conflict.* International Universities Press, Inc., New York.

Breuer, Josef, "Autobiography of Josef Breuer." 1953 Translated and edited by C.P. Oberndorf. *International Journal of Psychoanalysis.* 34: pp. 64-67.

Brown, Peter. 1988 *The Body and Society—Men, Women, and Sexual Renunciation in Early Christianity.* Columbia University Press, New York.

Clare, George. 1982 *Last Waltz in Vienna—The Rise and Destruction of A Family—1842-1942.* Holt, Rinehart and Winston, New York.

Clark, Ronald W. 1980 *Freud—The Man and the Cause.* Random House, New York.

Cornfeld, Gaalyeh and Freedman, David Noel. 1976 *Archaeology of the Bible—Book by Book.* Harper & Row, San Francisco.

Cross, Frank Moore. 1973 *Canaanite Myth and Hebrew Epic—Essays in the History of the Religion of Israel.* Harvard University Press, Cambridge, Mass. and London, England.

Ellenberger, Henri F. 1970 *The Discovery of the Unconscious.* Basic Books, Inc., New York.

Freeman, Erika. 1971 *Insights—Conversations with Theodor Reik.* Prentice-Hall Inc., Englewood Cliffs, N.J. p. 80.

Freud, Ernst L., Lucie Freud, and Ilse Grubrich-Simitis, eds. 1978 *Sigmund Freud, His Life in Pictures and Words.* Harcourt Brace Jovanovich, New York and London.

Freud, Martin. 1958 *Sigmund Freud: Man and Father.* The Vanguard Press, New York.

———. 1967 "Who Was Freud?" In *The Jews of Austria: Essays On Their Life, History, and Destruction.* Ed. by Josef Fraenkel. Valentine, Mitchell, London. pp. 197-211.

Freud, Sigmund. 1895 With Josef Breuer *Studies on Hysteria.* Standard Edition, II.

Freud, Sigmund. 1900 *The Interpretation of Dreams.* Standard Edition, IV-V.

———. 1901 *The Psychopathology of Everyday Life.* Standard Edition, VI.

———. 1907 *Obsessive Actions and Religious Practices.* Standard Edition, IX.

———. 1909 *Family Romances.* Standard Edition, IX.

———. 1912-13 *Totem and Taboo.* Standard Edition, XIII.

———. 1914 *The Moses of Michelangelo.* Standard Edition, XIII.

———. 1923 *The Ego and the Id.* Standard Edition, XIX.

———. 1925 *Letter to the Editor of the Jewish Press Centre in Zurich.* Standard Edition, XIX.

———. 1925 *An Autobiographical Study.* Standard Edition, XX.

———. 1927 *The Future of An Illusion.* Standard Edition, XXI.

———. 1928 *Dostoevsky and Parricide.* Standard Edition, XXI.

———. 1939 [1934-39]. *Moses and Monotheism.* Standard Edition, XXIII.

———. 1960 *Letters.* Selected and edited by Ernst L. Freud. Basic Books, New York.

———. 1985 *The Complete Letters of Sigmund Freud to Wilhelm Fliess—1887-1904.* Translated and edited by Jeffrey M. Masson. The Belknap Press of Harvard University Press, Cambridge, Mass., and London, England.

———. and Karl Abraham. 1965 *Letters, 1907-1926.* Edited by H.C. Abraham and E.L. Freud. Basic Books, New York.

Friedman, R.E. 1987 *Who Wrote the Bible?* Summit Books, New York.

Fromm, Erich. 1950 *Psychoanalysis and Religion.* Yale University Press, New Haven.

Gay, Peter. 1977 "At Home in America." *The American Scholar,* Winter Issue, pp. 31-42.

———. 1978 *Freud, Jews and Other Germans: Masters and Victims in Modernist Culture.* Oxford University Press.

———. 1987 *A Godless Jew—Freud, Atheism and the Making of Psychoanalysis.* Yale University Press, New Haven and London.

———. 1988 *Freud—A Life For Our Time.* W.W. Norton and Company, New York and London.

———. 1989 *Sigmund and Minna? The Biographer as Voyeur.* The *New York Times—* Book Review, January 29, 1989, p. 1.

Gicklhorn, Josef and Renee. 1960 *Sigmund Freud's akademische Laufbahn im Lichte der Dokumente.* Verlag Urban & Schwarzenberg. Wien-Innsbruck.

Gicklhorn, Renee. 1965 "Eine Episode aus Sigmund Freuds Mittelschulzeit." *Unsere Heimat.* 36: pp. 18-24.

———. 1969 "The Freiberg Period of the Freud Family." *Journal of the History of Medicine and Allied Sciences.* 24: pp. 37-43.

———. 1976 *Sigmund Freud und der Onkeltraum—Dichtung and Wahrheit.* Ferdinand Berger & Sons OHG, 3580 Horn, NO.

Gordon, Milton M. 1964 *Assimilation in American Life—The Role of Race, Religion, and National Origins.* Oxford University Press, New York.

Greenacre, Phyllis. 1963 *The Quest for the Father.* International Universities Press, Inc., New York.

Grinstein, Alexander. 1968 *On Sigmund Freud's Dreams.* Wayne State University Press, Detroit.

Grunwald, Max. 1936 *Vienna.* The Jewish Publication Society, Philadelphia.

Halevi, Mayer. 1958-59 "Discussion Regarding Sigmund Freud's Ancestry." *YIVO Annual of Jewish Social Sciences,* XII, pp. 297-300.

Halivni, Weiss David. 1986 *Midrash, Mishnah, and Gemara—The Jewish Predilection for Justified Law.* Harvard University Press, Cambridge and London.

Hardin, Harry T. 1988 "On the Vicissitudes of Freud's Early Mothering II: Alienation from His Biological Mother." *The Psychoanalytic Quarterly,* LVII: pp. 72-86.

Heller, Judith Bernays. 1956 "Freud's Mother and Father—A Memoir." *Commentary,* 12: pp. 418-421.

Helmreich, William B. 1986 *The World of the Yeshiva.* Yale University Press, New Haven and London.

Hes, Jozef Philip. 1986 "A Note on an As Yet Unpublished Letter by Sigmund Freud." *Jewish Social Studies—A quarterly journal devoted to contemporary and historical aspects of Jewish life.* XLVIII: pp. 321-324.

Hirschmuller, Albrecht. 1978 *Physiologie und Psychoanalyse im Leben und Werk Josef Breuers.* Hans Huber, Bern.

Jones, Ernest. 1953, I *The Life and Work of Sigmund Freud. Vol. 1: The Formative Years and the Great Discoveries, 1856-1900.* Basic Books, New York.

———. 1955, II *The Life and Work of Sigmund Freud. Vol. 2: The Years of Maturity, 1901-1919.* Basic Books, New York.

———. 1957, III *The Life and Work of Sigmund Freud. Vol. 3: The Last Phase, 1919-1939.* Basic Books, New York.

Jospe, Alfred. 1979 "German Jewry Was Different." *Judaism: A Quarterly Journal of Jewish Life and Thought.* 28: pp. 237-247.

Jung, Carl Gustav. 1965 *Memories, Dreams, and Reflections.* Ed. Aniela Jaffe; translated by Richard and Clara Winston. Vintage Books, New York.

Kaplan, Mordecai. 1949 *The Future of the American Jew.* The Macmillan Co., New York.

Klein, Dennis B. 1985 *Jewish Origins of the Psychoanalytic Movement.* The University of Chicago Press, Chicago and London.

Knoepfmacher, Hugo. 1979 "Sigmund Freud in High School." *American Imago,* 36: pp. 287-300.

Krull, Marianne. 1986 *Freud and His Father.* W.W. Norton and Company, New York and London.

Levine, Herschel M. 1987 "Three Talmudic Tales of Seduction." *Judaism: A Quarterly Journal of Jewish Thought.* 36: pp. 466-470.

Masson, Jeffrey M. 1984 *The Assault on Truth: Freud's Suppression of the Seduction Theory.* Farrar, Straus and Geroux, New York.

Meek, Theophile James. 1969 "Moses As Monolatrist." In *Monotheism and Moses — The Genesis of Judaism.* Ed. by Robert J. Christen and Harold E. Hazelton. D.C. Heath and Co., A Division of Raytheon Education Co., Lexington, Mass.

McGrath, William J. 1967 "Student Radicalism in Vienna." *Journal of Contemporary History.* 2: pp. 183-201.

———. 1986 *Freud's Discovery of Psychoanalysis — The Politics of Hysteria.* Cornell University Press, Ithaca and London.

Meissner, W.W. 1984 *Psychoanalysis and Religious Experience.* Yale University Press, New Haven and London.

Nadich, Judah. 1983 *Jewish Legends of the Second Commonwealth.* The Jewish Publication Society of America, Philadelphia.

Oring, Elliott. 1984 *The Jokes of Sigmund Freud.* University of Pennsylvania Press, Philadelphia.

Ostow, Mortimer. 1982 "Discussion of Martin S. Bergmann's Paper." In *Judaism and Psychoanalysis.* Ed. by Mortimer Ostow. Ktav Publishing House, Inc., New York.

———. 1988 "Four Entered the Garden: Normative Religion Versus Illusion." In *Fantasy, Myth, and Reality — Essays in Honor of Jacob A. Arlow, M.D.* H.P. Blum, Y. Kramer, A.K. Richards, A.D. Richards, Eds. International Universities Press, Madison, CT., pp. 287-301.

Pagels, Elaine. 1979 *The Gnostic Gospels*. Random House, New York.

Papo, M. 1967 "The Sephardi Community of Vienna." In *The Jews of Austria—Essays on their Life, History and Destruction*. Josef Fraenkel, ed. Vallentine-Mitchell, London, pp. 327-346.

Pappenheim, Bertha. 1930 *Zeenah U Reenah (Frauenbibel)*, "Ubersetzung and Anslegung des Pentateuch von Jacob ben Isaac aus Janow nach dem Judish— Deutschen bearbeited von Bertha Pappenheim." J. Kaufman Verlag, Frankfurt am Mein.

Patai, Raphael. 1988 *Apprentice in Budapest—Memories of a World That Is No More*. University of Utah Press, Salt Lake City.

Rabinowitz, Louis Isaac. 1980 "Piety and Honesty." *Judaism: A Quarterly Journal of Jewish Life and Thought*. 29: pp. 265-71.

Rainey, Reuben M. 1971 *Freud As Student of Religion: Perspectives on the Background and Development of His Thought*. Unpublished Ph.D. Dissertation, Columbia University, Department of Religion.

Rice, Emanuel. 1953 "Naturalism and Mordecai Kaplan—The Religious Philosophy of Reconstructionism, A Discussion of Its Contributions and A Critique." *The Student Zionist*. 10: pp. 20-26.

————. 1987 "The Jewish Fathers of Psychoanalysis." *Judaism: A Quarterly Journal of Jewish Life and Thought*, 36: pp. 109-115.

Ritvo, Lucille. 1965 "Darwin as the Source of Freud's Neo-Lamarckianism." *Journal of the American Psychoanalytic Association*, 13: pp. 499-517.

Roback, A.A. 1957 *Freudiana*. Sci-Art Publishers, Cambridge, Mass.

Robert, Marthe. 1976 *From Oedipus to Moses—Freud's Jewish Identity*. Translated by Ralph Manheim. Anchor Books, Anchor Press/Doubleday, Garden City, New York.

Rosenfeld, Eva M. 1956 "Dream and Vision—Some Remarks on Freud's Egyptian Bird Dream." *International Journal of Psychoanalysis*, 37: pp. 97-105.

Rosenfeld, Leonora Cohen. 1962 *Portrait of A Philosopher: Morris R. Cohen in Life and Letters*. Harcourt, Brace and World, Inc., New York.

Rowley, H.H. 1969 "Moses As The Source of Monotheism." In *Monotheism and Moses— The Genesis of Judaism*. Ed. by Robert J. Christen and Harold E. Hazelton. D.C. Heath and Co., A Division of Raytheon and Co., Lexington, Mass.

Rozenblit, Marsha L. 1983 *The Jews of Vienna—1867-1914—Assimilation and Identity*. State University of New York Press, Albany.

Samuel, Maurice. 1956 *The Professor and the Fossil*. Alfred A. Knopf, New York.

Sarna, Nahum M. 1987 *Exploring Exodus—The Heritage of Biblical Israel*. Schocken Books, N.Y.

Schultz, J.P. 1987 "The 'Ze'enah U'Re'enah': Torah for the Folk." *Judaism: A Quarterly Journal,* 36: pp. 84-96.

Schur, Max. 1972 *Freud: Living and Dying.* International Universities Press, Inc., New York.

Sellin, Ernst. 1922 *Mose und Seine Bedeutung fur die israelitisch-judische Religionsgeschichte.* A. Deicherstsche Verlagsbuchhandlung Dr. Werner Scholl, Leipzig-Erlangen.

———. 1924 *Geschichte Des Israelitisch-Judischen Vokes-Erster Teil: Von den Anfangen bis zum babylonischen Exil.* Verlag Von Quelle & Meyer in Leipzig.

Shengold, Leonard. 1972 "A Parapraxis of Freud's In Relation to Karl Abraham." *American Imago,* 29: pp. 123-59.

———. 1979 "Freud and Joseph." In *Freud and His Self-Analysis.* Edited by Kanzer, Mark and Glenn, Jules. Jason Aronson, New York.

Spiegel, Shalom. 1979 *The Last Trial—On The Legends and Lore of the Command To Abraham To Offer Isaac As A Sacrifice: The Akedah.* Translated from the Hebrew with an introduction by Judah Goldin. Behrman House, Inc., New York.

Spinoza, Benedict De. 1949 *Ethics.* Edited with an Introduction by James Gutmann. Hafner Publishing Co., New York.

Spitz, Ellen Handler. 1989 "Psychoanalysis and The Legacies of Antiquity." In *Sigmund Freud and Art—His Personal Collection of Antiquities.* Ed. by Lynn Gamwell and Richard Wells. State University of New York and Freud Museum, London. Harry N. Abrams, Inc., New York.

Sulloway, Frank J. 1983 *Freud—Biologist of the Mind.* Basic Books, Inc., New York.

Tanakh—The Holy Scriptures. 1988 *The New JPS Translation—Accoridng to the Traditional Hebrew Text.* The Jewish Publication Society, Philadelphia, New York, Jerusalem.

Toynbee, Arnold J. 1938 *A Study of History* (ten volumes). Oxford University Press, Oxford, England.

Trosman, H. and Simmons, R.D. 1973 "The Freud Library." *The Journal of the American Psychoanalytic Association,* 21: pp. 646-687.

Vitz, Paul C. 1988 *Sigmund Freud's Christian Unconscious.* The Guilford Press, New York and London.

Wagner-Jauregg, Julius. 1950 *Lebenserinnerungen.* Herausgegeben und Erganzt von L. Schonbauer und M. Jantsch. Springer-Verlag, Wien.

Wallace IV, Edwin R. 1978 "Freud's Mysticism and Its Psychodynamic Determinants." *Bulletin of The Meninger Clinic,* 42: pp. 203-222.

Waxman, Meyer. 1945 *A History of Jewish Literature.* Vol. III. Bloch Publishing Co., New York.

Wertheimer, Jack. 1987 *Unwelcome Strangers—East European Jews in Imperial Germany.* Oxford University Press, New York—Oxford.

Williams, Bill. 1976 *The Making of Manchester Jewry,* 1740-1875. Manchester and New York.

Wilson, John A. 1969 "Was Akhnaton a Monotheist?" In *Monotheism and Moses—The Genesis of Judaism.* Ed. by Robert J. Christen and Harold E. Hazelton. D.C. Heath and Co., A Division of Raytheon Education Co., Lexington, Mass.

Wolf, Gerson. 1861 *Geschichte der Israelitischen Cultusgemeinde in Wien (1820-1860).* Wilhelm Braumuller, Wien.

————. 1876 *Geschichte der Juden in Wien (1156-1876).* Wien.

Yerushalmi, Josef Hayim. 1989 "Freud on the 'Historical Novel': From The Manuscript Draft (1934) of Moses and Monotheism." *International Journal of Psychoanalysis,* 70: pp. 375-395.

Young-Bruehl, Elisabeth. 1988 *Anna Freud—A Biography.* Summit Books, New York and London.

Index

Aaron (Biblical), 80, 138, 155-157
Aaronid priest, 232
Abaye, Rabbi, 174
Abraham (Biblical): and the *Akedah*, 161-168; breaking of father's idols, 229; as champion of justice, 63; command of God to, 5; omission by Sigmund Freud, 162; origins of circumcision, 161-162; as our father, 162
Abraham, Karl: Freud on Polish Jewess, 11; origins of Monotheism, 162; Orthodox Jewish background, 216; as student of the Talmud, 93, 216n.6, 217n.7
Adler, Alfred, 125
Adler, Viktor, 15, 194, 195
Adolescence, 113, 115
Agamemmnon, 165
Aggadah, 93
Ahasverus, 25-26
AHU (Altona-Hamburg-Wandsbeck), 218
Akademische Leshalle, 194
Akedah, 161-168
Akhenaten, 132, 138-139, 140, 201, 205, 227
Albright, William Foxwell, 139, 140, 142, 198, 228n.10
Alexander Ephraim, 18, 211n.8
Alexander the Great, 18, 20
Alexander Ziskind, 18, 211n.8
Altmann, Rabiner, 38
Amarna, 139, 227n.4
Amenophis I, 228n.10
Amenophis III, 132, 228n.10
Amenophis IV, 132, 157
Amun, 132, 205, 228n.10
Amun-Re, 139, 231n.12

Andersen, Francis I. and Freedman, David Noel, 150, 154
Andreas-Salome, Lou, 124
Anna O: *see* Pappenheim, Bertha
Antiquity, study of, 16; *see also* Robert, Marthe
Antiquities, 119
Anti-Semitism: in Austro-Hungarian Empire, 15; in Austria, 46, 104, 193; and the 'blood libel', 233n.16; and Christianity, 205
Aphasia, On, 76
Aphrodite, 230
Apodictic-style set of laws, 93
Aramaic, 93, 94, 216n.5
Archaic heritage, 148
Archives, Sigmund Freud, 18, 39, 212n.2
Arlow, Jacob A., 149
Aron, Wily, 85, 121, 209n.2
Austro-Hungarian Empire, 87
Artemis, 165
Ashtoreth, 230n.12
Assimilation: definition of, 207n.1; and first-generation, 98; and status of Jacob and Amalia Freud, 65; and Jews of Vienna, 15
Association, Free, 102; *see* Free Association
Astruc, Jean, 197, 227n.7
Aten, 139, 140, 228n.10
Atheism, 115
Atkinson, J.J., 144
Auerbach, Elias, 136, 137
Augustine, Saint, 224n.8
Austro-Hungarian Empire, 3, 9, 85, 95, 103
Autodidact, 98
Aztecs, 233n.16

251

Index of References